COME, FOLLOW ME!
VOLUME 2

COME, FOLLOW ME!
VOLUME 2

A Worship
Program for
Teaching the
Gospel to
Children

ELAINE CLANTON HARPINE

ABINGDON PRESS / Nashville

COME, FOLLOW ME!: A WORSHIP PROGRAM FOR TEACHING
THE GOSPEL TO CHILDREN, VOLUME 2

Copyright © 2001 by Abingdon Press

This book is printed on recycled, acid-free, elemental-chlorine–free paper.

ISBN 0-687-09212-4

01 02 03 04 05 06 07 08 09 10 — 10 9 8 7 6 5 4 3 2 1

MANUFACTURED IN THE UNITED STATES OF AMERICA

To

David,

Virginia,

and

Christina

CONTENTS

Acknowledgments

A special thank you to my loving husband, Bill. Thanks for taking the pictures for the book, for your carpentry expertise, and for believing in me.

Special thanks to my three wonderful children, David, Virginia, and Christina. I created this program for you. You've now grown up and become my best helpers. Thanks; I couldn't do it without you.

A heartfelt thank you to all the children I've had the privilege and honor of working with over the years at the First United Methodist Church in Cuyahoga Falls, Ohio. I love each of you dearly.

Thanks to Kathy Walker for her never-ending love and encouragement, and to Dr. Steven Bailey for believing in the program. Special thanks to Dean Wagner and Tate Newland for taking time out of their busy schedules to lend their musical talents, and to Wendy Gillespie for her weekly devotion and music ministry.

Thank you to the parents. Your support helped make our children's worship program a fabulous success. Thanks also to our many friends. Thank you for believing in children's worship.

INTRODUCTION

The Best Way to Begin

"No, we can't go on vacation; we have to go to church." A pleased but somewhat perplexed mom recited her son's words to me over the phone. She explained that her son insisted on turning down a weekend vacation trip to California because my children's worship class was presenting a special children's service in the sanctuary on Sunday. Mom was pleased that her son had suddenly become so interested in going to church but couldn't believe he was skipping four days of fun for a church activity.

You, too, will receive phone calls from happy parents who are astounded at their child's new-found interest in church when you start a children's worship program with your congregation. It's easy. No prior teaching experience is necessary. The cost is minimal.

Come, Follow Me! A Worship Program for Teaching the Gospel to Children is a yearlong program with 53 thirty-five minute sessions, more than 300 Bible-related craft projects, 102 pages of full-scale patterns, and 371 different Bible verses. Each session comes complete with seven learning centers, a five-minute children's story, and a ten-minute worship service.

Come, Follow Me! is a two-volume set, but each volume may be used independently. If you want a complete yearlong program, then use volume 1 and volume 2 together. If you have never directed a children's worship program before, volume 1 gives step-by-step directions for starting a program. If you are simply looking to add on to your existing program with special emphasis for Easter and Pentecost, you may find everything you need contained in volume 2.

The sessions (as well as parts and chapters) in volumes 1 and 2 are numbered consecutively. Volume 2 takes up where volume 1 left off. There are no gaps, no weeks when you must make up an activity. Everything has been planned for you.

Consecutive session numbers will help when you are planning the Easter play and spring musical. Some programs may refer you back to Volume 1 for costumes, a clay water jar, lamb, or other biblical crafts made in an earlier session. If you are starting with volume 2 and the Easter play, simply substitute from your own closet or prop department.

Come, Follow Me! will easily adapt to fit your needs and help your children build self-esteem and ownership because each week they are creating their own worship service. Worship is no longer a dreaded time when children must sit still and not wiggle or talk. Worshiping God becomes exciting and takes on new meaning because the children are leading the worship service.

Each of the workstations used each week represents one of the seven parts of the worship service. All of the workstations teach the Bible verse being taught that particular week and stress teaching children how to share and work together in a spirit of Christian love.

There is no need to separate younger children. All ages may work together in one room side by side. Workstations are graded for educational and fine-motor-skill appropriateness.

So what are you waiting for? Turn your ordinary Sunday mornings into a wonderland of biblical adventure. Add to your existing children's worship program or create a whole new worship time for the children at your church. You, too, can set up a children's worship program that will encourage families to return week after week. It's easy, and it's fun. Open the door for the children at your church. Answer the call from Jesus to "come, follow me" (Matthew 4:19 NIV).

PART FOUR

....

GETTING READY FOR EASTER

12

••••••••••••••••••••••••••••••••••

From Ash Wednesday to Easter

Session 27
The Meaning of Ash Wednesday
(Intended for the Sunday
before Ash Wednesday)

The Bible Lesson

The Lord's Prayer

What the Children Will Learn Today

Children are compiling a Lenten prayer booklet that includes the Lenten Home Worship Program for the six weeks of Lent, a Lenten calendar, and The Lord's Prayer in Sign Language instruction sheet.

Time Needed

5 minutes for story
25 minutes for workstations
5 minutes for closing service from Lenten Home Worship Program

Supplies Needed (by Workstation)

Story: a bag of pretzels
1. Peanut butter, powdered milk, honey, and powdered sugar
2. Silver foil, cotton balls or stuffing, and blue paper
3. Lenten collection boxes and calendar, and purple paper
4. Brown and yellow paper and pattern for mountain and sun
5. Tan, green, and dark blue paper, and patterns

6. Frame and cover pattern, purple paper, and thin cardboard
7. Purple, pink, and lavender paper and patterns

Children's Meditation

GETTING READY

Have a pretzel for each child today at the end of the story.

STORY

Little Arms in Prayer

Long ago in the fifth century A.D., in a small German village, a baker worked at his bread table. This Wednesday would be Ash Wednesday and mark the beginning of Lent. Ash Wednesday was a very solemn time of prayer and fasting in the baker's church. People did not eat milk, eggs, or fats during the forty days of Lent. That's why the bakers in town were making "little arms of prayer" to give to the children. These "little arms" were nothing more than flour, salt, and water rolled and twisted into two little arms crossed one over the other in prayer.

The baker made a special "little arm," the prettiest of the batch, and placed it in his shop window with a sign that read, "Little Arms of Prayer Fresh from the Oven." The baker had to bake at least twelve trays of little arms that day.

Each year the palms from last year's Palm Sunday service were burned and the ashes saved. At the Ash Wednesday service during Holy Communion, the ashes were used to mark a sign of the cross on each person's forehead. The cross was a way to tell others you were sorry for any wrongdoings you had committed throughout the year and to ask for forgiveness from God. After the service, little arms were given to all of the children.

The baker whistled and mixed up more dough for the next batch of little arms. He thought how wonderful it would be if every time before people ate their little arms of prayer, they'd stop, bow their heads, and tell God "thank you" for something wonderful in their lives. The more little arms of prayer you eat, the more opportunities you have to pray. The baker became so excited with his idea that the shop was soon filled with clouds of flour as he busily mixed, rolled, and baked. The smells of the baking little arms filled the streets. The shop was soon crowded with people. A crowd standing in front pressed their faces closer to see in. The baker brought out tray after tray. The baker told the crowd that from this day forward little arms of prayer would no longer be sold in his shop. A sigh of disappointment arose.

The baker raised his hand for silence. "Today and every day, there will be a basket of fresh little arms sitting on my counter," said the baker. "Each little arm will be free to anyone who pauses for a moment in prayer."

The crowd cheered. The baker smiled. A hush fell over the entire crowd as they bowed their heads in prayer.

I have a basket of "little arms" for you today. The Germans later called these little arms of prayer "pretzels." As you know, pretzels are no longer eaten just on Ash Wednesday, but I hope that the next time you eat a pretzel, you'll remember our story and stop and silently say thank you to God.

Before we eat our pretzels this morning, we're going to bow our heads and join together in saying the Lord's Prayer.

Workstations

Workstation 1: Call to Worship

GETTING READY

Have peanut butter dough ready. Mix: 1 cup peanut butter, 1 cup nonfat dry milk, 1 cup powdered sugar, 1 tablespoon honey. Add more sugar as needed to roll dough into a pretzel shape. Makes 12 edible no-bake pretzels.

INSTRUCTION SIGN

Ash Wednesday marks the beginning of Lent and is a day of prayer observed by Christians around the world. Roll dough into pencil shape. Form "little arms of prayer." Before eating your pretzel, stop, read Matthew 6:9-14, and tell God "thank you" for something wonderful in your life. Sign up to read for worship today.

Workstation 2: Affirmation of Faith

GETTING READY

Start at any workstation but go to Workstations 6 and 7 last to make covers and assemble booklets. Workstations allow the children to work at their own ability levels. Some will make only a rainbow and sky, others will want to make every page. Any stage of completion gives a nice booklet.

INSTRUCTION SIGN

Today, you are making a Lenten prayer booklet to take home. The raindrops in the sunrise scene remind us that there are both happy and sad times in life. The rainbow represents God's love.

STEP 1: Start with a light blue piece of paper. Make fluffy cloud shapes with cotton and glue at the top of the page.

STEP 2: Cut raindrops from foil. Use pattern. Glue in place. Read Matthew 6:5. At bottom of blue paper, write:
For thine is the kingdom, and the power, and the glory, forever. Amen.

Proceed to next station. Volunteer to read for worship.

Workstation 3: Offering or Carpenter Shop

GETTING READY

Have boxes to use for collection boxes.

INSTRUCTION SIGN

Lent is a time of preparation. Glue a Lenten calendar onto a piece of purple paper. Then select a Lenten offering box. Decorate your box to remind you that our Lenten offering will be for the poor. You may bring canned goods for our Food Collection Basket and use this calendar to help you remember those who are hungry. Read Matthew 6:9-13. Place boxes on worship table for service. Go to next station.

Workstation 4: Sermon or Bible Study

GETTING READY

Have example of fringed sunrise.

INSTRUCTION SIGN

Cut out a mountain to represent strength. Read Matthew 6:7 and write the following sentence at bottom of mountain.

Give us this day our daily bread.

Cut sun with feather-edge sun rays; glue to back of mountain.

Workstation 5: Witness to Faith

INSTRUCTION SIGN

In the Ukraine, the egg was originally a pagan symbol adapted by the church to symbolize Jesus Christ as the Light of the World at dawn or sunrise.

Carefully trace and cut the lake, trees, and ground. Match corners of each pattern to corners of construction paper. Cut these pieces accurately or they will not fit together correctly. Read Matthew 6:14 and write on the very bottom of the lake page:

Our Father, who art in heaven,
hallowed be thy name.
Thy kingdom come,
thy will be done on earth
as it is in heaven.

Sign up to be a reader for service today. Go to next station.

Workstation 6: Prayer and Sewing Center

GETTING READY

Have children cut the front Easter lily cover from pattern outline together as you talk them through each step. Immediately glue flower petal cover onto egg-shaped frame. The cover is simple to cut if you fold and cut each step together. The only trick is to *always* cut from the folded center toward the edges. Most first and second graders can cut their own covers if you demonstrate the steps.

If you do not have poster board for egg-shaped frames, large cereal box panels or old folders also work well.

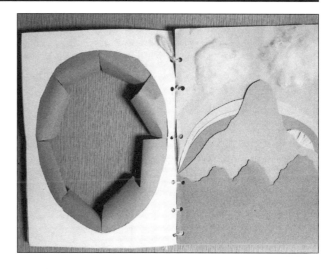

INSTRUCTION SIGN

Make cover for booklet. Follow directions exactly so that cover will turn out to be a beautiful purple lily with curled petals opening to show sunrise scene inside.

STEP 1: Place the egg-shaped frame pattern on a 9" x 12" piece of cardboard. Trace and cut. Write your name on the back.

STEP 2: Fold a piece of purple construction paper in half lengthwise. Match corners and crease all folds. The creases formed by folding the paper will become the lines you cut on to form the petals of the flower.

STEP 3: Fold in half again.

STEP 4: You are now ready to start cutting. Make all cuts starting in the CENTER of the folded side of the paper.
Unfold paper, one fold at a time. Cut creased lines in center. ALWAYS cut from the folded center on the creased line toward the open edges of the paper. Cut to 1/2" of edge. Do not cut through to open edge; otherwise, paper won't hold together.

STEP 5: You now have your paper cut into 4 rectangles. Lay paper flat on table. Draw a line from center of paper to each corner of the page. When finished, you will have 8 triangular flower petals. Cut from center of the paper toward eah corner point on the pencil lines you just drew to make triangle petals. Cut to 1/2" of edge. Curl each petal on a pencil. Glue flower cover onto frame. Sign up for service.

Workstation 7: Benediction

GETTING READY

Have all six weeks of the Lenten Home Worship Program and the Lord's Prayer in Sign Language sheets stapled and ready.

INSTRUCTION SIGN

The liturgical color for Lent is purple. Purple was a rare color in biblical times, worn only by the rich. Purple also reminds us to be humble. Being humble means not bragging.

Cut purple, lavender, and pink rainbows. Use patterns. Read Matthew 6:6. Write these lines at bottom of pink rainbow:

And forgive us our trespasses,
as we forgive those who trespass against us.
And lead us not into temptation,
but deliver us from evil.

If you went to each station and made the complete booklet, stack pages in order. If you only made a rainbow, staple rainbow to front of booklet and go to Workstation 1 to make a pretzel.

Assembling booklet: Your booklet represents sunrise on Easter morning. Start with the cover. Add ground, trees, and lake. Cut pieces accurately. Only small edges of the lake will show behind the trees. Next, add the mountain, rainbows (purple, lavender, and pink or smallest to largest), sky, and clouds. Now, add the Lenten Home Worship Program and the Lord's Prayer in Sign Language instruction sheet, and the Lenten calendar. Put together. You should be able to see each piece of your sunrise scene.

The Worship Celebration

SIGN-UP SHEET FOR TODAY'S WORSHIP CELEBRATION

Call to Worship (sing a favorite song):
Read "Witness for Jesus" from Home Worship Program:
Read "Symbol" from Home Worship Program:
Bible readers (Matthew 6:5-8; 22:36-40):
Lead the Lord's Prayer in sign language ("Our Father" portion):

ITEMS TO GO HOME TODAY: LENTEN PRAYER BOOKLETS

A Lenten Home Worship Program

During the Lenten season, the children in our Children's Worship program will be exploring the meaning of Lent and what it means to Witness. We will be making a Lenten Cross and lighting a new candle each week. Your family may choose to make a Lenten Cross at home or just arrange small candle holders in a cross shape.

This Lenten Prayer Booklet has a short worship service for each day in Lent. Start your service with a favorite song. Light a candle for each week of Lent as the Bible verse is read. Read the thought for the day that is listed. Close with the Lord's Prayer.

A calendar is attached to the Prayer Booklet to help us remember the poor and hungry of the world. Your family may wish to add more than the pennies listed on the calendar. We are teaching that even a seemingly worthless penny when multiplied by the work of others is significant. Canned goods may be brought each Sunday. Collection boxes return Easter morning.

Sunday Before Ash Wednesday: Matthew 6:5-8

Witness for Jesus: Lent is a time for Change. A time to change how we act toward others or treat other people. Think of a behavior you would like to change. Maybe you were sassy, threw a tantrum, rude, called someone a bad name, or yelled at someone in your family or at school. Go and tell that person you are sorry. Then show that person you are truly sorry by changing how you act toward them.

Symbol: Our symbol this week is the Pretzel. The pretzel reminds us to stop each day and say thank you to God for something or someone who is special in our lives.

Ash Wednesday: Luke 17:20-21

Witness: Lent begins today, and is a time of reflection. Think of a word you have been saying lately that may not be such a nice word to say. It doesn't have to be a curse word. Perhaps it is just an unkind word. Try to stop saying that word and in its place substitute a nice word.

Thursday: 1 John 4:7-8

Witness: Think of how you greet your family each morning. Do you smile and say something pleasant or do you grump at others because you did not want to get out of bed? Make it a point to say something nice to everyone you meet today.

Friday: Matthew 6:14-15

Witness: Tell someone in your family how you feel without saying anything negative.

Saturday: Colossians 3:12-17

Witness: If someone asked how your day went today, would you remember something nice that happened to you or would you immediately think of all the things that went wrong today?

First Sunday in Lent: Candle of Forgiveness: Luke 6:27-28 and 37-38

Act of Forgiveness: Lent is a time of Forgiveness a time to start over, a time to try and rebuild a friendship or relationship that has gone bad. Jesus taught mercy, forgiveness, justice, and love. It is often easier to see the faults of others than to say kind, loving words. Ask someone to forgive you and then try to show that you deserve forgiveness by how you change your behavior.

Symbol: Our symbol this week is a hollow Easter egg because our lives are empty without God's love and the love of friends and family. The egg is an ancient symbol of new life. When we have new life we seek forgiveness and extend forgiveness to others.

Monday: Matthew 7:1-5

Forgive: Lent is a time for repentance to say you are sorry and to genuinely try to change how you act or what you say. It doesn't do much good to say you're sorry if you do not try to stop making the same mistake. If you do not succeed in changing the first time, then try, try, try again. God always forgives.

Tuesday: Luke 6:43-45

Forgive: Often even loving families spend more time finding fault with the actions of each other than finding good. Share forgiveness. Think of one way you could be kinder to each member of your family. Make it a point to do something nice for each person in your family today or a friend.

Wednesday: Matthew 7:1-2, 7-12, and 14

Forgive: Sometimes we do nice things for others because we want them to do something nice for us. Share good things with others without expecting to be repaid. Do an act of kindness today without expecting anything in return. An act of kindness does not cost money. Sometimes the simple acts speak the strongest of love.

Thursday: John 8:7-11

Forgive: Think of how you would feel if others treated you the way you are treating them. Select one person in your life and make it your task during Lent to change how you treat this person. Forgive this person for any mean thing they have done to you.

Friday: Matthew 5:13-16

Forgive: Oil for a lamp was very costly in biblical time. What kind of an example do you set for others through your daily behavior? Share with someone in need today other than giving money.

Saturday: John 13:35

Forgive: Share love. Tell someone you love them and why. Today, share a hug with each person who is special in your life.

Home Worship for the Second Week of Lent

Second Sunday in Lent: Candle of Remembrance: Matthew 13:31-32

Stop and Remember: Remembering Jesus' life and teachings is one way we grow in our faith. Lent is a time to remember and grow in faith together.

Symbol: Our symbol this week is the cross. Remember the pain you cause others by your jealous acts and by thinking only of your own wants and needs. Think of a way this week to show others you are thinking kindly of them.

Monday: Matthew 6:24

Remember: Lent is a time for Remembering the good things you have in life, your family, daily kindnesses we take for granted, and for remembering to be grateful. Count your many blessings. Make a list of the ten most important people, things, or feelings in your life. Share your list with your family.

Tuesday: Matthew 6:19-21

Remember: The liturgical color for Lent is purple. Purple is symbolic of a time of spiritual preparation. Think of one way you are getting ready for Easter. Tell others in your family of one change you would like to make in your life and how they can help you.

Wednesday: Mark 2:13-17 and 1:14-15

Remember: As Christians, we are to witness for God in Christ's name. Tell one way you have witnessed for Christ today.

Thursday: Matthew 7:24-27

Remember: The scripture passages used throughout this week tell about the life and teachings of Jesus. Jesus used stories from daily experiences to teach the principles we need to live our lives by.

Friday: Luke 10:25-37

Remember: In biblical time people usually traveled on foot. It was the custom to wash your feet before eating. Usually a servant would bring a bowl and towel around and wash everyone's feet. Since there was no servant at the Last Supper, Jesus humbled himself to the task. Through this demeaning task, Jesus taught the lesson of humility. God knows our weaknesses and our strengths. Have each member of your family tell something you wish you could do better and something you do very well.

Saturday: Luke 11:5-10

Remember: Lent is a time of spiritual preparation for Easter. Tell about something nice that happened to you today. Remember a kindness shown you today. Tell each member of your family something special you enjoyed doing with them today.

Home Worship for the Third Week of Lent

Third Sunday in Lent: The Candle of Sharing: Matthew 22:36-40

Find a way to Share: As Christians, it is our challenge to share not just the things we do not care about or what is left over or not needed in our life. We are challenged to know and feel the needs of others and to share with those who are less fortunate than ourselves. We can share through the money we give, through our thoughts and actions toward others, through the little things we do to help our neighbors near and far, and by caring about our families and each other.

Symbol: Our symbol this week is the decorated Easter Egg. The egg is the symbol of new life. People all around the world decorate eggs at Easter time to share with others. In Ukraine, people make very elaborate eggs which are decorated with religious symbols.

Monday: John 8:31-32

Share: Lent is a time for sharing to give to others and to share the many good things you have in life with those who do not have life as easy as you do. Witnessing takes many forms: Using one's talents, sharing one's gifts through daily words, and even sometimes changing our daily actions toward others. As you follow your Lenten calendar and place your money in your collection box, think of other ways you can help others. Can you help a member of your family this week? Someone at school this week? A friend?

Tuesday: Luke 12:1-3

Share: Lent is a time for humbleness: to learn not to brag, to be proud without boasting, and to give without expecting something nice in return.

Wednesday: Romans 12:1-3

Share: Tell one way you can be more humble.
Thursday: 1 Corinthians 13:1-13
Share: We pray for understanding and help with our daily problems, world peace, and hope for tomorrow.

Friday: Mark 16:15

Share: Our theme this year is "Witnessing and what it means to witness." The Bible verses this week remind us to examine the actions and words we share with others. How did you witness today?

Saturday: Mark 9:34-37

Share: There are actually 46 days in the season of Lent. Lent begins on Ash Wednesday and ends on Easter Eve or the Saturday before Easter. The six Sundays in Lent are not actually counted as part of Lent. Sunday is always a day of CELEBRATION.

Home Worship for the Fourth Week of Lent

Fourth Sunday in Lent: The Candle of Action, Galatians 5:22-26

Taking Action: We all enjoy the feeling of being the best. Everyone likes to win. Humility is not easy, but we must learn to think of the feelings of others. We must stop and ask, "How would God feel about how I am acting and treating others right now?" We must also remember that God loves everyone and always forgives us for whatever we have done when we ask for forgiveness.

Symbol: Our symbol this week is the fish. The early Christians drew the simple sign of the fish on their doors, their dishes, or on the ground as a greeting and secret code to tell other Christians they were welcome and safe.

Monday: James 1:19-27

Action: It is wrong to get angry, but we all get angry. We must therefore find a way to show we are sorry for our anger and to help those we have hurt by our anger. Go to someone you have been angry with and talk about your feelings.

Tuesday: Matthew 5:33-37

Action: Have you ever made a promise you did not intend to keep? Have you ever broken a promise you truly intended to keep? Unfortunately, we all have. How can we improve? Make a special promise and work hard to keep it.

Wednesday: Matthew 5:1-12

Action: We tend to like people who are like us. We often dislike those who are different or who do not act as we want them to. Jesus shared His kindness and love with everyone. Think of a way you can share kindness and love this week with five people you do not like.

Thursday: Matthew 6:1-4

Action: How can we know and feel the needs of others? Think of a project you and your family can do together to help others.

Friday: Mark 7:20-23 and James 4:1-6

Action: Jesus was Jewish. The term Christian did not come into being until after Jesus' death. The name Christian is given to those who follow the teachings of Jesus. Think of a way you and your family can show that you follow the teachings of Jesus.

Saturday: John 13:34-35

Action: Eating together in biblical times was a sign of friendship, trust, and confidence. To betray someone after eating with him or her was unthinkable. How do you measure true friendship? What could you do to strengthen your friendship with a special friend or family member today?

Home Worship for the Fifth Week of Lent

Fifth Sunday in Lent: Candle of Commitment, John 8:12

Commitment: Each lesson this week encourages you to think about your commitment to God and how you can witness in your own life today. What does your "light" tell others? What do your actions say about your faith?

The 40 days of Lent should bring about a change in our daily lives. Think back to Ash Wednesday: has your family made any changes in how you act toward each other?

Symbol: The symbol this week is a disguised cross called the "anchor cross" that was used as a secret sign by the early Christians. The anchor cross can still be seen on the walls of the catacombs of Rome where the early Christians hid and worshipped in secret. The anchor cross is a symbol of hope (Hebrews 6:19).

Monday: Matthew 25:35-40 and 42-45

Commitment: Think of what it is like to be hungry. What can you do to help the hungry and homeless? How can you and your family help those in need in some way other than just giving money?

Tuesday: Luke 14:7-11

Commitment: Often we think we have to be the best, we have to win first place, or we have to be able to do things better than other people in our family. Jesus reminds us that all that is required is that we do our best. If we do the best that it is possible for us to do, others will notice and praise us. Compliment someone today. Be positive and sincere.

Wednesday: Luke 16:1-13

Commitment: Tell one way you can serve God instead of money. Make a family plan. Follow through on your plan. Can you think of a way to continue serving God even after Lent?

Thursday: Mark 10:17-21

Commitment: In the Bible verse, what is Jesus really asking the man to give away? Think of something you are willing to do without in order to help others. Donate a toy, clothes, or food to an organization that helps those in need. Put together a family donation, with each member of the family contributing.

Friday: Luke 6:31-36

Commitment: How can you show your love for your family every day? Think of a new chore or obligation you would like to undertake at home. Make this new chore your responsibility.

Saturday: Mark 10:13-16

Commitment: Alleluia means "Praise God" in Hebrew. Do you take time each day to "Praise God?" How do you show your love for God? Start a new family tradition to share each and every day.

The Sixth Week of Lent

Sixth Sunday in Lent, Palm Sunday: Candle of Faith, Mark 11:1-10

Have Faith and Trust in God: Lent is a time of growing closer to God and strengthening our faith. We are challenged to change the way we live our lives because of the teachings of Jesus. We witness to our faith every moment of our lives through our talents, our gifts to others, our daily words, and our daily actions. Worship is also a witness to our faith. You and your family are invited to write a Worship Service for Saturday evening to tell about your faith. Select a song or write a Call to Worship that invites others to come and celebrate God's love with you.

Symbol: The symbol this week is the butterfly which represents new life and the resurrection.

Monday: James 2:14-18

Faith: An Affirmation of Faith tries to explain what we believe. As a family write a statement of your faith.

Tuesday: Luke 12:15-21

Faith: Think of a special Lenten gift you can give to others who are less fortunate than your family. Perhaps you might offer your time instead of money.

Wednesday: Matthew 6:9-13

Faith: Write a family prayer.
Thursday: Matthew 13:24-30
Faith: How we react to the problems of daily life is a form of witnessing. The way we treat other people is witnessing. How we witness to others tells about our faith. Think of a way you could send messages to the members of your family about your faith. Make your witness statements part of your family worship service.

Friday: Matthew 13:3-8 and 18-23

Faith: The Parable of the Sower is thought to be one of the first parables told by Jesus. Sometimes a message comes in the form of a sermon, sometimes a song, and sometimes even the words of a child. Discuss such questions as, What is the kingdom of Heaven like? What is prayer important? What does the phrase "God's Will" mean? Think of a special way to share God's message with your family.

Saturday: Matthew 5:13-16

Faith: The benediction is the close of the worship service and a way of sending everyone out to share God's love. Think of a way for your family to continue sharing love and compassion together after this week closes. Celebrate the close of this week by celebrating the service you have written together as a family. Remember that the Benediction is not really the end of the Celebration but actually the beginning.

LENTEN OFFERING CALENDAR

Sunday	Monday	Tuesday	Wednesday	Thursday	Friday	Saturday
			Ash Wednesday for each glass of clear clean water you drink, pay 1¢.	For each cracker you eat today, pay 2¢.	If you eat a bowl of soup today, pay 3¢.	For each glass of milk you drink today, pay 5¢.
For each glass of milk today, pay 4¢.	For each cup of yogurt, pay 2¢.	For each snack today, pay 5¢.	For each carrot you eat today, pay 3¢.	If you ate beans today, pay 2¢.	If you drank orange juice today, pay 3¢.	If you eat an apple today, pay 2¢.
For each piece of hard candy, pay 20¢.	For each diet cola, pay 15¢.	If you eat peanut butter today, pay 5¢.	For every cookie you eat today, pay 5¢.	For each slice of cake today, pay 15¢.	For each doughnut today, pay 20¢.	If you eat popcorn today, pay 1¢ a piece.
For each potato chip you eat today, pay 2¢.	For each milkshake, pay 20¢.	If you eat tacos today, pay 15¢.	If you ate a hamburger today, pay 25¢.	If you had french fries today, pay 20¢.	If you eat a hot dog today, pay 25¢.	If you eat pizza today, pay 25¢.
If you eat pudding today, pay 7¢.	If you eat a brownie, pay 5¢.	If you eat spaghetti, pay 3¢.	If you ate a candy today, pay 30¢.	If you ate ice cream today, pay 20¢.	for each dinner roll today, pay 10¢.	For each slice of bread today, pay 1¢.
If you eat a banana today, pay 1¢.	If you eat pretzels, pay 4¢ each.	For each bite of cheese today, pay 2¢.	For each cola you drink today, pay 25¢.	If you did not eat rice today, pay 3¢.	If you eat cereal today, pay 5¢.	If you eat potatoes today, pay 5¢.
Palm Sunday For each food you eat today that has eggs in it, pay 3¢.	If you do not eat your vegetable at dinner, pay 8¢.	If you didn't eat breakfast today, pay 10¢.	For each crumb of food left eaten on a plate, pay 5¢.	Maunday Thursday If you wasted any water today, pay 1¢ for each time.	Good Friday If you didn't eat lunch today, pay 10¢.	Holy Saturday For each meal you have to eat today, pay 10¢.

Session 28
First Sunday in Lent:
Time-Traveling Reporters

The Bible Lesson

The Bible lesson tells how we are to forgive others and seek forgiveness for ourselves (Luke 6:27-28, 31-36, and 37-38).

What the Children Will Learn Today

Today's session focuses on forgiveness and introduces the Easter play. Turn to Session 43 for a complete copy of the play.

Time Needed

5 minutes for story
25 minutes for workstations
5 minutes for closing service from Lenten Home Worship Program

Supplies Needed (by Workstation)

Story: Tree branches and Christmas tree stand
1. Hollow plastic Easter eggs, scrap paper, and stickers
2. Hollow plastic Easter eggs, hole punch, and scrap paper
3. One real egg per person, sharp fingernail scissors, wax or old candles and crayons, foam egg carton
4. Play script and children's songbook
5. Hollow plastic Easter eggs, and colored string or yarn
6. Lord's Prayer sign language instruction sheet
7. Construction paper supply basket, stapler, and patterns

Children's Meditation

GETTING READY

Make a "Love Task Tree." Tape tree branches together at base. Place in Christmas tree stand.

STORY

The Unfortunate Note

Jackie was new at school and didn't have many friends. She wasn't part of the popular crowd. No one ever came up to her to say, "Jackie, will you sit with us at lunch?"

Jackie kept trying to make friends, but somehow it would turn out wrong. She was beginning to have hope, though, because two girls in her math class, Mary Frances and Judy, were sort of acting as if they might like her.

The next day, as Jackie sat in class, a note was passed up the row from the back of the room. The note was from Mary Frances and Judy. It said,

"Dear Jackie,
Please stop following us around. You're being a pest, and we're tired of being friends with you."

The note was signed by both girls. Jackie thought she'd start crying right there in class. What had she done wrong?

For the first time, she'd found a group, a place to belong. Now they were telling her to get lost.

To make matters worse, one of the boys gave the note to the teacher.

All three girls had to stay in at lunch. Mary Frances immediately defended herself by saying that the note was not her idea; it was Judy's. "I only went along with it because Judy begged me to," said Mary Frances.

The teacher pointed out that both girls had signed the note.

"You must stop and consider the other person's response to every word you say or write. You and only you are responsible for the words you say and the actions you take. If you participate, you're responsible."

As the day went on, Mary Frances thought about the teacher's words. Mary Frances couldn't believe she had let Judy talk her into signing that note. It was a cruel thing to do to Jackie.

After school, Mary Frances apologized to Jackie for the second time and invited Jackie over to her house. Judy overheard Mary Frances and became furious.

Judy stormed off and said she would never talk to Mary Frances again. Jackie and Mary Frances sort of smiled at each other and walked out the door together.

Like Mary Frances, we, too, often make mistakes because we do not think about the consequences of our words or actions. Like Mary Frances, we can go and ask for forgiveness. As you work at the different stations today, take a moment and make a forgiveness egg to hang on our Love Task Tree.

There are three options available: Workstations 1, 2, and 5 each have a forgiveness egg. Pick your favorite and make an egg. Your forgiveness eggs will hang on our tree till Easter to remind us of our need to seek forgiveness.

Workstations

Workstation 1: Call to Worship

GETTING READY

Have stickers or pictures from magazines available.

> INSTRUCTION SIGN
>
> Have you ever joined in when a group was teasing someone? Any time we hurt someone's feelings, we should say we are sorry and ask God for forgiveness. Think of something you have done that hurt someone's feelings. Read Luke 6:27-28. Then, write what you are sorry for doing on a scrap of paper and place it inside a plastic egg. Seal the egg shut with stickers or pictures cut from magazines. Attach a string to the top of the egg. Hang your egg on the Love Task Tree. Find a song for us to sing for worship today.

Workstation 2: Affirmation of Faith

GETTING READY

Use construction paper scraps. Make a few examples.

> INSTRUCTION SIGN
>
> Pretend you can travel back in time and write down on a piece of scrap paper a mistake you made and tell how you would do things differently if you had another chance. Read Luke 6:27-28, 31. Then, place your paper inside a plastic egg. Tape the egg shut. Punch circles from scrap paper. Tape a string to the top of your egg for a hanger. Cover egg with glue. Randomly sprinkle circles over the egg or place the circles in a pattern to form a picture or create a character. Hang your egg on the Love Task Tree before service today. Sign up to be a reader.

Workstation 3: Offering or Carpenter Shop

GETTING READY

Adult supervision required today.

Have children prepare eggshells or prepare eggshells at home before session. Make plain wax eggs or candle eggs.

If you make wax candle eggs at home, you can use them for your Lenten salt dough cross and worship service today. Melt wax or discarded candles in an old saucepan over low heat. Add bits of crayon to melting wax to create color desired. Use caution with hot wax. *Never let wax boil or mix with water.*

To turn the wax eggs into candles, punch a tiny hole in the top of the eggshell with a needle before you cut the opening in the bottom. Insert a small birthday candle inside the empty egg shell with wick poking through tiny hole on top. Place children's play clay around wick to prevent wax from leaking.

COME, FOLLOW ME!

INSTRUCTION SIGN

Jesus frequently talked about forgiveness. Read John 8:10-11. Think of someone who has treated you unfairly and find a way to show you forgive them. Make a wax egg as a reminder to offer forgiveness to others. Prepare eggshell today.

STEP 1: With a pair of fingernail scissors GENTLY poke a small hole in the bottom of an egg. You are only allowed one egg, so work slowly and carefully. Eggs, like people's feelings, are very fragile. You can't put a broken egg back together, and you cannot erase the pain you cause to others.

STEP 2: Cut a circle about the size of a dime in the bottom of the egg. Empty the contents of egg into a bowl. Rinse egg.

STEP 3: Write your name on the outside of the egg shell. Place in the waiting egg carton. Ladle melted wax into shells. Go make a forgiveness egg at Workstation 1, 2, or 5.

Workstation 4: Sermon or Bible Study

GETTING READY

Each week the cast for the Easter service will rehearse a portion of the Easter play during worship. Have scripts and puppets ready. The Easter play is divided into six 15-minute sections to reduce practice time. See Session 43 for the script.

INSTRUCTION SIGN

Practice Scene I from the Easter play today and show how to cooperate by working together in peace and harmony. Read Luke 6:27-28, 31-36, 37-38. Sign up to read for worship today.

Workstation 5: Witness to Faith

GETTING READY

Use plastic eggs, even leftover pieces that do not fit together anymore, because children are going to tape eggs shut. Multicolored cotton craft string works best, but yarn can be used.

INSTRUCTION SIGN

We witness every day with the tone of voice we use, by how we treat others, and by the activities we do with others. Read Luke 6:34-36. Write down on a piece of paper a mistake you've made. Then place your paper inside a plastic egg. Tape your egg shut. Attach a string to top of egg to use for a hanger.

Place glue on outside of egg. Start in the middle. Slowly wrap string over surface of egg. Use lots of glue. Keep string windings close together. Go slow. Hang your egg on the Love Task Tree.

Workstation 6: Prayer and Sewing Center

GETTING READY

The prayer station during Lent will be learning the Lord's Prayer in sign language. It helps if you have someone from your congregation who can come and work with the children.

INSTRUCTION SIGN

Our hands often show our feelings. By speaking to others through sign language, we express a desire to include everyone.

Your job during Lent is to learn to say the Lord's Prayer in sign language. Work on just a few lines each week. Read Luke 6:27-28, 31-36, 37-38. Be ready for today's service.

Permission granted to photocopy for local church use. © 2000 Elaine Clanton Harpine.

30

Workstation 7: Benediction

GETTING READY

Have supplies you would like for the children to decorate with: paint, glitter, stickers, or markers and crayons.

INSTRUCTION SIGN

Part of asking for forgiveness is changing how you speak and act toward others. Make a "Time to Change" egg as a reminder that we are trying to change during Lent.

STEP 1: Fold paper in half. Trace pattern. Cut 2 eggs.
STEP 2: Cut a zigzag line through middle of one egg.
STEP 3: Read Luke 6:37-38. On egg that is not cut in half, write 3 changes you would like to make in your life.
STEP 4: Staple the 2 cracked halves over the matching whole egg. Decorate the outside of the eggs. Take your egg home as a reminder of the changes you're working on.

The Worship Celebration

GETTING READY

For today's service, start with the "First Sunday in Lent" reading from the Home Worship booklet and light the 1st candle on the Lenten cross. You will use the Lenten cross, candles, and Home Worship booklet for the service each week.

SIGN-UP SHEET FOR TODAY'S WORSHIP CELEBRATION

Call to Worship (sing a song together):
Reader from Home Worship Program (light 1st candle while Bible verse is read):
Read "Symbol" (from booklet):
Person to lead the Lord's Prayer in sign language:

ITEMS TO GO HOME TODAY: "TIME TO CHANGE" EGGS

Session 29
Second Sunday in Lent:
The Parables of Jesus

The Bible Lesson

An Indian legend is used to remind us that we're all in need of God's grace (James 4:1-6; 5:7-12).

What the Children Will Learn Today

Although today's story is not a true Native American legend, many of the facts are true. The men of the Acoma tribe were known for their weavings and the women for their pottery. The Acoma lived in adobe pueblo dwellings two and three stories high. The God's Eye design, still used by many Native Americans in the Southwest, is often called "magic eyes." The Huichol tribe of Mexico is credited as being the originator of the God's Eye pattern or *"Ojos de Dios,"* Spanish for the "Eyes of God." Children will learn how to make a God's Eye today.

Time Needed

10 minutes for story (5 min. for Part I and 5 min. for Part II)

20 minutes for workstations

5 minutes for closing service from Lenten Home Worship Program

Tell story as one continuous ten-minute story or, if using story in the sanctuary service, stop after Part I. Part II, the actual making of a 3-D God's Eye, takes about five minutes depending on the size of your group.

Supplies Needed (by Workstation)

Story: Need multicolored yarn and cinnamon sticks (2 sticks per person). Plain or multicolored scraps of yarn can be used.

1. Empty detergent boxes, glue, brown paper bags or paper

2 and 5. Yarn and cinnamon sticks for God's Eyes

3. Wood or cardboard and supplies for building TV camera

4. Copies of play, puppets, and craft supply basket

6. Sign language worksheets

7. Construction paper supply basket

Children's Meditation

GETTING READY

The "God's Eye" yarn weaving is an old craft often used at camp and is a favorite with children. In presenting the 3-D God's Eye to your class, explain the actual history of the God's Eye.

History: High up in the western Sierra Madre mountain region of Mexico the Huichol Indians live much as they did during the time of the Aztecs. The remote, unreachable locations of the mountainous villages have left the Huichol secluded and unchanged. Their God's Eye or *tsikuri* is made on bamboo with wool yarn. Fathers make the God's Eye for each of their children to protect the children from harm and keep them in good health. The number of "rhombuses" or "lozenge" made on the bamboo cross signifies the age of the child (five god's eyes together for a five-year-old). The Huichol believe that their gods can see them through the center eye of the lozenge-shaped tsikuri or God's Eye, allowing the Huichol to communicate with their gods. After age five each child must make his or her own tsikuri to ensure good health. The God's Eye pattern is placed on belts, bags, necklaces, and even woven into blankets to protect the person wearing the tsikuri from harm. The God's Eye is a favorite with the Huichol children. Just as many spring rituals surrounding the egg were converted to Christian symbolism, the God's Eye pattern was given Christian significance by early Spanish priests. Today, the God's Eye is a favorite symbol of God's love made by children everywhere.

STORY

"Ojos de Dios" or the Eyes of God Part I

"Long, long ago," Miss Nema began, "when the rushing waters still flowed in the now dry riverbed, the Acoma lived proudly along the peaceful river in their three-story adobe pueblo. The young men farmed and the women made beautiful pottery, but it was the older men of the tribe who were the weavers. My grandfather would sit for hours weaving on long poles planted in the ground as his grandfathers had done before him.

"Each of Grandfather's blankets always started the same, a central crossing of the threads in the center to form an eye."

" 'Magic eye,' replied Grandfather. 'It is the eye of the universe and it brings good luck, good fortune, health, and a long and happy life.' "

Miss Nema sat, surrounded by the eager faces of her students at the Mission School, as she once again told her students a story about her life as a child growing up on a Pueblo Indian reservation.

Miss Nema reminded the children that Indian legends are not necessarily true stories; instead, they're stories told to teach a lesson. "Listen and see if you can tell me the lesson to be learned from this legend that my grandfather told me many years ago," Miss Nema said.

A Huichol youth from a tribe far to the south, in what is now called Mexico, was learning to weave from his grandfather. The young man was very impatient and didn't want to take the time to sit and carefully weave each tiny thread, yet he longed to do a weaving more beautiful than any he had ever seen so that his grandfather would be proud of him. The young boy rode his pony to the sun and reached out and grabbed a piece of its bright yellow radiance.

"This will be my center," he said. Then he placed the sun rays in his leather pouch and rode on, gathering green from the grass, blue from the river, red from the berries, and brown from the limbs of a nearby tree. The young boy's leather pouch looked as if it would split open at the seams. The young boy proudly rode back to his grandfather and told him all that he had gathered.

"Foolish boy," said the grandfather. "You cannot capture the sun."

"Yes, I can," replied the boy. "I have it right here in my pouch."

As the young boy emptied the contents of his pouch onto the ground the colors fell into the most beautiful pattern the boy had ever seen, but there was no yellow and there was no sun. [Show the God's Eye you made earlier.] The young boy was very disappointed.

"Everything has a place and a purpose," said the old man slowly. "It is not ours to know and understand. The Creator of the universe has shown favor with you by giving you this new pattern. The center shall be the eye of the universe and from this day forward we shall weave as he has shown you."

"And to this day," Miss Nema concluded, "there are still many in Mexico and throughout the Southwest who weave what we call the *Ojos de Dios* or the Eyes of God."

"I know," said Juan eagerly. "The eye in the center represents the eye of the universe or God's Eye."

"That's right," said Miss Nema. "The God's Eye reminds us that everything in God's world is interwoven. You are a special part of God's world, and you are important to God."

[If you want a 5-minute story, stop at this point. If you want to demonstrate how to make a God's eye, continue.]

Part II

"Teach us to make a God's Eye," said Juan.

"It's actually very simple," said Miss Nema. "You take two sticks and make a small hand loom," Miss Nema explained as she passed out sticks to each of the children.

STEP 1: Place the flat side of the cinnamon sticks together. Hold the two sticks together tightly in the shape of an X between your thumb and third finger. An "X" (the Greek letter *chi*) was often used by early Christians as a symbol for Christ. The teachings of Christ should always be at the center of our life.

STEP 2: Take the end of the string of yarn and place under your thumb. Wrap the yarn over the X pattern of the cinnamon sticks 5 times, forming an X pattern with the yarn. Pull the yarn tight so that it will hold the cinnamon sticks in place.

STEP 3: Begin weaving the God's Eye ornament by wrapping the yarn under and then back over the cinnamon stick. Pull yarn tight to make a pretty weaving.

STEP 4: Turn the cinnamon sticks in your hand like spokes on a wheel. Repeat the under and over weaving on each cinnamon stick. Weave over and under one stick and then turn to the next stick. Continue weaving under and over as you go around.

Make sure that each yarn woven lies flat on the stick right next to the yarn before and not on top of another piece of yarn.

Each strand of yarn needs its own special place, just as each of us has a special place and purpose in God's world. Go slowly. If you make a mistake, take the yarn off and start over.

Weave about ⅓ of the length of the cinnamon sticks. Flip the God's Eye upside down and continue weaving in the same manner on the back side. Weave until about ⅔ full this time.

Flip the God's Eye back over to the side you started with. Finish weaving out to the ends of the sticks.

STEP 5: Tie off the end of your yarn on the back.

"By flipping the God's Eye upside down, you create a three-dimensional God's Eye," said Miss Nema. "The idea for this 3-D effect grew out of a mistake made by a six-year-old girl. She became confused. Her God's Eye was different. Everyone wanted to make one. Her mistake led to a 3-dimensional God's Eye that reminds us of God the Father, God the Son, and God the Holy Spirit.

"Now to get back to our lesson," said Miss Nema. "Who knows what the lesson of the God's Eye weaving is for us today?"

Juan raised his hand. "Does the lesson have something to do with mistakes?"

"Yes, it does," Miss Nema said, chuckling. "So the next time you make a mistake"—Miss Nema paused—"remember the 3-D God's Eye. Instead of wading your mistake up or throwing it away, try to make something even more beautiful than what you started out to make."

Workstations

Workstation 1: Call to Worship

GETTING READY

Have brown paper bags to cover empty detergent boxes.

> INSTRUCTION SIGN
>
> In biblical times, Jerusalem was surrounded by a huge stone wall. We are building a wall and a gate for our Easter service. Our wall will be built from paper-covered cardboard boxes instead of large clay stones. Wrap boxes tightly as if you were wrapping a package. Use GLUE instead of tape. Read James 5:12. Place finished blocks in front of worship table for service today.

Workstations 2 (Affirmation of Faith) and 5 (Witness to Faith) Combined

GETTING READY

Have extra cinnamon sticks.

INSTRUCTION SIGN

Just as each strand of yarn has a special place in our God's Eye weaving, everyone is special to God and has a special talent to share in life. Make a God's Eye to go to nursing homes and hospitals for Easter. Read James 5:7. Hang your God's Eyes on the Love Task Tree for service today.

Workstation 3: Offering or Carpenter Shop

GETTING READY

The TV camera can be made from scrap wood or cardboard.

INSTRUCTION SIGN

Your job is to build a TV camera for our Easter play. Cover a box or build a box out of wood. Use lids or round cardboard circles for dials. Be creative.

Workstation 4: Sermon or Bible Study

INSTRUCTION SIGN

Jesus told parables using examples from everyday happenings in biblical life. As you practice Scene II from the Easter script today, see if you can remember parables that talk about bread, a merchant, or hungry guests. Read Luke 11:5-13.

Workstation 6: Prayer and Sewing Center

INSTRUCTION SIGN

Practice the Lord's Prayer in sign language for service. What did Jesus say to ask for in our prayers? Read Luke 11:3.

Workstation 7: Benediction

INSTRUCTION SIGN

Make a blanket using the God's Eye design.

STEP 1: Fold paper and trace patterns. You may use the same color or 3 different colors.

STEP 2: Glue diamonds onto another contrasting sheet of paper. We always remember kind words and deeds done to us by others. Think of a way to share kindness this week. Write kind deeds and words you plan to share with others on your blanket.

35

The Worship Celebration

SIGN-UP SHEET FOR TODAY'S WORSHIP CELEBRATION

Call to Worship (sing a favorite song):

Read from Home Worship Program (light 1st and 2nd candles on Lenten cross) and also read James 5:7:

Read "Symbol" (from Home Worship Program):

Sermon and Witness (hang extra God's Eyes on tree):

Benediction (Lord's Prayer in sign language):

ITEMS TO GO HOME TODAY: 3-D GOD'S EYES AND/OR GOD'S EYE INDIAN BLANKETS

Session 30
Third Sunday in Lent:
Why Jerusalem?

The Bible Lesson

Today's lesson (Mark 6:33-44) teaches that sometimes we don't need to sit and wait for God to perform a miracle because he already has: The miracle is within each of us when we reach out and share.

What the Children Will Learn Today

Preparations continue for the play this week, and the workstations emphasize ways to share God's love.

Time Needed

   5 minutes for story
   25 minutes for workstations
   5 minutes for closing service from Lenten Home Worship Program and play

Supplies Needed (by Workstation)

   1. Brown paper and large and small boxes for blocks (small boxes should fit together to form arch) and 12" pipe cleaners and colored beads for fish symbols (any size bead will work as long as it can be threaded on a pipe cleaner)
   2 and 5. Patterns, cloth, craft supply basket, cloth, glue, rubber bands, ribbons, stockings or socks, and sewing supplies
   3. Building supplies for TV camera
   4. Play skit and puppets or props for practice
   6. Salt dough (2 cups flour, 1 cup salt, and 1 cup water), foil-covered cookie sheet, coarse salt, and egg whites
   7. Construction paper supply basket with 2 shades of blue, 2 shades each of purple, pink, yellow, green, and sunrise egg patterns

Children's Meditation

STORY

SHOWING THAT YOU CARE

Mary Ellen hated the hot lunch served at school. Mary Ellen packed a sack lunch instead. Melinda, Mary Ellen's best friend, bought lunch. Mary Ellen liked to tease Melinda. Mary Ellen would hold her nose as if to avoid the smell when Melinda arrived with her tray.

"Will you stop that?" Melinda snapped. "I have to eat this stuff."

"I'm sorry," Mary Ellen giggled.

"Mother says a hot lunch is better for me. I don't have a choice," Melinda groaned. "At least I'm not eating yucky pimento cheese."

Both girls laughed. Mary Ellen and Melinda sat together every day at lunch, and without fail, teased and complained about each other's lunches.

One day as Mary Ellen sat waiting for Melinda, all of the children in the hot lunch line returned to the table empty handed. Melinda included. The principal made an announcement.

"It seems the main kitchen over at the middle school, where the cooks prepare the lunches, caught on fire."

A gasp sounded throughout the cafeteria.

"No one's hurt and the kitchen's not even damaged that badly, but today's lunch was burned to a crisp," the principal reported.

The children shouted, squealed, then grew quiet as the principal raised his hand for silence.

"We ordered pizza but it hasn't arrived yet. The pizza shop has had so many orders that it'll be at least another hour."

"Another hour," someone shouted. "I'm starving."

"I know everyone's hungry. We're doing the best we can. Those who brought their lunch may eat. Those buying a lunch may go outside and play. We'll call you when the pizza arrives."

No one moved. Mary Ellen broke off a piece of her sandwich and passed it to Melinda.

"Thanks, I think," Melinda smiled.

"It's better than nothing," Mary Ellen reminded her.

Jennifer sat at the end of the table. Mary Ellen and Melinda didn't know Jennifer very well. Jennifer was shy and didn't talk much.

Jennifer sat watching Mary Ellen and Melinda eat. Jennifer didn't say anything and she didn't go outside. Actually none of the kids went outside, not even the boys.

Mary Ellen broke off another piece of her sandwich and slid it over to Jennifer.

"It's pimento cheese. It's actually good. My mother makes it. Try some," Mary Ellen said as she slid the sandwich to Jennifer.

"Thanks," Jennifer whispered.

At that moment, the most remarkable thing happened. Those who had brought their lunch started breaking off parts of their sandwiches and sharing with those sitting around them.

Mary Ellen had grapes. She plucked small handfuls of grapes and passed them out to everyone at her table, even the boys.

People were passing food back and forth. Not one child without a bite to eat.

'When the pizzas finally arrived, the students who were buying their lunch returned the favor. By the time lunch was over, everyone was stuffed full.

"You know," Melinda began. "That pimento cheese sandwich wasn't so bad after all."

"It was fabulous," grinned Jennifer.

"Your pizza wasn't bad either," Mary Ellen laughed. "Come on, we'd better go to class."

Mary Ellen and Melinda started down the hall. Jennifer didn't move.

Mary Ellen turned back toward Jennifer. "Aren't you coming? You can walk with us if you like."

Jennifer looked as if she had been given a trophy. She was beaming with pride as she walked down the hallway with Mary Ellen and Melinda.

It seems the girls at Mary Ellen's table did more than simply share their lunch with each other. They shared friendship too.

The three girls remained best of friends through elementary school, middle school, and high school. They still write to each other, call on the phone, and get together when they're home from college.

It all started the day the kitchen caught on fire and lunch was late. When you care enough to share, wonderful things can happen.

Workstations

Workstation 1: Call to Worship

GETTING READY

The number of blocks needed will depend on whether you are presenting the play in your fellowship hall and want a complete wall, or in the sanctuary and only want a gate. You will need at least twenty blocks for the gate. You also need small boxes for the arch. Have beads and pipe cleaners ready for fish.

INSTRUCTION SIGN

King David chose the city of Jerusalem to be the capital of Israel. In King David's time, the city was small. The entire city was surrounded by a stone wall. Before Jesus was born, the city was expanded and the walls rebuilt several times.

Our wall and gate need at least 20 blocks. If each person wraps one block, we will soon have more than enough blocks to build our wall of Jerusalem. When you finish, make the early Christian sign of the fish to hang on our Love Task Tree. You will take your fish home Easter morning. String beads on a pipe cleaner. Count four beads from end. Twist ends together. Shape to make fish. Read Mark 6:33-44. Hang fish on tree for service.

Workstations 2 (Affirmation of Faith) and 5 (Witness to Faith) Combined

GETTING READY

Have the patterns, cloth, and pop bottles. Have children make clothes for puppets from scraps of fabric.

INSTRUCTION SIGN

Many of us get new clothes at Easter. Maybe you buy something new or maybe you just get out spring clothes and put away winter clothes. In the parables, Jesus frequently told people to change how they were living their lives. What change was Jesus asking the people to make in Mark 6:33-44?

Make a puppet for our Easter play. We need 9 puppets for the Easter service. Don't worry if you can't finish today. This station will be set up for several weeks. Sign up to read today.

Girl Puppets Needed: Alexandria (dressed for Easter), Mary, Megan, Jody, and Sally

STEP 1: Cover bottom of bottle with flesh-colored stocking. Pull stocking over bottle. Use more than one stocking if necessary. Decorate facial features with buttons, sequins, or felt eyes and mouth.
STEP 2: Add yarn, fuzzy fabric, or stuffing for hair.
STEP 3: Glue cloth around pop bottle to form clothing. Make sure that the cloth is longer than your bottle so that cloth will cover your hand when you are holding the puppet. Glue in place. Use neck of bottle for handle.
STEP 4: Add arms by rolling fabric. Add flesh-colored hands, a Bible, or gloves. Attach arms at edge of

---

face with a tight rubber band. Tuck top of arm inside top edge of dress. Glue and pin in place till dry. Add biblical headpiece for Mary. Add lace or a ribbon around neck for others. Add hats or other features as desired.

Boy Puppets: Maxwell (dressed for church), Joseph, Jack, and Sam

STEP 5: For boys, make suits and ties and shorter hair. Felt works best for suits. Let cloth hang down over neck of bottle to cover hand. Cover small box for TV camera for puppet.

Workstation 3: Offering or Carpenter Shop

INSTRUCTION SIGN

King Solomon, King David's son, built the first Jewish Temple in Jerusalem on the highest point in the city. Solomon's Temple was very expensive to build and was one of the main reasons the city of Jerusalem continued to be so important in the lives of the people of Israel throughout history. Read Luke 19:45-46. Continue making the TV camera and have it ready for Easter. Sign up to read for service.

Workstation 4: Sermon or Bible Study

GETTING READY

The play is written as a newscast and participants may read or memorize their parts. Schedule rehearsals before Easter.

INSTRUCTION SIGN

As you practice Scene III from the Easter play, remember that the city of Jerusalem survived many years of destruction. Solomon's Temple was completely destroyed. Under Roman rule, King Herod the Great decided to rebuild the Temple as a peace offering to the Jews. Herod built a Temple twice as large as Solomon's. It was to this Temple that Jesus made many journeys during his lifetime. Read John 2:13-17.

Workstation 6: Prayer and Sewing Center

GETTING READY

Mix salt dough.

INSTRUCTION SIGN

Continue practicing Lord's Prayer in sign language today. Also make salt dough pretzels to hang on Love Task Tree as a reminder to pray. Roll dough into long pencil shapes. Then form pretzels. Place on foil-covered pan, brush with egg white, and sprinkle with coarse salt. Bake before hanging on tree. Read Mark 6:33-44. Sign up to lead prayer.

Workstation 7: Benediction

INSTRUCTION SIGN

Before the reign of King David, Jerusalem was often called "Yara-Salem," referring to its beauty at sunrise and dawn. The Jews under David's rule changed the name of the city to "Ieru-shalom" or "City of Peace." Jerusalem became the center of the Jewish faith during the life of Jesus. People would travel for weeks to go to the Temple to worship. Read John 2:13. Create an Easter Sunrise Egg to show that Easter begins at sunrise. Place eggs on worship table for service.

STEP 1: Read Luke 6:37-38. Write verse on back of egg. Cut egg, grass, colors of sunrise, and sun using patterns.

STEP 2: Start with the sky and glue each piece in place: light blue, purple, pink, sun, and grass. Glue only the ends of the sun rays and tuck in behind the sun.

The Worship Celebration

GETTING READY

Children will hang beaded fish and baked pretzels on tree before service.

SIGN-UP SHEET FOR TODAY'S WORSHIP CELEBRATION

Call to Worship (sing a favorite song):
Read from Home Worship Program (light 1st, 2nd, and 3rd candles as Bible verse is read):
Read "Symbol" (from Home Worship Program):
Read Bible verses (Mark 6:30-44):
Lead the Lord's Prayer in sign language:

ITEMS TO GO HOME TODAY: EASTER SUNRISE EGGS

Session 31
Fourth Sunday in Lent:
The Significance of Passover

The Bible Lesson

Love is presented as the answer instead of fighting.

What the Children Will Learn Today

Molding hollow sugar Easter eggs and making the house of love take patience and allow children to help one another.

Time Needed

7 minutes for story to allow for cutting house
20 minutes for workstations
8 minutes forclosing service

Supplies Needed (by Workstation)

Story: Jasmime and Jared's house, paper, and scissors
1. Boxes, brown paper, glue, and clear mailing tape
2. Puppet-making supplies from last week continued
3. TV building supplies
4. Easter play script, puppets, and props to be used
5. Sugar (2 cups of sugar needed for each group of 5 children), water, and plastic mold(s) for eggs (inexpensive hollow sugar egg molds from craft or cake decorating stores)
6. White and green paper, scrap paper, and lily pattern
7. Craft supply basket, pattern, and supplies to decorate house

Children's Meditation

GETTING READY

This is an action story but may be told without house. Practice so you can cut as you tell story. Have scissors and paper ready for children to cut along with the story.

STORY

Jasmine and Jared's House of Love

Jasmine and Jared, like many brothers and sisters, did not always get along. [Fold paper in half, 5 1/2" x 8 1/2".]

One day on the way home from church, Jasmine screeched from the backseat that Jared had his foot pointed toward her side of the car. Jared naturally retorted that there wasn't any other place for his foot to go. The two pushed and shoved, yelled and screamed so loudly that their dad almost drove the car off the road into the ditch. [Cut 2 V-shaped notches from the middle of the fold. See pattern.]

Upon arriving home, both children were promptly sent to their rooms to think about their behavior. Jared slammed the door as he went into his room, knocking down a picture from the wall and breaking the frame. [Cut off a *rounded* corner. It doesn't matter which corner you cut first. You're going to cut four. Remember, you are making an egg-shaped card.]

Jasmine, not to be outdone, slammed her door even harder and not only knocked a picture off the wall but broke the glass. [Cut off another *rounded* corner.]

Both children were given extra chores to do to pay for the broken picture frames. Jared cleaned a space in one corner of the garage large enough to park his bike, and then announced that he was done. Jasmine, who was busy sorting items for the recycling bins, promptly announced that her bike belonged there and pushed her bike right into Jared's. Naturally, the fight was off and going again. [Cut third *rounded* corner.]

Such a ruckus you've never heard. The yelling and screaming could be heard all around the neighborhood. [Cut fourth corner.]

Mother and Father stormed out the door. [Cut a front door.]

Mom, Dad, Jasmine, and Jared sat down to have a talk. Dad said that Jared's and Jasmine's behavior had to change because they were destroying the peace and happiness of the entire household. [Fold top of card over and cut window. See pattern.]

"You must talk about your problems and differences," said Mother, "not look for excuses to blame one another or try to get the other one in trouble."

"You can spend the same amount of energy having fun that you're spending fighting," said Dad.

Mom passed out paper and pencils. "I want each of you to make a list of five things you're sorry for doing. [Hold up first piece cut from window.]

"Then I want both of you to write down five activities you would enjoy doing together. [Hold up other window piece.]

"Now, say you're sorry, and stop fighting." [Fold paper in half and cut half a heart.]

It was hard at first. It took a while, but finally Jared and Jasmine stopped fighting.

Jared cleared a space large enough for both bikes. Jasmine concluded that it didn't really hurt anything for Jared's feet to sort of poke onto her side of the car because she was smaller and didn't need all the space anyway.

Life still isn't perfect. After all, Jared and Jasmine are brother and sister. On those occasional days when Jasmine and Jared get a little grumpy, they sit down and make a list of all the reasons they like each other. The likes always outweigh the problems and fill their home once again with love. [Show house from Workstation 7.]

Workstations

Workstation 1: Call to Worship

GETTING READY

The location of your Easter play will determine the size of gate you want to build. Remember to consider heights of children.

INSTRUCTION SIGN

Jesus, like most other Jews of his time, traveled each year to Jerusalem for Passover. Everyone entered or left Jerusalem through one of the city gates. Read Luke 19:37-38.

Start building the gate for our play today. Assemble arch on the floor where it can be left undisturbed till next week.

STEP 1: Stack and glue boxes. Form 2 columns. Make the base wide at the bottom for support.
STEP 2: Put glue between the blocks and tape the back of the arch together to hold it in place. Leave arch on floor to dry till next week. Sign up to read for worship.

Workstation 2: Affirmation of Faith

INSTRUCTION SIGN

Passover is a celebration of freedom from bondage or slavery in the Jewish religion. A roasted egg is used in the Seder or Passover meal to symbolize new life in the promised land. Read Matthew 26:20-21. Sign up to read for worship service.

Continue working on your puppet.

Workstation 3: Offering or Carpenter Shop

INSTRUCTION SIGN

Camera must be finished by Easter. Think of colors to paint the KTBT camera: White stands for purity, joy, and happiness; yellow reminds us that Easter begins at sunrise, and purple indicates a time of preparation. Read Matthew 27:15-18.

Workstation 4: Sermon or Bible Study

GETTING READY

Schedule extra rehearsals as needed this week.

INSTRUCTION SIGN

"Easter" comes from the ancient Norse word "Eastar," meaning the "growing" or rising sun in the East. Practice Scene IV of the play. Read Mark 15:16-20. Sign up to read for the worship service today.

Workstation 5: Witness to Faith

GETTING READY

Have egg molds and sugar mixture ready.
Hollow sugar Easter eggs are an old English tradition that your children will beg to make every Easter. Mix 2 cups of granulated sugar and *exactly* 4 teaspoons of water together right before you are ready to mold eggs. Mixture makes 5 eggs.

After church, scoop eggs about 2 hours after molding. Schedule a rehearsal to coincide with egg-molding day. Then actors can help scoop out eggs.

Let eggs dry for at least 2 hours. If you try to scoop out eggs too soon, eggs crumble. If eggs sit too long, they harden.

Take a teaspoon and carefully scoop out each egg. The soft scooped-out sugar mixture can be used to mold more eggs. Keep extra sugar mixture in tightly sealed container. Let eggs dry.

INSTRUCTION SIGN

Make a hollow sugar egg. You will take your egg home on Easter morning. A hollow egg reminds us of the resurrection.

STEP 1: Fill and pack each half of the egg mold with the prepared sugar mixture. Pack tightly.

STEP 2: Place a plate or piece of heavy cardboard over the molds and flip egg upside down as you would flip a cake out of a cake pan. Gently lift molds. If your egg cracks, remold. Set aside to dry for 2 hours. Read 1 Corinthians 13:4-7.

Workstation 6: Prayer and Sewing Center

GETTING READY

Have patterns available.

INSTRUCTION SIGN

In biblical times, purple dye was made from shellfish. Each fish supplied only a small speck of coloring. The color purple was expensive to make and was mostly used to make cloth for the wealthy. The soldiers used a purple robe to mock and make fun of Jesus after the trial. Read Mark 15:16-17. We use purple in church to remind us to be humble. Continue practicing the Lord's Prayer. Be ready for the service. Trace pattern and cut pieces for Easter lilies. We'll put them together next week.

Workstation 7: Benediction

GETTING READY

The egg house used in today's story may be brought to this station and decorated or children may trace pattern. Have stickers show through open window. (You might place a picture of child inside to share with Mom and Dad on Easter morning.)

43

INSTRUCTION SIGN

The first Easter basket was shaped to resemble a bird's nest. As time passed, the grass birds' nests were replaced by woven baskets filled with straw and eggs on Easter. Today, we fill baskets with artificial grass and eggs of every color.

Decorate Jasmine and Jared's egg-shaped house from the meditation today. If you did not cut a house as the story was told, simply trace the pattern provided. Copy the following sentences onto your house and fill in the blanks:

1. I will show I care for others by_____.
2. I have _____ that I can share with others.
3. I will do _____ during Lent to share God's love.

Take Jasmine and Jared's house home with you as a reminder to share love in your house this week.

The Worship Celebration

SIGN-UP SHEET FOR TODAY'S WORSHIP CELEBRATION

Call to Worship (sing a favorite song):
Read from Home Worship Program (light 1st, 2nd, 3rd, and 4th candles during reading):
Read "Symbol" from Home Worship Program:
Bible reader (Matthew 26:20-21; 27:15-18; Mark 15:16-20; and 1 Corinthians 13:4-7)
Lead the Lord's Prayer in sign language:

ITEMS TO GO HOME TODAY: JASMINE AND JARED'S HOUSES

Session 32
Fifth Sunday in Lent:
The Story of the Last Supper

The Bible Lesson

John 13:34-35 teaches the commandment from the Last Supper.

What the Children Will Learn Today

Workstations teach about Maundy Thursday.

Time Needed

5 minutes for story
25 minutes for workstations
5 minutes for closing service from Lenten Home Worship Program

Supplies Needed (by Workstation)

1. Brown paper blocks for gate
2. Tissue paper, glue, and hollow plastic take-apart eggs
3. Painting supplies for TV (tempera is suggested)
4. Easter play, puppets, and props needed
5. Royal icing (4 cups powdered sugar, 3 egg whites, and 1/2 teaspoon cream of tartar), butterfly pattern, pipe cleaners, and sugar eggs from last week
6. Green and brown paper, tubes for trees, and patterns
7. Construction paper, craft supply basket and small egg pattern

Children's Meditation

STORY

This Is God's World

Everywhere you look, God has created a beautiful world for us to enjoy and take care of. In the woods, trees are growing, changing, and some even dying to make room for others. It takes about one hundred years for a forest to grow and replace itself. If you didn't mow the grass for a couple of months in your backyard, tall grass and weeds would move in. If you continued not to mow, low bushes, berries, and seedlings would take over.

In about five years, quick-growing pines and tiny sweet gum and maple seedlings would sprout up. These "pioneer trees" are the first trees to reclaim the land. Birds and small animals return. Where once your backyard was home only to insects and your family, in ten short years, your backyard would be covered in trees and provide shelter for birds, rabbits, and even skunks.

If you left your backyard untouched for about twenty years, your backyard would transform itself from a neatly mowed, manicured lawn to a tall pine forest. In fifteen more years, if no one bothered the trees in your backyard, maple and sweet gum trees would replace the pines. The pines would die.

Hardwoods such as oaks and elms would take root. By your fiftieth birthday, the old sweet gum trees would begin to die to make room for the new young elm trees.

As year after year went by, the forest would become thicker and thicker with hardwood trees. Where once, some one hundred years ago, your backyard was green, grassy, and filled with a sandbox and swing, there would now be a forest filled with mountain lions, wolves, deer, squirrels, chipmunks, and opossums.

Just as God has a special job, time, and place for every tree, God has a job for you and me. God has given each of us a talent. It may be ours and ours alone or shared with many.

Use the talents you've been given to the best of your ability. Regardless of whether you're the grass in the backyard, a pine tree, a maple or a sweet gum, or a mighty oak or elm, each of us has an important job to do in God's world.

Workstations

Workstation 1: Call to Worship

GETTING READY

Finish blocks for the gate. Do not attach the arch to the columns until right before the play. Then tape the arch to the back of the columns with clear mailing tape so that you can disassemble the gate for moving and storage afterward. You will use the gate again during the summer for the biblical village.

INSTRUCTION SIGN

When Jews came to Jerusalem for Passover, the city was so crowded that travelers would stay in nearby towns. Jesus and his disciples stayed in Bethany at night and then traveled to Jerusalem during the day. Finish work on the gate. Read Matthew 26:36-41. Sign up to read for service.

Workstation 2: Affirmation of Faith

GETTING READY

This is a fun but messy project. Have cover-ups. Use regular plastic take-apart eggs for molds. Use scraps of leftover tissue paper. Cover hardened egg with tiny circles, glitter, sequins, paint, or papier-mâché into special shapes.

INSTRUCTION SIGN

The practice of giving eggs as presents started in Egypt, Persia, Greece, and in Rome during the spring festivals. An old Latin proverb says that "all life comes from an egg." Early Christian missionaries added color to eggs and transformed the egg into a symbol for the resurrection. In Germany, it is the custom to blow out eggs and hang them on a tree branch. Make a tissue-paper egg to decorate and give as a present or hang on our tree.

STEP 1: Place a strip of construction paper inside a plastic egg. Make sure ends of paper stick out for handle.

STEP 2: Squash tissue paper into egg mold. Add glue. More tissue. More glue. Add glue each time you add paper and squash paper tightly. Small pieces of tissue paper work better than big wads of paper. Make a top and bottom for your egg.

STEP 3: Before paper has a chance to dry, lift egg out of plastic mold by scrap paper handle from Step 1. This paper may be taken off or glued down once egg has been lifted out of mold.

STEP 4: Glue two halves of egg together. Let dry.

Workstation 3: Offering or Carpenter Shop

GETTING READY

Have tempera paint, cover-ups, and brushes ready for TV.

INSTRUCTION SIGN

The biblical account of Jesus washing the feet of the disciples has led to the tradition of helping the poor, homeless, and hungry on Maundy Thursday. Read John 13:4-5.

In England, gifts are sometimes given according to your age. If you are 10, you must give 10 gifts. If you are 50, you must give 50 gifts of food, clothing, or money. Your gift today is to paint TV neatly or decorate with paper. Remember to share.

Workstation 4: Sermon or Bible Study

INSTRUCTION SIGN

Maundy Thursday was first celebrated in fourth-century Jerusalem. The day is also referred to as Holy Thursday. The Passover meal was one of the preparatory steps for the Jews in celebrating Passover on the Sabbath. Read Mark 14:12-16.

A Maundy Thursday service today usually includes holy Communion. Continue practicing today so that we are ready to present our play on Easter morning. Sign up to read for service.

Workstation 5: Witness to Faith

GETTING READY

Use royal icing. Mix right before using. Recipe: 3 egg whites, 4 cups confectioners' sugar, ½ teaspoon cream of tartar. Beat with mixer at highest speed for 10 minutes. Divide into small bowls, add food colors desired, and place in cake-decorating bags. Decorating bags are inexpensive and available at cake decorating or grocery stores. Have butterfly pattern and an example for children to see.

INSTRUCTION SIGN

The word "Maundy" comes from a Latin word meaning "commandment." Maundy Thursday services often trace the events of the Last Supper, prayer in the Garden of Gethsemane, and the arrest of Jesus. Read Matthew 22:34-40.

Decorate the inside of your sugar egg today. Take turns and share with your neighbor. Make 3 designs on your egg, then pass the decorating bag to the next person.

While you wait, use pattern and make a paper butterfly. Color the butterfly with bright colors or decorate with sequins and glitter. Glue butterfly to pipe cleaner. Add butterfly to inside of egg before icing dries. Decorate just the inside of each egg half today. Do not touch icing until it is completely hard and dry next week. Sign up to read for worship today.

Workstation 6: Prayer and Sewing Center

GETTING READY

Have patterns and an example of a finished palm leaf.

INSTRUCTION SIGN

The date palm was a popular tree for its fruit and its leaves. The leaves were used as a symbol of victory. Read Matthew 8:8-11. Make 15 palm leaves for trees needed for play.

STEP 1: Cut leaves using pattern. Follow pattern carefully and cut slashes for leaves in the direction indicated. Smaller slashes look best for leaves. Cut carefully because we want our leaves to look as nice as possible.

STEP 2: Use glue instead of tape to put leaves together.

Be ready to lead the Lord's Prayer for our service today.

Workstation 7: Benediction

INSTRUCTION SIGN

Egg rolling, such as the event on the White House lawn each year, is symbolic of rolling the stone away from the tomb. Read Mark 16:1-4. Use pattern. Make egg that will turn and spin.

Cut 9 paper eggs from different colors of paper.

You may match and coordinate colors. Use scrap paper. Fold each egg in half down the center. Staple eggs together in center. Glue string between folds. Open folds of egg so that they stand out and show the different colors. Sign up to read.

The Worship Celebration

SIGN-UP SHEET FOR TODAY'S WORSHIP CELEBRATION

Call to Worship (sing a favorite song):

Read from Home Worship Program (light 1st, 2nd, 3rd, 4th, and 5th candles as Bible verse is read):

Read "Symbol" (from Home Worship Program):

Read Bible verses (John 13:34-35):

Lead the Lord's Prayer in sign language:

ITEMS TO GO HOME TODAY: SPIRAL EGGS

Session 33
Sixth Sunday in Lent:
A Visit to Old Jerusalem on
Palm Sunday

The Bible Lesson

The meaning of humbleness (Matthew 5:5)

What the Children Will Learn Today

Easter traditions and celebrations around the world

Time Needed

5 minutes for story
20 minutes for workstations
10 minutes for closing service

Supplies Needed (by Workstation)

1. White, yellow, and green paper, green and yellow chalk, green pipe cleaners, white tissue paper, lilies from Session 31
2. Cloth, felt, vinyl, netting, or scrap material. String, old shoelaces, plastic lacing, or heavy thread for drawstring, and craft supply basket with glitter, sequins, or paper circles
3. Buttons and lids for TV camera knobs and dials
4. Easter play
5. Royal icing and decorating supplies for sugar eggs
6.Leftover sturdy cardboard tubes from carpeting or vinyl flooring to make trees, green and brown construction paper
7. Construction paper supply basket

Children's Meditation

STORY

The Old Man and His Donkey

In a small farming community lived a man who was bent and stooped from years of heavy farm labor. He had worked since his youth to grow wheat to make bread, but now most of his fields lay empty because he was too old to plow and plant crops anymore. Everything was changing, too. In the city of Noah, most of the farmers now used large tractors. Unlike the big farms, the old farmer only had a little old donkey.

No one paid much attention to the old farmer except to honk their car horn and say, "Get out of the way, old man."

One day a man drove up to the farm in a big, long, fancy car. The salesman gave the old farmer a check for five million dollars and told the old farmer that he was rich and could go wherever he wished. The old man's farm was to become a fancy new shopping mall, the first in the city of Noah.

The old farmer sat on his front porch rocking back and forth in his rocking chair, staring at the check. What would he do? Where would he go?

The next day the old farmer loaded his possessions in two cloth bags, slung them across the donkey's back, and headed for town. Everyone in town had heard about the salesman and the new shopping mall. As the old farmer got close to town, people came running out to greet him.

A crowd of people now swarmed about the old farmer as he plodded on with his head bent down and his hand steadily tugging the donkey along. The town's people talked excitedly. Some offered the old man a new coat, others a new hat. Some of the younger men offered to carry the old farmer high up on their shoulders in victory and triumph.

The old farmer stopped, looked around at all of the people, and slowly climbed up on his little old donkey's back and rode on into town. The town's people looked confused but followed, shouting for joy and eagerly offering to sell the old farmer this or that.

The old farmer stopped in front of the bank, tied his donkey to the parking meter, and went inside. The old farmer handed the banker the check and sat down in a soft cushy chair. "I want to build a house," said the old farmer. "I want to build a big house."

"You can build the biggest, fanciest house in all of Noah with a check like this," the banker replied.

"It doesn't have to be fancy," said the old farmer. "All I ask for is a warm, dry room for myself and a little barn out back for my donkey. The rest of the house is to be filled with the homeless who don't have a place to live, the hungry who need a hot meal, abandoned children who are lost and confused, angry souls who need a chance to start over, babies who are sick and have no one to care for them, and anyone else who is searching and in need. Do I have enough money to build such a house?"

"Well, yes," the banker said slowly, and then went on in a puzzled sort of voice to say, "But why? You could have anything you want."

The old farmer sat quietly for a moment, then slowly rose to his full five-foot height. "Because we need one," he replied and slowly walked toward the door.

A few months later, the house sat high on a hill at the edge of town. There's a barn where the children go to pet and ride the old donkey. And a room is always kept ready and waiting for anyone and everyone in need. The sign above the door reads:
The Old Farmer's House
Everyone Welcome Don't Bother to Knock, Just Come on In

Workstations

Workstation 1: Call to Worship

GETTING READY

Make a simple wooden cross on a stand or use a cross from a Sunday school classroom. Cover the cross with flowers for the Easter play.

Put purple egg dye or food coloring into small bowls for children to dye the carnation-type tissue-paper flowers.

INSTRUCTION SIGN

The triumphant entry of Jesus to Jerusalem was not celebrated by early Christians until the fourth century. We celebrate today and remember his message of humbleness.

Work together in Christian fellowship today. Read Romans 12:16. Then make a tissue flower to dip in egg dye or make an Easter lily to decorate our cross for Easter.

Work together in peace and harmony. Help your neighbor.

Tissue Flower:
STEP 1: Cut twelve 4" x 4" squares of white tissue paper. Fold as you would to make a fan. Twist green pipe cleaner around middle. Open sheets of paper and separate to make flower fluffy.
STEP 2: Dip the tissue-paper flowers in the prepared egg dye. Wear a cover-up to protect your clothes. We need 12 tissue flowers to cover our cross for the play. While the tissue flowers are drying, make Easter lilies for the cross. Purple reminds us to be humble. White reminds us of the joy and happiness of Easter.

Easter Lily:
STEP 1: Use lilies already cut or make more using patterns.
STEP 2: Glue Easter lilies together on tab. Attach pipe cleaner for stem. Add green and yellow paper centers and leaves.
STEP 3: Curl ends of Easter lily with a pencil. Take cross to worship. Once cross is finished, make an Easter lily on a paper stem to take home as a reminder to get ready for Easter.

Workstation 2: Affirmation of Faith

GETTING READY

Use scraps of netting, vinyl, felt, or other cloth scraps.

INSTRUCTION SIGN

On Monday we celebrate the return of Jesus and his disciples to Jerusalem and remember his reaction to the money changers in the temple. Read Matthew 21:13 and remember that the money changers were cheating the poor by overcharging the people and keeping the profits.

STEP 1: Use pattern. Cut a circle for a cloth money pouch.

STEP 2: If your fabric has holes or a large weave, use shoelace or vinyl lacing for drawstring. Sew in and out through fabric. Gather up fabric. If the fabric does not have holes or a large weave, use thread.

STEP 3: Make paper coins for bag. Place on worship table.

Workstation 3: Offering or Carpenter Shop

INSTRUCTION SIGN

In Greece and Romania, Easter eggs are colored red to express the joy of Easter. When friends see each other on Easter Sunday, they knock two red eggs together. One person says, "Christ is risen." The other responds, "Truly, he is risen." We won't be knocking any eggs together, but make sure the TV camera is finished. Add dials. Read Galatians 5:23.

Workstation 4: Sermon or Bible Study

GETTING READY

Announce final rehearsal schedule this week.

INSTRUCTION SIGN

Many cities and even small towns around the world present plays about the life of Jesus for Easter. In Oklahoma, a small town named "Holy City" performs a six-hour outdoor passion play each year surrounded by the beauty of the Wichita Mountains. The play, the "Oklahoma Oberammergau," begins at midnight and ends at sunrise Easter morning. The little town of Oberammergau, Germany, in the Bavarian Alps is the setting of the original Oberammergau Passion Play. The play started in 1634 after a terrible plague the year before. It is performed every 10 years and tells the story of the last week of Jesus' life. Thanks for working hard on our play each week. Special rehearsal times will be announced today. Read James 4:6. Sign up to read for worship today.

Workstation 5: Witness to Faith

GETTING READY

Have royal icing and decorating tubes ready.

INSTRUCTION SIGN

In Bethlehem, Pennsylvania, the Moravians have a tradition of getting up early on Easter morning. Trombones are played at 3:00 A.M. to announce the resurrection. An outdoor sunrise service follows. A Moravian sugar cake breakfast at the church is served after the service. Read Matthew 5:5.

Finish your sunrise hollow sugar egg today. Use icing to draw a sunrise on top of egg and decorations around the edges.

Workstation 6: Prayer and Sewing Center

GETTING READY

Find or make tall cardboard columns for palm trees. Carpet stores have leftover cardboard tubes and are often happy to donate. Make tree stands and tree trunks before session. Make two tree stands by nailing 2" x 4" scraps to sturdy 2" x 8" boards that are approximately 14" long. Your carpet or flooring tube should fit right over the 2" x 4" post. Make any adjustment needed for a secure fit. Glue tree in place.

INSTRUCTION SIGN

Today, on Palm Sunday, we celebrate the return of Jesus to Jerusalem. The people gathered to welcome Jesus with shouts of "Hosanna!" and laid palm branches on the ground as they would for a king. Read Mark 11:7-10. Finish palm tree(s) for play.

STEP 1: Make sure you have at least 15 complete palm branches for each tree. The more branches the better.

STEP 2: Make the bark for our palm tree. Fringe one side of an 8 ½" x 11" brown piece of construction paper. Fringe enough brown sheets of paper to cover the cardboard tube for the trunk of the tree. Cut fringe only to middle of paper. A thin fringe looks best. Then glue paper onto cardboard tube, starting at the top. Overlap. Make sure cardboard does not show.

STEP 3: Glue leaves to top of tube. Be ready to lead the Lord's Prayer in sign language for Easter.

Workstation 7: Benediction

INSTRUCTION SIGN

In Italy, families may dye as many as 200 eggs to exchange because everyone they see on Easter Sunday is given an egg as a symbol of the resurrection. The Ukrainians wax and dye beautiful Easter eggs. Their designs are very elaborate. Each egg takes many hours to make and conveys a message. Read 1 Peter 5:6.

STEP 1: Use pattern and cut 2 paper eggs. Draw and color a design.

STEP 2: Stuff wads of leftover tissue paper or polyester stuffing inside. Glue edges of egg together.

The Worship Celebration

GETTING READY

Today's service comes from Mark 11:1-10, Jesus' triumphant entry into Jerusalem. If children have palms, they may wave them gently as Bible story is read during lighting of the candles.

SIGN-UP SHEET FOR TODAY'S WORSHIP CELEBRATION

Read Sunday statements from Home Worship Program:
  1st candle—reader:
  2nd candle—reader:
  3rd candle—reader:
  4th candle—reader:
  5th candle—reader:
  6th candle—reader:
  Read "Symbol" from Home Worship Program:
  Lead the Lord's Prayer in sign language:

ITEMS TO GO HOME TODAY: PAPER-STUFFED EGGS

Session 34
Easter Sunday:
A Celebration of Love

The Bible Lesson

The play teaches about the meaning of Easter (Matthew 28:19-20). The theme throughout the play is that Easter is a celebration of love (Galatians 5:22-23).

What the Children Will Learn Today

The service is a make-believe TV show. It is easy to incorporate scripts into the play because TV reporters often read from scripts; therefore, children who may not be experienced in drama or with memorizing lines may still participate.

Time Needed

The service is written to be one hour long. You may adjust the length by merely removing one of the reporters or leaving out a song or two.

Sets and Staging

The Easter service may be staged as a chancel drama in your sanctuary with no sets or minimal sets such as the trees and gate of Jerusalem. Lecterns and the pulpit may be used as puppet stages for children to hide behind.

The play is also appropriate for a fellowship hall. Create a biblical village. Use puppet stage from volume 1. Have a TV studio. Pictures can be drawn on large pieces of paper or cloth. Room divider screens could be carried on and off stage to change the setting.

If your church has a stage area, the curtain opening and closing gives you a wonderful way to travel back and forth to biblical times. If not, you may create the scene changes by dimming and brightening the lights. Many sanctuaries have dimmer switches. Be creative. Use what you have.

Props

Many of the props are items made during previous sessions.

1. microphones (use real mikes for sound system) and TV camera (made during Lent) or use a video camera
2. puppet stage from volume 1 and puppets (see cast list)
3. desk with KTBT studio sign (You may also use a lectern if you are in the sanctuary.)
4. block wall, well, and gate of Jerusalem (Lent)
5. tree(s) (built during Lent)
6. sleeping mats (from Christmas play in volume 1)
7. bread dough and bread board (recipe from Thanksgiving)
8. weaving loom (from Session 7 in volume 1)
9. biblical house (Cover cardboard boxes for clay bricks and build a house.)
10. play clay for pottery
11. fishing net and bread to eat
12. papier-mâché clay hand lamp (Session 13, volume 1)
13. travel bag for traveler (Session 3, volume 1)
14. clay water jars
15. wooden cross (build from wood scraps)
16. palm leaves or make paper leaves
17. paper TV camera for puppet show
18. Easter hat for Alexandria to wear
19. heavy winter coat, gloves, boots, and such for Lacy
20. papier-mâché dinner bowl and cups (Session 13, volume 1)

Costumes

Everyone will wear Easter Sunday clothes, except for those in biblical scenes: Lindsey, Rachel, traveler, weaver, head of household, village merchant, pottery maker, bread maker, and fisherman (see biblical costumes from Christmas play, volume 1).

Weekly Workstations

Each week during Lent the sermon workstation will practice part of the play. It works best if you have one adult who will take charge of the sermon workstation each week and the Easter service as well. This adult will be in charge of assigning parts, leading rehearsals, and directing the play.

Practicing the play one section at a time makes it easier to manage a large cast and allow individual time with each part of the play. Schedule at least two complete rehearsals.

The Worship Celebration

If your church presents the play at a time other than on Easter morning, videotape and replay the service for the children.

Children's Easter Service

KTBT's Easter Morning Celebration
(A TV Studio Play About
the Meaning of Easter)

Adjust parts to fit number of participants. Many parts may be combined. Entire play can be done with only 10 children.

SPEAKING PARTS FOR ACTORS

TV studio crew:
    KTBT announcer, Christopher Michaels (major speaking role):
        Camera operator (small speaking part):
        Director (small speaking part):
        Offstage KTBT voice (small speaking part):

TV reporters:
    Lindsey Warren (major speaking role):
    Rachel Horton (major speaking role):
    Lacy Simmons (medium speaking part):
    Casey Lewis (medium speaking part):
    Sam Goodman (medium speaking part):

Costumed biblical actors:
    Merchant (small memorized speaking part):

Traveler, Rebecca (memorized lines):
    Head of the household, Joseph (memorized lines):

SPEAKING PARTS THAT REQUIRE NO ACTING

(All speakers for puppets read but are not seen by audience.)

Speakers for puppets:
    Maxwell (medium reading part):
    Alexandria (has a singing part too):
    Megan (small reading part):
    Jack (small reading part):
    Jody (small reading part):
    Sam (small reading part):
    Salley (small reading part):
    Mom (small reading part):
    Dad (small reading part):

ACTING PARTS THAT REQUIRE NO SPEAKING

(People of village in biblical costume)
    Person 1: weaving
    Person 2: pottery
    Person 3: bread
    Person 4: marketplace
    Person 5: fishing boat

PUPPETEERS WITH NONSPEAKING PARTS

    Alexandria:
    Megan:
    Jody:
    Sally:
    Maxwell:
    Jack:
    Sam:

SCRIPT

(*Note:* Play is divided into scenes to organize workable sections to use each week for rehearsals.)

KTBT's Easter Morning Celebration

Prelude
[Music by children on the piano, violin, cello, flute, or other instruments that they have learned to play.]

SCENE I
(This portion of service is practiced during 1st week of Lent.)

Call to Worship

DIRECTOR:	Places everyone. We're on in five minutes. [Chris and choir get into place.] Choir on stage. Chris, straighten your tie. Choir, you're first on the program. We lead in with a song and then we'll cut to Chris. Six seconds . . . three, two, one . . . you're on the air . . .
OFFSTAGE KTBT VOICE:	Good morning and welcome to KTBT's Easter Morning Celebration with your host Christopher Michaels.

[Special music for Call to Worship]

SPEAKER FOR ALEXANDRIA:	[Sings along with closing lines of choir's song]
SPEAKER FOR MAXWELL:	What's all the noise out here?
ALEXANDRIA:	[big sigh] Oh! I just love Easter with all the fancy hats and wonderful songs to sing. And what do you mean, "noise"? I was singing. KTBT just so happens to have a special Easter program this morning, and I was singing along.
MAXWELL:	Sorrrrry!
ALEXANDRIA:	For your information, Christopher Michaels is about to come on with a really neat Time Travel Report.
MAXWELL:	Time Travel?
ALEXANDRIA:	You know, when they travel back to biblical times to explain about something that happened in the Bible a long time ago. Shhhhhh! It's starting.

[Camera operator moves into place. Puppets disappear behind puppet stage as Chris begins to talk.]

KTBT ANNOUNCER, CHRISTOPHER MICHAELS:	Good morning on this beautiful Easter morning. Did you know that every Sunday is a day of celebration? Every Sunday we get together here at church to celebrate God's love. Today is extra special, though, because today it's Easter, and we have a fantastic show just for *you* today. Our studio here at the Key to Bible Times network is pleased to travel back in time with Lindsey and Rachel, our dynamic time-traveling duo. We'll have special reports on what's happening this morning in your neighborhood and around the country. So fasten your seat belts. We are off to Jerusalem. [Curtain opens or lights go up. Lindsey and Rachel appear in biblical costumes.]
LINDSEY:	Good morning, this is Lindsey Warren.

RACHEL: And Rachel Horton reporting live from Jerusalem in the year a.d. 6 on the eve of the Feast of Passover. Can you imagine walking for five straight days to get here?

LINDSEY: My feet hurt walking around the mall.

RACHEL: Lucky for you, we didn't have to walk.

SCENE II

(This part of the play is practiced 2nd week of lent. Actors in the village scene may need extra practice.)

LINDSEY: It's dawn and things are beginning to happen around here. [Curtain opens or return lights. Actors start coming through the door of the house and from offstage saying "Peace be with you" when they pass.]

      [Person 1] comes out door of house stretching and yawning as they wake up. Shakes off sleeping mat, sits down on mat, and begins to weave in front of the house.

      [Person 2] picks up water jar, goes to the well, pretends to fill jar and then takes it over to potter's stand. Potters go to work making clay bowls.

      [Person 3] also goes to the well to get water but then goes over with a friend to make bread under the shade of a tree.

      [Person 4] goes and sets up a table in the marketplace for selling oil lamps.

      [Person 5] fisherman sits to mend fishing net.

      [Travelers start walking in from back of room. Travelers continue walking toward gate.]

RACHEL: Look, Lindsey, I see some weary travelers coming down the road toward the gate. [Reporters pause to wait for travelers.]

TRAVELER: Jerusalem! Let us go to the house of the Lord. [Spoken loudly from back of room]

      [Rachel and Lindsey step forward and talk into microphones as if reporting back to Chris at studio.]

LINDSEY: Chris, we'll see if we can get an on-the-spot interview as they get closer to our location.

RACHEL: [Talk as travelers arrive at gate.] Excuse me! I'm Rachel Horton from KTBT News. Are you here for the festival?

TRAVELER,
REBECCA: [Standing outside gate] Yes, we come every year to celebrate Passover with my cousin and her family. Jerusalem and even nearby Bethany are filled with people who have made the journey. Come in peace and join us.

LINDSEY: Thank you, we will.

      [Travelers go through gate. Lindsey and Rachel step forward alone as if talking to Chris at studio.]

LINDSEY: Chris, we're back to you for a quick station break, while we make our way into Jerusalem. [Lindsey and Rachel turn and walk through the gate as curtain closes or lights dim.]

CHRIS: Thank you, Lindsey and Rachel. [Have piano music playing in the background.] We'll be right back after this message from our sponsors. [Continue quiet music in background. Focus switches to puppet stage as stage goes dark or curtain closes.]

ALEXANDRIA: Wow, is this exciting! It's even better than I thought it was going to be. I wish I could be a time-traveling reporter like Lindsey and Rachel. I can hardly believe my eyes.

MAXWELL: It's not so great. All they've talked about is walking back and forth so far.

ALEXANDRIA: Give 'em time Maxwell.

DIRECTOR: [Spoken loudly from side stage and studio] You're on the air, Chris.

CHRIS: And we're back.

MAXWELL: Shhhhhhh! You'll miss your program.

      [Puppets disappear behind puppet stage. Attention returns to TV studio, and then stage for time report.]

SCENE III

(This part of the service is practiced the 3rd week.)

CHRIS: Lindsey and Rachel have been invited to join the travelers entering the gate of Jerusalem. Let's return to our live report from inside the city. [Lindsey and Rachel reappear.]

RACHEL: Thank you, Chris. We have stopped here in a cluster of small one-room houses at the edge of the city.

LINDSEY: The houses are built close together, and the streets are very narrow. Many of the merchants are already out selling the items they've made this morning.

MERCHANT: Hand lamps! Clay hand Lamps! Wick and olive oil. Hand lamps! [Walks across stage calling out as he walks]

[You may either construct a house or just have actors point offstage in the distance as if looking at a house. Cousin comes out of house or off stage area to greet travelers. Cousin does traditional greeting: (1) place right hand on traveler's left shoulder and bow your head over the traveler's right shoulder, (2) then, place left hand on the traveler's right shoulder and bow head over left shoulder and say, "Peace be with you" each time. Traveler answers, "Peace be with you."]

LINDSEY: As we look around, the family has already been busy grinding grain to make today's bread.

RACHEL: Most of the people's houses are one room with a raised platform on one end for the family to eat and sleep. The sheep and goats occupy the lower level of the house.

LINDSEY: Do you mean they sleep in the house with their sheep?

RACHEL: Well, you have a cat that sleeps all over your bed.

LINDSEY: That's different.

RACHEL: Maybe you can sleep up on the roof. I heard someone say that if the weather is nice tonight, we might all take our mats up on the roof to sleep.

LINDSEY: This? You expect me to sleep on this? [Picks up mat and shakes it]

RACHEL: Shhhhh! Someone will hear you.

DIRECTOR: Chris, get ready for a station break.
[Focus switches back to TV studio.]

CHRIS: Lindsey, Rachel, we are going to pause for a moment for a word from our sponsors. Then we'll be back to conclude your report from Jerusalem. [Close curtain or dim lights.]

CAMERA
OPERATOR: We're clear. [Have piano play softly.]
[Puppets return. Stage goes dark or curtain closes.]

ALEXANDRIA: Can you imagine what it must have been like for Jesus to grow up in a house like that?

MAXWELL: I'd demand my own room.

ALEXANDRIA: Your own room? There weren't any rooms. Everybody lived in one small room together.

MAXWELL: No running water? No beds? No refrigerator? No electricity for your TV show?

SCENE IV

(This part of the script is practiced the 4th week.)

DIRECTOR: [Spoken from offstage and TV studio] Places . . . people . . . three . . . two . . . one. [Puppets disappear.]

CHRIS: As we return, we join Rachel and Lindsey sharing dinner with a family. Everyone sits around a large bowl of vegetable stew. Meat was only served on special holidays. Everyone dips their bread into the stew as a sort of spoon. Let's return now and see how Lindsey and Rachel like the goat's milk that is often served with dinner. [Curtain opens or lights are brought up with everyone pretending to wash hands and feet. Everyone is seated in a circle around the bowl. Everyone faces the audience. Begin with Hebrew grace.]

HEAD OF
THE HOUSE-
HOLD, JOSEPH: Blessed are you, O Lord God of the universe, who brings bread out of the earth. [Everyone repeats verse.]

RACHEL: [Pretend to eat so you'll still be able to talk.] This is very different but good.

LINDSEY: No, thank you, I don't care for any goat's milk. I'll just eat some bread.

EVERYONE: [Everyone repeats blessing.] Blessed are you, O Lord God of the universe, who brings bread out of the earth.

JOSEPH: Tomorrow, we will take you to the market area outside the Temple.

RACHEL: Then what?

JOSEPH: Since it is the day before Passover, the entire house must be cleaned and readied for the "Mitzva." Passover is a celebration of freedom. It reminds us that our people have not always been free. We were once held as slaves in Egypt. Passover celebrates their release to freedom. It is a very special day. There will be much to do, we must all sleep.

[Everyone prepares to go to sleep. Lindsey and Rachel rise and walk forward as they talk to Chris. Lindsey picks up her mat and stands staring at it.]

RACHEL: We'll be here to report on the festival tomorrow.

LINDSEY: [Stands holding and staring at mat] I'm not so sure about this, Chris, but I suppose it's good night from Jerusalem. [Curtain closes or lights dim.]

CHRIS: And good night to both of you in Jerusalem. The second half of our program today focuses on what is happening around town. Finish your breakfast and get dressed and ready for church while we tell you what is going on around town this beautiful Easter morning.
[Puppets appear at puppet stage.]

MAXWELL: Speaking of getting dressed, you'd better stop watching TV and get dressed before Mom and Dad come downstairs.

ALEXANDRIA: For your information, I am ready. See, I have my hat, my Bible for Sunday school, and unlike you, I even know where my shoes are.

SCENE V

(This part of the script is practiced on the 5th week.)

[Focus returns to TV studio.]

DIRECTOR: Camera one, give me a close-up on Chris.
[Puppets disappear as Chris begins to talk.]

CHRIS: We turn next to our on-the-spot reporter, Lacy Simmons in Chicago. Good morning, Lacy. How is the weather this morning in Chicago?

LACY
SIMMONS,
ON-THE-SPOT-
REPORTER IN
CHICAGO: [Reporter appears on stage in heavy winter coat and boots] The weather is awful here in Chicago this morning, Chris. We are caught in the middle of an unexpected ice storm. But somehow, people are still managing to make their way. The youth group has been working hard for weeks preparing a play for this morning's sunrise service. It's still dark outside, and according to the schedule, the play will end right at sunrise. [Workers walk behind reporter carrying wooden cross. Place wooden cross where it can be easily seen. Costumer tries costumes on an actor. One is too short. The other too long. Finally one fits as reporter continues to talk. Director comes out shuffling papers. Throws hands up in frustration.]

LACY: As you can see here backstage, last-minute props and costumes are still being put in place.
The play is very dramatic and based upon Jesus' trial before the council as told in the book of Matthew.

CHRIS: Sounds great Lacy. We'll return to Chicago as the play gets started. Stay warm.
LACY: I'll try, Chris.

AFFIRMATION OF FAITH

[Puppets break in.]
ALEXANDRIA: An ice storm for Easter!
MAXWELL: Sure, you could hide Easter eggs in the snow and behind the icicles.
ALEXANDRIA: I want flowers for Easter. I want sunshine. I want all of the wonderful signs of spring that make me feel warm and happy
MAXWELL: Are you saying that if it's not a beautiful spring day, we have to cancel Easter?
ALEXANDRIA: No, of course not! It's not flowers, my new hat, or even getting to wear my new spring dress that makes today Easter. It would still be Easter even if we were having a blizzard outside. Easter is a feeling.
MAXWELL: [Spoken very sarcastically] E a s t e r! is that warm, loving feeling you get . . .
ALEXANDRIA: Oh, stop it; you know what I mean. Easter is a time to start over. The flowers, the trees, everything just seems to get started again at Easter.
                We can start over too. If you have been mean, rude, or even sassy, then Easter is a time to go and say you're sorry.
MAXWELL: Save the lecture. You're missing your program. Shhhhhhh!

[Puppets disappear after Chris begins to speak.]

WITNESS TO FAITH

CHRIS: Our next on-the-spot report comes from Casey Lewis, who is standing by at an outdoor passion play that reenacts the last week of the life of Jesus. Did you tell me earlier, Casey, that this play is performed every year?
                [Children are being lined up with palms as reporter talks. Children practice waving palms standing in line.]
CASEY: That's right, Chris, and the play is very well attended. Everyone is gathering on a hill here overlooking the set below. Just as the pink and purple hues of dawn begin to show in the sky behind the set, white doves are released as a sign of the resurrection. The children are lining up here behind me, and the play is scheduled to start in about fifteen minutes.
CHRIS: Casey, we'll check back with you at the start of the play. It's time for a station break. When we return, we'll have a special about town report from Samuel Goodman. So, stay tuned. [Music plays in background.]
DIRECTOR: Stay alert! We're back in sixty seconds. (TV crew yawns with a loud noisy yawn, but stays in place.)
OFFSTAGE
VOICE: This is KTBT, your Key to Bible Times station, bringing you a special Easter Morning Celebration.
CHRIS: We return now to the local scene to find out what your friends and neighbors are doing this Easter morning. We turn first to Sam Goodman, our about town reporter, for a report on what's happening locally. Let's go to Sam live down on Third Street and see what he has found.
SAM
GOODMAN,
ABOUT TOWN
REPORTER: Thank you, Chris. We have been traveling all over town, and we want to highlight a few of the services you can attend today.

[Have stage crew set up for puppet play as Sam talks. Put Love Task Tree and flower-covered cross in place.]

This morning, if you're looking for a place to worship, the Church on the Hill invites you to celebrate Easter with them. They have built a flower stand in the shape of a giant cross that covers the entire front of the sanctuary. The cross is made of white Easter lilies. After the service, each of the lilies will be taken to a shut-in or nursing home. Each lily is delivered with a little basket full of cookies made by the children in Sunday school. The lilies will be carried out of the sanctuary as a part of the benediction.

If you don't want to fight the lines at the restaurant but really would enjoy not having to go home and cook after church, then come on over to the Church of the Master. They're serving an Easter luncheon from 12:30 to 2:00. Tickets are available at the door, and they will be presenting puppet plays all afternoon. The proceeds from the luncheon will go to the Food Bank. And we have a free sample this morning of one of the puppet plays.

SCENE VI

(This part of the script is practiced on the 6th week.)

Sermon

[Switch to puppet stage.]

MEGAN:	Hurry up! We have to be finished in five minutes.
	[Puppet is constantly looking in every direction to see if anyone is coming.]
JODY:	If you'd done your part, we wouldn't be in trouble.
MEGAN:	We aren't in trouble yet.
JODY:	We're going to be though, if we don't get this finished. And besides, why aren't you helping?
MEGAN:	I am helping. I'm keeping a lookout to make sure no one's coming.
SAM:	[Spoken very sarcastically] That's real important.
SALLY:	Will the two of you quit arguing? We need help.
SAM:	What question are you on?
JODY:	Number 1, of course: What's the meaning of Easter?
SAM:	We talked about how Jesus died on a cross.
JACK:	He's not really dead. He's alive! Through his death, Jesus taught us that death is not the end but actually the beginning, the beginning of a whole new life with God.
SALLY:	Does that mean Easter is a celebration of death?
JACK:	No, Easter is a celebration of *life*. That's why we use the butterfly and Easter lily as symbols of Easter. The caterpillar looks dead and lifeless in its chrysalis. Then, when it's time, the chrysalis cracks open and out comes not a caterpillar, but a beautiful butterfly. The same is true of the Easter lily. If you plant the bulb, it just sits in the ground and seems to decay and rot away, but then come spring, up from seemingly nowhere pops a beautiful, tall Easter lily plant whose green blooms burst open into gorgeous white flowers.
MEGAN:	When did you learn about butterflies and Easter lilies?
SALLY:	Isn't there a shorter answer? I can't write all that stuff down.
MEGAN:	He doesn't know what he's talking about.
JODY:	Yes, he does; you're just feeling jealous, Megan, because Jack had a big, fancy answer and you didn't.
MEGAN:	For your information, I already have my whole entire paper filled out. [Shakes paper out over puppet stage curtain]
JODY:	Can we go on to Number 2? I have no idea why people give something up for Lent.
SALLY:	I gave up eating chocolate.
SAM:	Lent is supposed to be a time of change.

JACK: Actually, Lent is a time of preparation. In the early church people wouldn't eat certain foods for forty days before their Baptism on Easter Sunday. They were to evaluate their life and totally change the way they lived.

MEGAN: [Spoken sarcastically] The new and improved you!

JODY: I get it, you get a new life. You start to act and talk differently. You get rid of your bad habits.

SALLY: Does that mean I have to give up more than just chocolate?

JODY: I think it means we all do; I think it means that we all have to start being a lot nicer to each other too.

MEGAN: All this talk about change makes me nervous. I like making smart remarks and teasing people. I don't want to change.

SAM: We all have to change.

MEGAN: Why?

JODY: Sometimes the way we act or the words we speak hurt other people, and if our actions are hurting someone else, then we have to change even if we don't want to.

SAM: If our actions hurt others, they hurt us too. It's impossible to hurt someone else without hurting yourself in the process.

JACK: That sounds like a good answer to Number 3. Lent is a time to start over, forgive and be forgiven.

SALLY: Does anyone have a shorter answer?

MEGAN: Sally! Write the word [spell out] F-O-R-G-I-V-E, because if you forgive others, you will be forgiven.

SAM: We have to stop talking so much. Look at Number 10. It says to put together a short skit. I got the TV camera out [have puppet hold up a paper TV camera], but if we don't quit talking, we'll never get to use it.

SAM: Let's hurry! Number 4 says: If you were going to change your life this Easter, what would be your first step?

MEGAN: I'd dye my hair purple.

JODY: Megan, would you please be serious?

MEGAN: All right, don't be so grumpy. I put down that my first step toward change would be to sit down and make a list of all my good behaviors or things I do well. Then, I'd make a list of all the things I do that I actually know I shouldn't be doing, like yelling, fighting, throwing tantrums, losing my temper, telling people I hate them when I'm angry, slamming my bedroom door, pinching . . . the usual.

SAM: That's it! Megan, you've given me the perfect idea for our script. We'll do a story telling how a group of kids decided to change their lives and follow Jesus.

JODY: And the change could start on Easter morning.

MEGAN: I like it.

SALLY: What about the rest of these questions?

SAM: We'll let Megan speak for our group.

JODY: That's a good idea.

SALLY: Thank goodness! [Crumbles up paper and throws it over the puppet stage]

SAM: I'll be the camera operator. Megan, you come down and be over here with everyone else. You'll speak first.

      [All puppets go offstage. Quietly, clear away puppet show as focus switches back to Chris. Alexandria and Maxwell speak but do not appear at this point. Have puppets speak loudly from off stage, as if they are yelling upstairs to Mom and Dad.]

MAXWELL: Mom, Dad, can we go there too? It sounds super.

ALEXANDRIA: And the money goes for a very good cause.

DAD: Sure, why not?

ALEXANDRIA AND MAXWELL:	[In unison] Yeah!
MOM:	Turn off the television and let's get in the car. If we don't get going, we'll never make it to church, much less lunch. [Sound of feet running across stage or floor]
CHRIS:	If you're staying with us for the next hour, we will be returning to Dallas and Chicago. If you're heading out the door to church, we wish you a peaceful Easter.
	Keep us in mind each and every week. Same time. Same station.
	We'll close this hour with music and a special presentation in sign language. Thank you for tuning in and remember to "share a smile with someone today."

Prayer

[Follow with the Lord's Prayer in sign language. Make sure audience can see children signing the prayer. Bow heads briefly after "Amen." Then exit.]

Benediction

[Hold microphone next to machine that clicks on and off. Make *click* noise. Have director speak loudly from offstage.]

DIRECTOR:	We're clear. Good show, everyone. Take a short break; I'll signal you when it is time to come back.
	[Dim lights. Pause with silence as TV crew walks off.]

Postlude

PART FIVE

....

THE MEANING OF PENTECOST

13

Teaching Clown Ministry to Children

Even if you have absolutely no experience in clown ministry, the following sessions give the step-by-step details you need to organize a clown troupe. The Getting Ready sections tell you exactly how to teach clowning to your group.

Children are fascinated by the idea of being clowns. Age is not a barrier. My youngest daughter started clowning when she was three. The children in my "Penny Clown Troupe" range in age from six to sixteen. Both boys and girls enjoy clowning. Workstations provide the perfect atmosphere in which to develop a clown character who gives to others without thinking of the rewards to oneself.

Go out into every corner of the world and share God's message of loving acceptance with everyone you find. Once you start, you'll never want to stop.

Session 35
A Story Brought to Life:
Learning to Speak Through
Your Movements

The Bible Lesson

Galatians 6:1-10 tells how we are to treat others.

What the Children Will Learn Today

Children are challenged to explore ways of expressing faith.

Time Needed

5 minutes for story
20 minutes for workstations
5 minutes for closing worship service

Supplies Needed (by Workstation)

Story: large mailing envelope, copy of story, and book

1. Bibles, bell, or whistle
2. Long sheets of construction paper, pop bottles, paper streamers or ribbon, jingle bells, string, magazines to cut from, gravel, popcorn, beans, or rice
3. 2" x 6" boards and plywood scraps to build bookshelves
4 and 6. Paper plate to make clock, feather duster, permanent marker to write on balloon, and a large balloon
5. Plastic 2-liter pop bottles, newspaper or scrap paper, rubber bands, hole punch, string, plastic bags, and masking tape
7. Construction paper supply basket and tulip pattern

Children's Meditation

GETTING READY

Copy story and place it in a large envelope. If you have an envelope you received through the mail that's even better. You may also make a balloon animal from Session 37 during story. Start by saying, "I received a letter. Would you like for me to read it out loud?"

STORY

A Letter from Happy Penny

Greetings, my friends!

I'm so excited this morning. I want to tell you about clowning. Clowning is more than just putting on funny makeup. Clowning is a ministry.

I became convinced that clowning was for me one morning after a recent trip to the hospital. No, I wasn't a patient. I was a hospital clown. I went with thirteen children called the "Penny Troupe."

When you think about going to visit sick people in the hospital, it can be sort of scary. I wasn't at all sure what to expect. What would I say? What would I do?

It was actually easy. We walked into room after room sharing the cards and gifts we had made and performing silly skits. Lonely patients were obviously moved by our abundant energy. The nurses even commented on how one man never smiled, yet sat laughing and clapping along with us. We were truly God's messengers of joy and hope.

One patient sent us a thank-you note that said over and over again how our visit had brightened her day. The staff begged us to return.

If you're saying, "I've never tried anything like this. I'm not a professional clown," welcome aboard, neither are we. As for myself, I'm far from it.

The only requirement is to genuinely "love your neighbor." If God's love is your message, his love will shine through.

The first step to clown ministry is to decide on your costume. A clown minister doesn't need the traditional polka dots and ruffly collar. You don't even have to buy anything; dress-up clothes will do. Dad's old shirt and a baggy pair of pants with suspenders work fine. Mom's old skirts and shoes are always a big hit. Pick a washable costume that's comfortable and easy to get on and off. Be creative but practical.

All you need to get started in clown ministry is *you*. Welcome to clowning. You'll love it.

Peace and love
from your friend,
Happy Penny

Workstations

Workstation 1: Call to Worship

INSTRUCTION SIGN

STEP 1: Give a clown handshake. Be creative! Shake hands facing backward, with a foot and a hand, by thumbs. Make an arch with your left hands. Then shake right hands underneath the arch. Once you get started, the creativity will flow.

STEP 2: Have everyone demonstrate a clown walk. Put something distinctive into the way you walk.

STEP 3: Clowns must also learn to say good-bye. A bow can be grand and showy or timid. Practice! These are the first three characteristics of your clown personality.
Remember, we are clown ministers. You witness to your faith by how you present your clown personality. We will NOT use costumes or makeup today. We'll only pantomime our actions.

STEP 4: Read 2 Timothy 1:7-8. Then, practice and use the following routine for the Call to Worship for today's service.

CLOWN ROUTINE FOR SERVICE TODAY

Everyone Is Welcome in God's Church

Scene I: Blow a whistle or ring a bell when you are ready to start. Walk in using your clown walk. Have everyone sit in a circle. Whiteface clowns do not talk, so you have to form a circle WITHOUT WORDS. Use only motions.

Scene II: Once you have everyone sitting in a circle, greet everyone with your silly handshake. Go around the circle trying to think up as many different handshakes as possible. After a while, everyone will have a fun handshake waiting for you when you get to them. Clowning catches on quickly.

Scene III: After everyone has been greeted, take your bow and join the circle because everyone is welcome in God's church. Open your Bible and sit down to read silently.

Workstation 2: Affirmation of Faith

INSTRUCTION SIGN

As a clown minister, you want to make a statement of faith or tell others what you believe. You might say, "God is Love," "God loves everyone," or "Happy are the peacemakers." Read 1 Corinthians 1:27-28 and Matthew 5:7 for more ideas.

STEP 1:   Draw a picture or cut pictures from old magazines to explain the message that you want to send to others through clown ministry. Remember, you must be able to explain your message without speaking words. For example, Happy Penny uses a simple, seemingly worthless penny as a token of friendship.

STEP 2:   Tape finished pictures around bottle. Keep picture right side up when holding neck of bottle as handle.

STEP 3:   Fill your pop-bottle noisemaker with rice or pebbles. Tape streamers or ribbons to cap. Take to worship.

Workstation 3: Offering or Carpenter Shop

GETTING READY

Have scraps of wood and tools ready.

INSTRUCTION SIGN

Joseph's Carpenter Shop is building clown benches and/or Bible bookshelves. The bench is sturdy enough to sit on, and an excellent place to keep your Bible at home. Read Luke 17:20-21.

STEP 1: Cut 3 pieces from a 2" x 6" board. Cut two 6" long boards and one 12" long board. Sand smooth.

STEP 2: Add glue and nail 2" x 6"'s together, forming a U shape. Set aside to let glue dry. Make several benches.

Workstation 4 (Sermon or Bible Study) and Workstation 6 (Prayer and Sewing Center) Combined

GETTING READY

This simple lesson in motion can easily become your opening or closing for a program. You could start with everyone pretending to be asleep and then awakening to form the clown machine or reverse action and walk in with motion. Then pretend to collapse exhausted onto the floor at the end.

INSTRUCTION SIGN

In a clown troupe, everyone works and acts together. Since clowns traditionally do not talk once they put on whiteface, everything must be done by motions. You must learn to watch, understand, and follow the actions of others and create actions that can be easily interpreted by your audience.

STEP 1: The prayer, sermon, and benediction are combined today. You are in charge of leading all three. Read 1 Corinthians 4:10 and Galatians 6:3-5, 7, and 9-10. You need:

1 sound effects person (Hidden in puppet stage or such—
1 person to lead Lord's Prayer in sign language
2 (or more) people pretending to sleep

STEP 2: Trace patterns and have props ready before you practice. Make: (1) Time for Worship Clock (Use a paper plate. Make simple clock. Write in large letters on clock: "Time for Worship.") and (2) write LOVE on an inflated balloon.

STEP 3: Practice the following clown routine for today's service:

Wake Up, It's Time for Worship

Scene I: Sit or lie down in the center of the circle and pretend to be asleep. Add snoring sounds.

Scene II: Prayer person, enter late with alarm clock and a feather duster. Make clock noises (*tick, tock, rinnnnng*). No one wakes up. Snoring continues. Prayer person throws up hands in disgust and starts leading Lord's Prayer in silence. Say prayer silently as you sign.

Scene III: After the prayer, a sleeping clown wakes up and starts an action. It can be any action. The clown might pretend to pull a rope or be a wheel that turns. Make the motion with your body and hands. Remember, you want the audience to figure out what kind of action you're making.

Scene IV: Another sleeping clown wakes up and adds to the first action. The second person might be the wheel pretending to wind up the rope. The sleeping clowns wake up one at a time, see the clown machine going, and go over and add a new motion to the clown machine. The third child might be the piston that moves up and down to make the wheel turn that winds up the rope and so on.

Scene V: When all of the clowns sleeping on the floor have joined the clown machine (if you have more than 10 clowns, make more than one machine), have prayer clown go and one by one add every member of your class to the clown machine. Have those who made noisemakers at the call to worship station use their noisemakers as part of their action. Continue adding actions until you have everyone involved with the clown machine.

Have a balloon with the word "LOVE" written in large letters. Float balloon above clown machine to symbolize that we are able to work together as one when we share God's love.

Scene VI: Have machine stop action and freeze. Read Bible verse. Start with lead clown. If lead clown freezes in place, everyone else will follow example. When quiet, read.

Scene VII: Close with clown handshakes and special "clown bow."

Workstation 5: Witness to Faith

GETTING READY

Show pictures in book. Cat is easier to make than dog.

INSTRUCTION SIGN

Clowns often have toys, gimmicks, or props that introduce them. You can make a papier-mâché pop-bottle dog or cat. You might carry your dog or cat in your arms and pretend to pet it as you walk up to meet someone. The dog or cat's collar could read, "God loves you." In this way, the dog or cat helped you to make an introduction and tell your mission or purpose in coming. Read Psalm 100:2. Then, make a pop-bottle papier-mâché dog or cat.

STEP 1: Place a wad of plastic bags inside another plastic bag to form the head, or smash and shape newspapers for the head. Shape head for a dog or cat depending on which you are making. Attach head to NECK of pop bottle with a strong rubber band. Do not use tape or head will fall off when wet.

STEP 2: To make stand-up legs for the dog, punch 2 holes at the end of 4 tissue holders. Run string through holes. Stuff tissue rolls with leftover plastic bags so that they do not become soggy from papier-mâché. Tie in place.

STEP 3: For cat (lying down), shape legs from newspaper or plastic bags and rubber-band in place.

STEP 4: Trace ear patterns on scrap cardboard. Glue and tape in place.

STEP 5: Shape tail from newspapers. Tape in place.

Workstation 7: Benediction

INSTRUCTION SIGN

Clown ministers typically present their message in silence. Make a tulip card to share. Share God's message of love.

STEP 1: Trace tulip and leaf patterns on fold.

STEP 2: Fold a sheet of green paper to make stem.

STEP 3: Glue stem to back of tulip so that tulip will stand straight. Glue leaves in place.

STEP 4: Write inside tulip : "1 John 4:7-8: God is love. God loves everyone."

The Worship Celebration

GETTING READY

The call to worship and sermon workstations have clown scripts to follow for leading today's service.

SIGN-UP SHEET FOR TODAY'S WORSHIP CELEBRATION

Call to Worship ("Everyone Is Welcome in God's Church"):
Sermon ("Wake Up, It's Time for Worship"):
Benediction (clown handshakes and clown bow):

ITEMS TO GO HOME TODAY: AFFIRMATION NOISEMAKERS; TULIP CARDS

Session 36
Your Story Is Written on Your Face

The Bible Lesson

Clowns show God's love through their actions (1 John 3:18 and 2 Corinthians 9:6-15).

What the Children Will Learn Today

Principles of clowning as taught by minister Floyd Shaffer in his book *If I Were a Clown* (Augsburg, 1984)

Time Needed

5 minutes for story
20 minutes for workstations
10 minutes for closing worship service

Supplies Needed (by Workstation)

Story: White oval poster for face, markers, and envelope

1. Newsprint, white office-paper scraps, large pan, papier-mâché, cover-ups, and pop-bottle animals from Workstation 5

2. White paper (each person in your group will make a name tag), heart and bow tie patterns, markers, and Happy Penny's face

3. Bible bookshelf building supplies

4. Clown machine instructions from Session 35

5. Construction paper, yarn, stapler, masking tape, empty pop bottles, and a needle and thread for sewing wig

6. Cloth scraps, needles, thread, and travel bag pattern

7. Construction paper supply basket and glasses pattern

Children's Meditation

GETTING READY

Each week you will have another letter from Happy Penny that tells the children about clown ministry. Use the same envelope and read the letter. Draw a picture to help tell today's story.

STORY

Second Letter from Happy Penny

Dear Children:

I am so happy to hear that you have decided to become clown ministers. Clowning is a fun way to tell others about God.

There are many kinds of clowns. A hobo clown is always sad and lonely, the august clown can never seem to get things to work out right, and the whiteface clown's mission is to go around sharing love, happiness, and joy. I'm a whiteface clown because it's the easiest.

The white face represents the resurrection, new life in Christ. The clown's face tells a story. Each clown's face is different. Create a clown face to fit your personality.

I'm not a circus clown. I don't do magic tricks or funny stunts. I can't even blow up a balloon or make a balloon animal, but I do love to have fun and make people smile. I use a silly feather duster to clean away all of the frowns and sad faces of the world. I always have a mission to accomplish when I put on my clown face. I'm a messenger for God. My job is to tell others that God loves them. I use a simple penny to remind those who are sick and lonely that everyone is important in God's world.

Your next step to becoming a clown is to decide what you want to tell others about God. What do you want to accomplish?

Since whiteface clowns don't talk, your face makeup, costume, and actions become very important. Design a face that tells something about your faith and what you believe.

Keep your face simple and emphasize a smile. You may also change your clown face as you become more experienced with clowning. Start with a white face.

I always place a perky red smile on my right cheek [draw smile on poster] because smiling is the right thing to do to make myself and others happy. I also place a blue teardrop on my left cheek [draw blue tear] because life is not always happy. My tear and smile are a statement of faith or affirmation because life is full of both sad and happy moments. I always strive for happiness but can handle sadness when it comes because I know that God loves me and accepts me just the way I am. I don't have to be perfect or even happy for God to love me.

By painting colorful rainbow eyebrows on my face [draw two colorful rainbow eyebrows], I remind myself that God forgives me when I make mistakes, lose my temper, do things I shouldn't, or forget to help someone else in need. The rainbow is God's symbol of hope that appears on even the gloomiest of days.

With a bright red clown stick, I put on my final symbol, a smile. I don't paint a permanent smile on my face. I simply paint my lips with clown lipstick [draw red smile]. Then, I have to make my lips smile for my makeup to be complete.

Now, it's your turn. Workstation 2, the affirmation, will help you create your clown personality. Remember, you are a messenger for God. Let your face tell a story. Build upon a key phrase: "God is Love" or "God offers hope." I say, "God loves everyone." Develop your statement of faith. Work at all seven stations, but make sure that you stop by Workstation 2 before the service today. Go in peace and tell others about God's love.

Peace and love
from your friend,
Happy Penny

Workstations

Workstation 1: Call to Worship

GETTING READY

Make clown wigs and hats or put hair up in a special way.

INSTRUCTION SIGN

Floyd Shaffer, known also as "Socataco" the clown, says the word "silly" originally meant "blessed, merry, innocent, or holy." We don't think of something simple or innocent being "holy," but perhaps we should. Jesus led a simple life and talked about the beauty of nature and innocence of children. Read Matthew 18:1-5. Clowning builds upon childlike innocence.

Create a "silly" hat or yarn wig to wear when clowning. Keep in mind the overall clown person you are creating.

Simple Hat with Hair Attached

Make a paper-cone hat by curling and stapling a piece of paper. Decorate your hat with a message from God: "Everyone is welcome in God's church" or "God loves everyone." Staple hat together. Cut about fifty 12" pieces of yarn and tape them evenly around the inside of hat so that the yarn will hang down when the hat is placed on your head. Don't let yarn cover your face.

More Complicated Yarn Wig

If you want to be more sophisticated, you can make long straight or braided yarn wigs.

STEP 1: Set up 2 chairs back-to-back approximately 45" apart. Vary distance of chairs by how long you want your wig.

STEP 2: Wrap skein of yarn around chairs. Keep tension on yarn. Place the strands of yarn side by side, not lumped together.

STEP 3: Measure the size of your head by placing tape, STICKY SIDE UP, from forehead and measuring over the top of the head and down to the base of the neck.

STEP 4: Place masking tape, STICKY SIDE TOUCHING YARN, on individual strands of yarn to hold them together in one line.

STEP 5: Sew down the middle of the tape with needle and thread or use extra tape to hold the yarn in place. Tape marks the center of head. Cut yarn to make both sides even. Yarn can then be placed on head as long straight hair or braided on each side. A hat or cap works nicely to hold hair in place.

Workstation 2: Affirmation of Faith

GETTING READY

Children may clown without makeup. Children who do not want to wear makeup may simply dress up in a costume.

INSTRUCTION SIGN

Design a clown name tag. What will your clown name be? How will you decorate your face? Read 1 John 3:18.

Happy Penny uses colorful rainbow eyebrows because they symbolize hope, a commitment, and a loving relationship with God. The smile on her right cheek indicates that she wants to be happy. The teardrop on her left cheek says she's not always happy. Sometimes she's sad and worried. It is only through God's help and guidance that she can find her way back to happiness. Think of symbols as you create your clown face.

STEP 1: Trace hearts, hat, and bow tie patterns.

STEP 2: Draw your clown face on the white heart. The heart reminds us that our mission is to go and share God's love. Glue whiteface heart to large heart used for body. Write your clown name on large heart. Glue bow tie in place. Add a hat or hair.

STEP 3: Cut 4 paper arms. Use pattern. Fold arms as if you were making a paper fan. Add arms and heart hands to name tag. Explain your name tag during worship today.

Workstation 3: Offering or Carpenter Shop

INSTRUCTION SIGN

Clowns were used in worship services in the twelfth century. Clowns were used for what was called a "holy interruption." The clown reminded the congregation of something that was wrong with the world. Then the clown would disappear and the service would continue. Read 1 John 3:18 and continue working on bookshelves.

Workstation 4: Sermon or Bible Study

INSTRUCTION SIGN

Use your clown handshakes and the clown machine to start off today's worship service. Remember to include everyone. Review instructions from last week if needed.

Then have everyone sit in a circle and share their clown faces and names from Workstation 2.

Workstation 5: Witness to Faith

GETTING READY

Mix 1 cup white glue and 1 cup water for papier-mâché. Make a thick but workable paste. Use old recyclable white office paper for the last layer. White paper is easier to paint than newsprint. Have cover-ups and covers for table.

INSTRUCTION SIGN

Clowns create an environment of acceptance, love, and simple joy. Your pop-bottle animal will help you create an atmosphere of acceptance and joy as you go out to tell others that God loves them. Read 2 Corinthians 9:6-9. Put on a cover-up.

STEP 1: Cover dog or cat with papier-mâché. Make sure all parts are covered smoothly with papier-mâché.
STEP 2: Your last layer of papier-mâché should be old white office paper so that the newsprint will not show through.
STEP 3: Let dry for one week before painting.

Workstation 6: Prayer and Sewing Center

GETTING READY

Have large scraps of cloth for making clown bags.

INSTRUCTION SIGN

Clowns share hope. During hospital visits and worship services, you will need a clown travel bag to carry balloons, cards, and other treats.

STEP 1: Read 2 Corinthians 9:10-13. Make a 12" x 12" cloth bag. Cut cloth on fold. Sew side seams.
STEP 2: Fold under top edges so that edges do not unravel. Sew side seams. Add cloth or braided handle.
STEP 3: Sew clown name on bag or decorate with felt.

Workstation 7: Benediction

INSTRUCTION SIGN

Perhaps you wear glasses or know someone who does. Children often make fun of those who wear glasses. Make a big pair of funny paper clown glasses to hand out to others when clowning. Trace pattern. Decorate your glasses using today's Bible verse from 2 Corinthians 10:17-18. Wear your glasses to worship.

The Worship Celebration

SIGN-UP SHEET FOR TODAY'S WORSHIP CELEBRATION

Call to Worship (handshakes and clown machine):
Bible reader (1 John 3:18):
Sermon (explain clown faces):
Lead the Lord's Prayer:
Benediction (clown bow):

ITEMS TO GO HOME TODAY: CLOWN GLASSES; CLOWN FACE NAME TAGS

Session 37
Preparing for Pentecost:
Clowning as Outreach
Ministry

The Bible Lesson

Today's lesson comes from the parable of the good Samaritan.

What the Children Will Learn Today

The children will learn clowning techniques but not actually apply makeup during today's session.

Time Needed

5 minutes for story
20 minutes for workstations
10 minutes for closing worship service

Supplies Needed (by Workstation)

1. Pop-bottle dogs and cats, cover-ups, and paint
2. Watering can and water drop patterns, juice cans, construction paper supply basket, stapler, tape, and shiny paper
3. Balloons for balloon animals, pump, and instruction book
4. "The Unwanted" script, bandages, radio, mirror for snob
5. Bible and biblical costumes (if desired)
6. Clown Travel Bag and card making supplies
7. Car pattern and construction paper supply basket

Children's Meditation

GETTING READY

Today's story talks about visiting a hospital. Since trips to hospitals must often be planned for Saturday or Sunday afternoon, today's session lays the groundwork for your trip.

STORY

Third Letter from Happy Penny

Dear Children:

I've heard that you are going clowning at a hospital. You will have a wonderful time. People in hospitals are often very lonely and sad. You can brighten their day just by walking in with your silly costume.

Clowns normally do not talk, but you may find that people in the hospital really want to talk to you. So take a puppet along and let your puppet talk for you. Also, plan a funny but simple routine. It's very important to know what you want to do before you walk into the patient's room.

I like to pretend to clean the hospital room with my feather duster. I dust the person's hands and feet. If I'm visiting a child, I also dust the patient's hair and sometimes pretend their feet stink. Before I leave, I give the patient a "Have a Nice Day" card, a bouquet of paper flowers, or a small gift I've made. My goal when visiting the hospital or nursing home is to spread joy and happiness.

On one visit to a local children's hospital, I went with twenty-four children. We divided into four teams so we could visit more rooms. We had made forty paper-bag fish to give as gifts, and we packed bubble-making kits and puppets.

As we walked into the first room, a teenager sat all alone. She was bored and staring at the TV. I quickly put Sunshine Share-a-Lot on my hand. Sunshine passed out bubble wands, even to the patient, and we had a wonderful bubble party. When we left the teenager was smiling and laughing with us. We had definitely served as messengers of God's love.

I must admit, I still get a little nervous when I walk into a hospital, but I remember the words of an eight-year-old clown who said, "The people were so sad when we walked in, and when we left they were all smiling."

Remember your mission—we're God's messengers. Go and tell everyone that God loves them.

Peace and love,
your friend,
Happy Penny

Workstations

Workstation 1: Call to Worship

GETTING READY

Today's workstations give tips on applying makeup with children. The children are not actually applying makeup today, just learning what to do.

INSTRUCTION SIGN

You'll soon be putting on clown makeup for the first time. Working with makeup can be very exciting. To help you get ready, make a list of things you'll need. First, you need the picture of your clown face.

Before Happy Penny puts on her makeup, she pulls her hair back from her face. You'll need to do this, too, so you don't get makeup in your hair. Bring headbands or pins to use.

Happy Penny doesn't speak while applying her makeup. Sitting and working in silence gives Happy Penny time to think about her mission. Read Luke 10:36-37. Think about your mission as a clown minister.

We aren't painting our faces today, but we are painting. Put on a cover-up and paint your dog or cat.

After painting, plan a routine to use at the hospital. The clown machine works well. Include your dog or cat.

Workstation 2: Affirmation of Faith

INSTRUCTION SIGN

The early Christians often talked about what it meant to be a follower of Jesus and how they should act as followers. A clown's white face is symbolic of the resurrection and is a reminder that we, too, are followers of Jesus.

We'll be working with makeup soon. Here are a few makeup tips to remember.

When you apply white clown makeup, you cover your entire face, eyebrows, and eyelids. Just close your eyes and gently smooth makeup around your eyes. Anytime your clown white makeup will not smooth out, put a drop of water on your finger.

Once the whiteface is smooth, you'll add your colors. Keep your face simple. Read Luke 10:27.

While you think about the colors you'll paint on your clown face, make a watering can that reminds people that God loves everyone. Place on worship table for today's service.

STEP 1: Trace pattern for can, handle, and spout.
STEP 2: Write a message on the side of the watering can: "10 Ways to Make Friends" or "Do's and Don'ts for a Happy Day."
STEP 3: Glue paper to empty frozen-juice can. Staple handle at top. Tape other end of handle to bottom of can. Glue and staple spout in place. You don't have to be a professional clown to go out and share God's message of love.
STEP 4: Cut water drops on fold of shiny wrapping paper. Use pattern. Write one way to be a good friend inside each raindrop.

Workstation 3: Offering or Carpenter Shop

GETTING READY

Clowning allows the shyest of children to reach out in love. Everyone accepts a clown, but some children do not want to be clowns. Balloon animals are an excellent alternative.

INSTRUCTION SIGN

Even when you're not clowning, you can share God's love. Remember to smile and think of the needs of others. Read Luke 10:27.

Make balloon animals. Everyone loves balloons.

STEP 1: To make a mouse, inflate a long balloon-animal balloon about half full. Tie shut. Twist balloon into 4 round balls, starting at the valve end.

STEP 2: Bend the balloon in half between the second and third balls. Twist first and fourth ball together. Mouse should hold.

STEP 3: Draw face with permanent marker. From this simple beginning, you can go on to make a dog with short legs or a giraffe. Place a balloon animal on the worship table today.

Workstations 4 (Sermon or Bible Study) and 5 (Witness to Faith) Combined

INSTRUCTION SIGN

Sign up for characters in "The Unwanted." Practice and be ready for the worship service today. Since clowns tell their stories without speaking, have a narrator read the story as you act out the actions. Read Luke 10:25-37. The skit is the entire service today. Remember, clowns don't hit or ever hurt anyone.

Clown Actors Needed:

1. Lucy, who likes to dance and listen to her radio

2. Gang Members, who attack Lucy (2 gang members)

3. The Snob, who is too busy fixing her hair to help Lucy

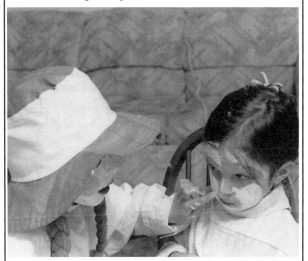

4. Ms. Wonderful, who was going to help

5. The Unwanted, person whom nobody likes

6. The teasing, sassy group that makes fun of the Unwanted (2 to 8 sassy members)

7. The Nurse, who is busy counting bandages

The Unwanted

Once upon a time, there was a girl named Lucy. Lucy spent all of her time, day and night, listening to her radio. She kept the radio close to her ear. Lucy danced and sang wherever she went. One day she was playing her radio particularly loud. She danced along, not paying any attention to where she was going. I mean, Lucy was really into her music and dancing all over the place. She danced to the right, and then she danced to the left. Lucy knew all of the latest dance steps. As Lucy danced along, she danced right into the middle of a gang meeting. Well this made the gang so mad that they decided to attack Lucy. The gang was vicious and cruel. They took her radio and left her lying in a heap. Lucy was crying. Lucy tried to get up and walk, but her foot hurt too much. Lucy called out for help. No one came. Lucy cried out for help again, but still no one came.

Then, all of a sudden, along came the Snob. The Snob, as usual, had her mirror and her hairbrush. The Snob was so busy admiring herself that she didn't even notice as she stepped right over the top of poor Lucy.

Lucy felt abandoned and forgotten. She cried out for help again. This time, Ms. Wonderful came running to the rescue. Ms. Wonderful came running up and began to brag about how wonderful it was that she, Ms. Wonderful, was going to help this poor, forgotten child. Ms. Wonderful started to help Lucy up. Lucy was so happy and grateful. Then, just as Lucy started to get up, Ms. Wonderful dropped Lucy back down on the ground in disgust. Ms. Wonderful looked at her hands and dress. Ms. Wonderful forgot all about Lucy and ran off in horror. It seems that Lucy got some dirt on Ms. Wonderful's freshly pressed dress.

Lucy was really beginning to feel abandoned when she saw the Unwanted over on the playground. The Unwanted was being teased by a group of the most popular kids in school. These kids, of course, always did everything right, had all the right answers, and, as you would expect, wore all the right clothes. And if you didn't do exactly what they said to do, well, then you couldn't be in their group of friends. Which meant, of course, you were *unwanted*.

The Unwanted slowly walked away with her head hanging down. As a matter of fact, the Unwanted walked right into Lucy and almost fell on top of her. The Unwanted got up and immediately began to apologize. The Unwanted shook Lucy's hand and said "I'm sorry" about ten times before she even noticed that Lucy was hurt. The Unwanted knelt down next to Lucy and helped Lucy up. Together they hobbled over to the school nurse, who was busy counting bandages. As the nurse counted, the bandages flew first over her right shoulder and then over her left. It was a terrible mess. The girls had to stand there weaving from side to side till the nurse had finished her counting. The nurse took one look at Lucy and took them both into the clinic.

Well as you might have guessed, the Unwanted isn't unwanted anymore. The Unwanted has a new best friend named Lucy. And the two girls dance and play together all day long.

Workstation 6: Prayer and Sewing Center

INSTRUCTION SIGN

Write or sew a message on outside of clown travel bag. Make cards or simple gifts to fill bag. Read Luke 10:27.

Workstation 7: Benediction

INSTRUCTION SIGN

Circus clowns drive tiny cars or do funny stunts. We don't have fancy trick cars or gimmicks. We simply walk from room to room at the hospital sharing God's love with everyone we meet. Our message is simple: God loves you.

Fold a sheet of paper, trace pattern on fold, and make a car to take to the hospital. Make sure your car has a happy face. Read Luke 10:27. Write "God Loves You" on the inside.

The Worship Celebration

GETTING READY

The skit is the entire service today (Workstation 4).

SIGN-UP SHEET FOR TODAY'S WORSHIP CELEBRATION

Sermon ("The Unwanted"):
Benediction (lead the Lord's Prayer):

ITEMS TO GO HOME TODAY: DOG OR CAT BALLOONS; WATERING CANS; CLOWN BAGS; CARDS

Session 38
Writing a Clown Ministry
Worship Service

The Bible Lesson

The parable of the mustard seed (Matthew 13:31-32) [Dupe Session 42?]

What the Children Will Learn Today

The parable of the tower builder (Luke 14:28-30) defines the cost of being a follower of Jesus.

Time Needed

  5 minutes for story
20 minutes for workstations
10 minutes for closing worship service

Supplies Needed (by Workstation)

  1. Pop-bottle cats and dogs, collar pattern
  2. Pop bottles, paper sacks, masking tape, markers, balloons, construction paper, and patterns
  3. Bookshelves and tempera paint and supplies
  4. Clown wigs and hats (no makeup today), clown costumes, and props for skit: feather duster, wagon with blocks, a triangle block, handkerchief, paper airplane, soccer ball
  5. Tissue paper in a variety of colors, pipe cleaners
  6. Clown travel bags
  7. Cardboard butterfly tracing pattern and craft supply basket

Children's Meditation

STORY

Fourth Letter from Happy Penny

Dear Children:

I'm pleased to hear that you're planning a worship service. Worship is a joyous time when clown ministers have a chance to teach from the Bible.

Will you present your service on Pentecost Sunday? Will your service be for the children or for the entire congregation? Will your clown service be a service in silence?

Sorry, I'm suddenly filled with questions. Like the vineyard owner from the parable of the tower builder, you need to make some plans.

Being a clown minister is a big responsibility. If we're to be messengers for God, we have to control our anger and think of the needs of others. Being a messenger for God is really a lot harder than it sounds, but I can do it, and so can you because God loves us.

I know I'll make mistakes, but I also know that God forgives. Every time I make a mistake, I'll start over, say I'm sorry, and then try to talk in kind words.

If I'm going to be a happy clown who spreads joy and happiness wherever I go, I think I'll start at home. I'll think of something nice to say to each member of my family today. I'll also think of something helpful and nice to do.

I can't pretend to change for only one day. I have to make this change permanent. I can't be a messenger for God just on days when I have on my clown makeup. If I'm truly to be God's messenger, I have to be a messenger even when I don't have on clown makeup.

What do you think? Should we try it? I'm going to, and I hope you will too. I know I won't be perfect, but I'll do my best.

Peace and love,
Happy Penny

Workstations

Workstation 1: Call to Worship

GETTING READY

Have craft supplies for decorating collars.

INSTRUCTION SIGN

The purpose of the call to worship is to create a worship atmosphere or set the stage for worship. Worship is a time of joyous celebration. Read Mark 4:30-32. Practice your clown handshake and bow.

Dress your dog or cat for worship. Work with your neighbor. Trace collar pattern. Write a message on the collar: "God loves everyone."

Workstation 2: Affirmation of Faith

GETTING READY

I have the children draw their clown face several different times before I introduce them to makeup. This helps them to think of the statement of faith they are making with their face.

INSTRUCTION SIGN

You are in charge of creating a Statement of Faith for our Pentecost worship service.

First you will need to make some equipment to work with.

STEP 1: Wrap white paper around an empty pop bottle. Draw or cut out pieces from scrap paper to make your clown face.

STEP 2: Make paper clown hat. Write your goal or what you hope to accomplish through clowning on your hat. Glue on top.

STEP 3: Make a big clown bow tie. Write your clown name on bow tie. Glue bow tie to bottom of pop bottle. Use your clown pop bottles and practice the skit.

STEP 4: Practice Statement of Faith

1st: Set up the pop-bottle clown faces like bowling pins.

2nd: Give several clowns different size balloons to blow up. Write the word "Faith" on each balloon in large letters.

3rd: Have clowns try to knock down the pop-bottle bowling pins with balloons. Throw balloons. Roll balloons. Even get down on the floor and blow the balloon along. Nothing works.

4th: Have clowns tightly squash together 3 paper bags. Place bags inside a fourth paper bag and shape into a round ball. Children can mash bags with their feet and hands on the floor. Keep bags in round shape with masking tape. Write in BIG BOLD LETTERS: FAITH. Have your smallest child knock down the bowling pins. With faith, you can do anything. Read Matthew 13:31-32.

Workstation 3: Offering or Carpenter Shop

GETTING READY

Use tempera paint.

INSTRUCTION SIGN

Finish bookshelves today. Wear a cover-up when painting. Read Luke 14:28-30. Place bookshelves on worship table to dry.

Workstation 4: Sermon or Bible Study

GETTING READY

Children enjoy telling a story by acting out the words. If you have someone read a story, then the children feel comfortable playing make-believe and acting out what is being read. Use the story presented or have the children write stories.

INSTRUCTION SIGN

The word "clown" came from the Anglo-Saxon word "clod," meaning one who is considered to be the lowest in a class of people. Read Luke 20:9-17.

As clown ministers, we come as lowly servants or followers of Jesus to tell others about God's love. We use our clown costumes and makeup to hold people's attention so they will listen to the message from the Bible.

Present "The Tower" for our service today. Listen for action words; they appear in capital letters in the story. Act these action words out with facial expressions and movement. Remember to move slowly and never turn your back to the audience. Help the congregation feel the sadness, frustration, and finally the happiness and joy described in the story.

Clowns Needed:
Candy, cries a lot
Sparkplug, pulls wagon
Dusty Musty, has a feather duster
Sweety Pie, very sweet and smiles a lot
Jingle Bell, can wear bells on shoelaces
Soccer, needs a triangle block for tower

CLOWN SKIT FOR SERMON

The Tower

One day a group of clowns were SITTING AROUND BORED. Then, Candy had a brilliant idea, "I know what we can do," she said, "Let's BUILD a tower."

"That's a great idea," said Sparkplug as he RAN OFF to get the wagon full of blocks.

Candy GAVE a block out of the wagon to each of the clowns. Candy felt so PROUD for sharing her blocks, she SMILED from ear to ear.

Everyone was CLEARING OFF a space to build. Dusty Musty took out a feather duster and began to SWEEP the place clear. Sweety Pie got down and BLEW ACROSS THE FLOOR to make it clean. Jingle Bell just STOMPED the dirt into the floor.

Everyone SAT DOWN IN A CIRCLE, except Candy. Candy was still BEAMING and STRUTTING to and fro across the floor. Candy was very PROUD of herself for having shared her blocks so nicely.

Sparkplug STARTED TO PUT his block down first. "No," CRIED Jingle Bell, "that's not fair; I want to be first." While they were ARGUING, Dusty Musty SILENTLY PUT her block down in the CENTER. A second block was PLACED ON TOP. The tower had begun. One by one, block by block, the clowns very CAREFULLY PLACED each and every block they could find on the tower. The tower was getting tall. The clowns were getting NERVOUS. No one wanted to be the one to knock down the tower.

About this time, Candy LOOKED IN THE WAGON to get her block. There were no blocks left. Candy began to CRY. Dusty Musty BROUGHT OVER a block to share with her, but no, Candy WANTED HER ONE SPECIAL BLOCK. Unfortunately, the block Candy wanted WAS ALREADY ON THE TOWER. In order to give Candy the block she wanted they would HAVE TO KNOCK THE TOWER DOWN AND START OVER. That would SPOIL everyone's fun. Candy CRIED UNCONTROLLABLY.

It was also about this time that Soccer RETURNED. Soccer had been outside PLAYING. Soccer was JEALOUS AND ANGRY. No one had even asked him if he wanted to HELP BUILD a tower. And now the only blocks that were LEFT were little tiny ones, because several of the clowns had used most of the remaining blocks to BUILD roads leading to and from the tower.

Soccer got ANGRIER and ANGRIER as he thought about how he had been LEFT OUT of all the fun. When NO ONE WAS LOOKING, Soccer SNATCHED a block from one of the roads. NO ONE EVEN NOTICED.

He'd SHOW THEM who was in charge around here. Since they hadn't noticed when he STOLE a block, Soccer went over and KNOCKED DOWN one of the houses. Soccer STEPPED BACK TO WAIT and see what would happen. Sweetie Pie, a very happy and cheery clown, SMILED and WENT OVER AND REBUILT the house. Soccer was FURIOUS.

EVER SO SLOWLY, Soccer PICKED UP a triangular, pointed block and PLACED it on top of the tower. The tower DIDN'T FALL, but now no one could place any more blocks on the tower. The clowns, who HAD BEEN SO HAPPY with their tower, SAT IN TOTAL SILENCE, STARING AND POINTING at the tower. Even Candy STOPPED CRYING.

Then, from out of nowhere a paper airplane FLEW right near where Soccer was STANDING. Soccer LEANED OVER AND PICKED UP the airplane. He OPENED it and BEGAN TO READ:

Is it fair for you to spoil everyone's fun just because you weren't here at the beginning of the game? Do you really always have to be the "star"? Can you let someone else feel important and be in charge without feeling jealous? YES, YOU CAN."

Soccer FOLDED the airplane and FLEW it off over the top of the tower where his triangle block still sat. Soccer WALKED OVER AND LIFTED the triangle block from the top of the tower. The tower WOBBLED and tumbled to the floor. For a moment, no one spoke, no one moved.

Then, the clowns began to DANCE. They GRABBED Soccer's hand and PULLED him into their circle. They brought Candy with her tearstained handkerchief along too. The clowns DANCED all around the room. They DANCED AROUND AND AROUND IN A CIRCLE.

You see, it wasn't the tower that was important, and it wasn't the HEIGHT of the tower that made the clowns HAPPY. It was when they PLAYED AND WORKED TOGETHER that they were HAPPY. If the tower fell, so what—they could build another one. They could even build an entire city. The important thing was that everyone was WORKING TOGETHER now. Candy had STOPPED CRYING. Soccer TOOK THE TRIANGLE OFF and everything was right with the world once again. The clowns had learned an important lesson today, so they wanted to DANCE AND CELEBRATE.

Workstation 5: Witness to Faith

INSTRUCTION SIGN

You don't have to get dressed up to be a clown or talk with God. When I'm clowning, I wear a silly mix-matched outfit because God loves us no matter how we're dressed. I wear a long skirt with pockets, an orange vest, a blue blouse with yellow flower, and a long braided-yarn wig and a western hat. Absolutely nothing in the costume goes together.

Make a multicolored paper flower to wear on your wrist, lapel, or in your hair when you clown to remind you that everyone is welcome and an important part of God's world. Read Luke 14:28-33.

Then, use the pattern and cut 12 different colors of tissue paper. Stack and fold to make a paper fan. Twist a pipe cleaner around middle. Gently separate tissue layers to make a flower.

Workstation 6: Prayer and Sewing Center

INSTRUCTION SIGN

Finish clown bags. Read Matthew 13:31-32.

Workstation 7: Benediction

GETTING READY

Make a butterfly cardboard tracing plate before the session. Cereal-box cardboard works well.

Make a butterfly out of cardboard. Cut circles and ovals out of cardboard to glue on top of cardboard butterfly. Make a pretty pattern. Let dry before children use butterfly.

If you do not want to make construction paper sticks for butterflies to sit on, simply glue butterfly onto Popsicle stick.

INSTRUCTION SIGN

The butterfly is a symbol of new life. Make a butterfly.

STEP 1:   Place paper over cardboard tracing plate. With the side of a crayon, color over paper.

STEP 2:   Cut out butterfly. Fold green construction paper to form stick, staple and glue to butterfly. Let your butterfly flap its wings and bring happiness to others on the way to worship. Read Matthew 13:31-32.

The Worship Celebration

GETTING READY

Skit is entire service today.

SIGN-UP SHEET FOR TODAY'S WORSHIP CELEBRATION

Sermon ("The Tower"):

ITEMS TO GO HOME TODAY: CLOWN POP-BOTTLE FACES; BUTTERFLIES

Session 39
Pentecost Sunday

Use the different parts of the worship service from this chapter to present a Pentecost "Clown Worship Service in Silence." The theme of the service is "Change your life and become a follower of Jesus."

TIME NEEDED: approximately 1 hour

SUPPLIES NEEDED (by Workstation)
1. Puppet stage, bells, whistle, Lord's Prayer in Sign Language sheet, Bible, Workstation 5 Session 33 instruction sheet
2. Water-based clown makeup, costumes, red balloon, Affirmation written in Session 8, volume 1, or write affirmation
3. Props for clowning, cards, balloon animals, and wagon to collect canned food offering if used
4. "The Unwanted" script and props from Workstation 4, Session 37
5. "The Tower" script and props from Workstation 4, Session 38; musical instruments if being used
6. Prayer written by children from Session 9, volume 1 or have children write a prayer
7. Hospital skits developed by children and props used

Pentecost
Clown Ministry Service in Silence

Call to Worship

1st: Start by banging metal pans, blowing whistles, or ringing bells.

2nd: Use handshake and greeting developed.
3rd: Follow with bowling skit.

Affirmation of Faith
At the end of the bowling skit, have child hold up a card saying "FAITH."

Have someone read an affirmation they wrote.

Affirmation
Instead of asking for an offering, the clown minister always gives to others. Have children take their pop-bottle cats and dogs and go out into the congregation. Clowns should mingle among congregation, giving cards, flowers, and balloon animals to as many as possible. Use animals and cards to convey message that "God loves you."

It's also nice to incorporate a collection of canned goods for the needy. After clowns have given to congregation, congregation may come forward and place food in the empty baskets and bags of the clowns. You may even use a child's wagon and put a sign on the side that says "Food Wagon, Give to Those in Need". The clowns can fill the wagon as food is brought forward and then it can be rushed out of the service as if it is going directly to feed those who are hungry.

BIBLE LESSON
Pantomime parable of the good Samaritan as story is read from the Bible.

SERMON
Use the story "The Unwanted" as the sermon. Have a strong, loud reader or use a microphone so that clowns can hear words being read.

WITNESS TO FAITH
Use "The Tower." Have a reader in the puppet stage.

PRAYER
Do Lord's Prayer in sign language or a written prayer.

BENEDICTION

Use clown machine for benediction. If you are in the sanctuary with pews, you cannot put everyone in a circle. If you have a large congregation, select a few people for clown machine. Remember, everyone in circle is included in clown machine.

Have children present skit as silent clown walks around room carrying sign saying "Go Ye Into All the World." Close service with a love circle or your traditional closing.

Add Bible reading from Luke 10:25-37 at end.

PART SIX

A CHILDREN'S MUSICAL: THE LIFE AND TEACHING OF JESUS

14

·····························

How to Put Together a Children's Musical

Some may ask, "Why should we go to the extra work to put on a children's musical?" People who have directed musicals before know the advantages of putting together a musical at the end of the year: excitement, increased attendance, a sense of purpose, and a new understanding of what it means to be a follower of Jesus. You may also remember the headaches of trying to teach children an entire set of new songs in late spring and holding rehearsal after rehearsal when children would rather be outside playing. "Tell Me a Story" combines the best of both situations. The acting is simple and doesn't require hours of rehearsal time. The music comes from the songs you have sung and practiced all year. The story comes from Bible verses the children have studied throughout the year at the weekly workstations. You simply take the story of the life and teachings of Jesus, add the children's favorite songs, and have an easy-to-plan musical.

Session 40
His Life Began in a Manger

The Bible Lesson

The parable of the Pharisee and the tax collector

What the Children Will Learn Today

The lesson of humility (Luke 18:9-14)

Time Needed

5 minutes for story
20 minutes for workstations
10 minutes for closing service

Supplies Needed (by Workstation)

1. Paper grocery bags, fish pattern, paper, Bibles, scrap paper for stuffing, and craft supply basket with stapler
2. Red, black, and white construction paper, patterns, silver paper for bell, and craft supply basket
3. Pop bottles, silver duct tape, pattern, and cereal boxes
4. Script from musical, Bible, and props to be used
5. Pop bottles, silver duct tape, cereal boxes, and cardboard boxes (size to hold 5 pop bottles), and craft supply basket
6. Embroidery banner, needles, and crewel embroidery yarn in colors for flowers and leaves
7. Construction paper supply basket and art supplies: colored pencils, markers, charcoal pencils, chalk, or crayons

Children's Meditation

STORY

The Early Life of Jesus

None of us remember the actual day we were born, but ask your parents to tell stories of your birth and watch smiles of joy light up their faces. Their voices will be filled with pride as they once again tell the story of your arrival.

And so it must have been in the early worship services, the early Christians' faces filled with hope and joy as they retold over and over how Jesus was born in a humble cave with only the animals, some lowly shepherds, and finally wise men from the east. There were no brass bands, parades, or fancy parties. Jesus didn't even have his own bed to sleep in; he had to borrow a feeding trough filled with straw from the animals.

The humble, lowly circumstances surrounding the birth of Jesus were echoed throughout his ministry. Jesus grew up as the child of a carpenter in a poor, common, and humble household. He lived a simple life without fancy clothes or labels of greatness and started his ministry at the age of thirty. He traveled from town to town teaching and preaching without receiving any money or payment for his services, often trusting in the generosity and love of others for food and shelter for the night.

The example Jesus gave us through his own life gives us a guideline to follow. We should not be concerned with how much money we have; we should instead concern ourselves with helping others and showing God's love and kindness with everyone we meet. You're important to God regardless of whether you live in a simple one-room house without heat or a mansion.

Do you respond with a sarcastic comment when others tease you about how you are dressed?

Do you make up wild and exotic stories to impress others with your list of possessions?

Do you shy away from inviting friends home from school because you're embarrassed that your house is not as fancy as theirs might be?

Do you beg and plead to wear the same clothes as everyone else at school so that others won't think you're different?

Well, Jesus did the opposite. Jesus intentionally dressed differently, lived differently, and taught the common people of his day in a way totally different from the traditionally accepted, "popular" leaders of his time. Jesus said not to worry or get upset when others make fun of you or tease you, because that's to be expected. Jesus said that the important thing for you to do is to love God and to go out and share God's love with everyone you meet.

Permission granted to photocopy for local church use. © 2000 Elaine Clanton Harpine.

Workstations

Workstation 1: Call to Worship

INSTRUCTION SIGN

Many churches today use a bell to call people to worship. The early Christians drew the secret sign of the fish to announce or mark the place of worship. You're going to make a fish.

STEP 1:   Fold the bottom of a large brown grocery bag to form tail fin of fish. Trace pattern and cut out paper-bag fish.

STEP 2:   Copy memory verse, Luke 10:27, on the clear blank side of the fish. Decorate to cover any writing on side of bag. Use colorful markers and your best handwriting. Take your time.

STEP 3:   Stuff fish with scrap paper, seal edges with glue, and staple shut. Do NOT staple tail fin flat or your fish cannot pretend to swim.

STEP 4:   Trace pattern for tail. Make 4. Cut thin slits in each construction-paper tail fin. Glue in place.

Sign up to read Luke 10:27 for service today.

Workstation 2: Affirmation of Faith

GETTING READY

Make an example for children to follow. Do not staple booklets. Children will add more pages next week. Save booklets.

INSTRUCTION SIGN

God knows and hears each word you say, whether it be kind, rude, or hurtful. When you go out of your way to hurt someone else or someone else's feelings, you actually hurt yourself just as much as you hurt them. Read Luke 12:3, 15-21.

Sign up to help with the musical. Make a church as a reminder to say nice words to everyone you meet each and every day.

STEP 1:   Trace pattern and cut 3 churches. Cut 2 from white paper and 1 from red. Red is the liturgical color for the Holy Spirit and Pentecost. God is always with us.

STEP 2:   Cut a fish design from the red church page. Trim edges to fit neatly inside white pages. You're making a booklet. White pages are the cover. Write Bible verse and 5 ways you plan to be a better follower of Jesus on last white page.

STEP 3:   Trace and cut door opening and steeple window on cover. ONLY cut openings from 1 white page for front cover.

STEP 4:   Cut silver or white bell but glue down only the edges so that the bell stands up on red page. See example.

STEP 5:   Cut black doors, windows, and steeple roof using patterns. Glue in place as marked on pattern. Create stained-glass effect by gluing tiny strips of colored scrap paper into patterns and shapes.

You may also use stickers for windows or color windows on white paper and glue on top of the black frame.

Decorate puppet stage or worship table with booklets.

Workstation 3: Offering or Carpenter Shop

INSTRUCTION SIGN

A Jewish tax collector was one of the most hated people in any town. The tax collector worked for the Roman government and collected taxes from his fellow Jewish neighbors for a profit.

There was a "poll tax" just for being alive, a land tax, a tax for entering a walled city, an import and export tax on everything, a road tax, a tax for owning a cart, and even a tax for crossing a bridge. The poor often could not pay their taxes.

Read Luke 18:9-14 and sign up to help with the upcoming musical.

Jesus said that he came to bring peace (John 14:27) to all people. We're going to make a peace rocket to help us send his message of Peace out into the world. Build a peace rocket.

STEP 1: Stack and tape 3 or more pop bottles together. Cut open a cereal box and tape box around pop bottles. Use silver duct tape. Masking tape won't work.

STEP 2: Trace pattern for nose cone on cardboard and tape in place on top of rocket. You'll decorate rocket next week.

Workstation 4: Sermon or Bible Study

GETTING READY

Each week the sermon workstation will practice the musical.

INSTRUCTION SIGN

Jesus used the Pharisees as examples of how we shouldn't live our lives. The Pharisees were the ultimate snobs. They considered themselves better than everyone else and would not have anything to do with the poor. Jesus said we should not think of ourselves as better than someone else, for God will judge us with the same kindness that we judge others (Luke 6:37-38).

Read Luke 18:9-14 and remember to think of the feelings of others as you practice and work together. God never thinks one person is more important than another. God loves everyone equally and forgives our many mistakes. We should do the same.

Practice the "Call to Worship" section of the musical today and the pantomimed "Bible Reading." See script in Session 43.

Workstation 5: Witness to the World

GETTING READY

You'll need long scraps of fabric to make skirt for Session 43. Heavier fabric works best. Ask for donations ahead of time.

INSTRUCTION SIGN

Does your mom ever complain about how you wash your hands? To eat without washing your hands was a sin under Jewish law. You also had to wash your hands in a certain way. Special water was kept for handwashing. First, about 3 tablespoons of water were poured over your hands while you scrubbed with your fist. Then, hands were held up high and water was poured down from the tips of the fingers to the wrists. Finally, the process was repeated, but the second time the hands were to be held with fingers pointing down. It was almost impossible for anyone to completely follow the exact rules and procedures for washing hands. Jesus said it was more important to be honest and sincere than it was to follow every single petty rule. Read Luke 18:9-14 and sign up to be in the musical today.

We are making a stand-up puppet for the musical. Follow the step-by-step directions carefully so that your puppet will stand up when complete. It will take 3 weeks to finish.

STEP 1: Stack and tape 5 pop bottles together with duct tape. Cut open a cereal box and tape box around pop bottles, connecting them together. Use the silver duct tape. Masking tape won't work. Make sure pop bottles will stand.

STEP 2: Select a cardboard box that will hold 5 pop bottles standing up. This should be a tight fit.

STEP 3: Place glue on bottom of pop bottles and place 4 pop bottles into cardboard box. Slide stack of 5 pop bottles taped together into the center of box. Put glue on bottom pop bottle before placing in box. Let dry till next week, but make sure pop bottles fit tightly into the box and are drying straight. Sign up for musical.

Workstation 6: Prayer and Sewing Center

INSTRUCTION SIGN

Jewish law included all sorts of rules and regulations. The Pharisees, meaning the "separated ones," believed themselves to be better than other Jews because they followed every detail of Jewish law. Jesus, on the other hand, said that God wanted us to be humble and not filled with boastful pride. Sewing is a peaceful activity that gives you time to think. Read Luke 18:9-14 and think of ways that you can act more humbly in your daily life. Sign up for the musical and to lead the prayer.

Then, learn to sew a simple flower on our embroidery banner.

STEP 1: First draw an "X" on the cloth with a pencil. With a single strand of crewel embroidery yarn, start at the right-hand top point of the X. Stitch from right to left, leaving a loose, puffy thread sticking up.

STEP 2: Continue sewing right to left between the 2 top arms of the X, until you arrive at the center. Tie ends. Move to the bottom of the X and repeat process.

STEP 3: Fill in the 2 sides following the same procedure. Remember you want a puffy flower, so do not pull thread tight.

STEP 4: Once your flower is finished, you may add a center to your flower in a contrasting color. You may also sew leaves and stems for your flower.

Workstation 7: Benediction

INSTRUCTION SIGN

Jesus was Jewish. He lived in a hot, dry region. Most of the Jewish people had dark black or brown hair, and even the men wore their hair long. Jewish men often wore beards too. We do not have any photographs of Jesus. All of the drawings and pictures you see today are just an artist's idea of how Jesus might have looked.

STEP 1: You are the artist. Draw a picture of Jesus.

STEP 2: We are going to write a book during the next 3 weeks. We will start with the cover and first chapter today. Your picture of Jesus is the cover. Chapter 1 of your book will tell about the birth of Jesus. Read Luke 2:1-12 and Matthew 2:1-2. Draw a picture of the Nativity.

STEP 3: Staple pages together. Take booklets to worship.

The Worship Celebration

SIGN-UP SHEET FOR TODAY'S WORSHIP CELEBRATION

Call to Worship (sing a favorite song from musical):

Bible reader (Luke 10:27):

Sermon (practice Call to Worship from musical):

Bible readers (pantomime Bible readings from musical):

Lead the Lord's Prayer:

Benediction (share pictures of Jesus):

ITEMS TO GO HOME TODAY:
ART BOOKLETS

Session 41
The Parables Today

The Bible Lesson

Parable of the workers in the vineyard (Matthew 20:1-16)

What the Children Will Learn Today

God does not give more love to one than to another. Like a loving father, God loves us all the same.

Time Needed

5 minutes for story
20 minutes for workstations
10 minutes for closing service

Supplies Needed (by Workstation)

1. Scrap construction paper for cutting scales, paper-bag fish from last week, patterns, and craft supply basket
2. Church booklets, patterns, and brown construction paper
3. Wide roll of old wrapping paper (even brown wrapping paper can be used) or any paper that will cover peace rockets; craft supply basket, foil or shiny paper, and nose pattern
4. Complete script for musical and props to be used
5. Paper plates, craft supply basket, pop-bottle puppet, and supplies to be used for hair (yarn, fake hair, or paper)
6. Crewel embroidery yarn, banner, and needles
7. Construction paper supply basket and art supplies

Children's Meditation

STORY

The Strawberry Patch

Granny was known in the mountain area for her strawberries. She worked in her strawberry patch year-round. She would say, "You can't just sit around and wait for strawberries to happen. If you want the best strawberries, you have to work and tend them every day."

In winter, Granny gingerly placed straw around every strawberry plant to protect it from the cold snow. In early spring, Granny went out daily to pull weeds. When the strawberries were ripe, Granny gently picked every berry, being careful not to hurt the plant. In late spring and early summer, she transplanted and carried water to the plants. All year long, you could find Granny working in her strawberry patch.

One winter, as Granny grew older, she became very stiff with arthritis and was unable to climb the mountain path behind her house to the strawberry patch. She worried all winter, wondering if her strawberry plants would survive. Come spring, Granny still could not walk. There was no way she would be able to tend the strawberries this year, for it was all she could do to move around the house. Granny wondered what she would do. If she didn't sell strawberries this spring, she wouldn't have money to pay her bills.

Two boys came by early one morning wanting to buy strawberries. Sadly, Granny told the boys she wasn't able to pick strawberries anymore. The boys offered to work all day for two baskets of strawberries each. Granny was delighted. She sent the boys out to the patch to work. At noon, the boys brought the strawberries they had picked and placed them on the front porch. It was amazing; the front porch was almost covered with strawberries, and the boys said that there were still hundreds more. After lunch two other children came by Granny's and she sent them out with the first two boys to pick strawberries. Just before sundown, two other children happened by Granny's house looking to buy strawberries. Granny said in a pleading sort of voice, "Please go out and help the other children gather in all of the ripe strawberries, for there is a rainstorm coming tonight. If we do not gather the strawberries tonight, they will ruin before it is dry enough to work in the strawberry patch again."

As the glow of evening was setting in, all of the children returned to the house with ripe strawberries. The harvest was better than Granny could ever remember. As the parents arrived to call the children home, Granny told each child who had worked to select not two as she had promised that morning but four baskets of the best strawberries.

Well, the children who had arrived before sunset were delighted, and so were the children who went to work after lunch, but the two boys who had worked since morning were angry. The boys said, "That's not fair! We worked longer than they did. We deserve more than they do."

Grandma looked kindly at the boys and said, "Didn't I pay you more than you agreed to work for?"

The boys nodded their heads in agreement. "Then you should never be greedy and demand more than someone else. As long as you have been given the payment you agreed to, it does not take away from you or your work if I am generous with the others who happened to come along and help at the last minute. Everyone is important. If it had not been for the extra help, many of the strawberries would have been lost in the rainstorm. I needed everyone to bring in the harvest."

Granny smiled her usual loving smile and served everyone strawberries and cake before they headed for home. In the days that followed, all of the children returned early each morning to Granny's strawberry patch. The children gathered the ripe strawberries, tended the plants, and were always paid in equal amounts of strawberries.

Workstations

Workstation 1: Call to Worship

GETTING READY

Have paper-bag fish from last week and scrap paper for scales.

INSTRUCTION SIGN

The fish was the secret sign of the early Christians. They used the sign of the fish on their pottery and as decorations on their houses. The sign of the fish would announce to another Christian that it was safe because friends lived within.

Just as Jesus calls us to be friends to other Christians, we are also reminded to care for all of God's creation. Use scrap paper today as a way of recycling leftover paper from other projects. Read Matthew 23:11-12 and then continue working on your fish. We want to finish the fish before the musical.

STEP 1: Trace and cut scales for fish. Remember to use only scrap paper. You need about 30 scales.

STEP 2: Trace mouth pattern on paper-bag fish to show where mouth will be placed.

STEP 3: Glue scales in place. Start at tail. Glue scales in place, overlapping edge of tail fin and overlapping line for mouth. You do no need to glue scales where mouth will go. Overlap scales as you glue. Completely cover brown bag.

STEP 4: On the side where you have written your memory verse, place scales only along edges so that you frame your writing but do not cover up any of the words.

Workstation 2: Affirmation of Faith

GETTING READY

Keep booklets together by tacking them on bulletin board.

INSTRUCTION SIGN

In late August and early September, the grape harvest must be gathered before the September rains start. Hired servants or day laborers gathered at the marketplace in hopes of being hired for the day. A Jewish day was from approximately 6:00 A.M.. to 6:00 P.M. Landowners would go to the marketplace in search of workers in the morning, at noon, in the afternoon, and sometimes even an hour before quitting time if they needed extra workers. It was very likely that the owner of a vineyard would go back to the marketplace and hire more workers with only one hour left to work, if all of the grapes had not been gathered. Read Matthew 20:1-16. The lesson is that we should not compare ourselves to others or be jealous of what others may receive. Add to your booklet from last week or start a booklet today.

STEP 1: Cut blue carpeting and brown pulpit pages using patterns. Blue is a liturgical color used in the church to represent truth. You will often see blue used near the altar.

STEP 2: Fold steps leading to fish symbol like a paper fan.

STEP 3: Make red liturgical paraments to hang on pulpit. Fringe edges and put a small gold or yellow fish on the front.

STEP 4: Cut altar or communion table. Glue directly underneath fish on red page. Glue ONLY ends of table so that steps can slide in and out from underneath. Do NOT glue steps.

STEP 5: Glue just the edges of the brown and blue pages together to strengthen the page when turned. On carpeting, write "Welcome to God's House." Do not staple or glue your booklet together yet, because you will add the last page next week. Remember, you are making a book. The pages are to turn. Today's service will use the Bible verses from the "Affirmation" section of our upcoming musical. Sign up to read today.

Workstation 3: Offering or Carpenter Shop

GETTING READY

The purpose of the peace rocket is to teach the Bible verses. Make sure the children read and copy the verses.

INSTRUCTION SIGN

Hired servants were hired by the day and were always paid at the end of the day, for they were very poor and needed money to buy food. Jesus said that God does not love those who are rich more than those who are poor. God loves everyone equally. Read Matthew 20:1-16. Then finish working on your peace rocket.

STEP 1:   Trace pattern and cut paper to cover nose of rocket. You may use foil or shiny paper for metal effect. If you wish to decorate the nose of your rocket, do so before gluing paper in place. Remember your purpose is to "go in peace."

STEP 2:   Cover bottom of rocket with silver paper too.

STEP 3:   Cut paper to cover the sides of the peace rocket. Don't glue paper on rocket yet. Read one of the following Bible passages and select a Bible verse(s) to write on the side of your rocket: Ephesians 4:2-3; James 3:16-18; Galatians 5:22-23, 26; Romans 12:15-18; Psalm 34:14; and John 14:27. Draw pictures explaining each Bible verse. Take your time and work neatly. Decorate your rocket and make it look very fancy. Your rocket will take a special peace message out into the world. Peace rockets will be on display at the musical. Place peace rocket in worship area when finished.

Workstation 4: Sermon or Bible Study

INSTRUCTION SIGN

The parables talk about helping those in need and sharing God's love. Jesus explained that it was important not to just sit and listen to the words he spoke but to take the ideas he talked about and put them into action to help others.

Read Matthew 5:16. Many of the followers of Jesus continued to teach the principles Jesus taught and put them into practice in daily life after his death. Read Matthew 20:1-16 and practice the "Affirmation" portion of the musical today.

Workstation 5: Witness to Faith

INSTRUCTION SIGN

At age eighteen, Jewish boys who wanted to become scribes or doctors would find a teacher to follow. These students were called disciples. Jesus was such a teacher. His followers listened to many stories or parables. We can still learn from the teachings of Jesus. Read Matthew 20:1-16. Then continue working on your pop-bottle puppet.

STEP 1: Glue 5 paper plates together to make 1 stiff plate for the face. It is easier to make your pop-bottle puppet a girl than a boy. A long skirt can easily be draped around the pop bottles, so draw a girl's face.

STEP 2: Make hair for the puppet. You may use yarn, fake hair, or curl long strips of construction paper to make paper curls. Glue hair along edges and top of plate. The paper-plate face is the head for your pop-bottle puppet.

STEP 3: Tape paper-plate face to top of pop bottles for head of puppet. Use duct tape to hold plate in place.

STEP 4: Make and glue more hair to a second plate for the back of the head. Staple or glue second plate to face plate after it is taped to pop bottle. Cover staples with hair. Make sure pop-bottle top does not show. Do not glue plates to pop bottles because you will be adding cloth next week.

Workstation 6: Prayer and Sewing Center

INSTRUCTION SIGN

Prayer and sewing both take patience. If you learned how to sew a flower last week, find a friend or someone you do not know and teach them how to sew. Teaching someone else how to sew a flower is like having a prayer chain. You keep God's love flowing from person to person. Read Matthew 20:1-16 and sign up to lead the Lord's Prayer for our service today.

Workstation 7: Benediction

INSTRUCTION SIGN

Jesus worked as a carpenter and knew the problems of earning a living wage. Read Matthew 20:1-16. If the owner of the vineyard reduced a worker's wage for arriving late, there would be hungry children at the laborer's home that night. As Christians, we must think of the needs of our neighbors. It is not right for one person to eat while another goes hungry.

Jesus frequently taught large crowds of people as they gathered by the Sea of Galilee. Draw a picture of Jesus sitting in a small fishing boat in the water with a crowd of people standing and listening to him teach. Add page to art booklet.

The Worship Celebration

GETTING READY

Worship this week is the "Affirmation" portion of musical.

SIGN-UP SHEET FOR TODAY'S WORSHIP CELEBRATION

Sermon (Affirmation portion of musical): Lead the Lord's Prayer in sign language:

ITEMS TO GO HOME TODAY: ART BOOKLETS

Session 42
He's Alive in Our Church

The Bible Lesson

The lesson comes from the parable of the mustard seed (Matthew 13:31-32; Mark 4:30-32; and Luke 13:18-19).

What the Children Will Learn Today

The fancy, expensive things of the world are not the most important. Instead, the simplest, smallest acts of kindness rank with God as most important.

Time Needed

5 minutes for story
20 minutes for workstations
10 minutes for closing service from Lenten Home Worship Program

Supplies Needed (by Workstation)

1. Construction paper, patterns, fish, and craft supply basket
2. Brown and yellow paper, patterns, and church booklet
3. Pop-bottle rocket, paper for sides, red and orange streamers, and craft supply basket
4. Musical script and props being used
5. Large pieces of cloth to make skirt and blouse for puppet, fabric glue, sewing pins, duct tape, needle, and thread
6. Embroidery banner, crewel yarn, and needles
7. Construction paper, art supplies, and art booklet

Children's Meditation

STORY

Miss Never-Thinks-of-Anyone-but-Herself

One day, Miss Sally Never-Thinks-of-Anyone-but-Herself was going over to visit her friend Marcy. Sally put on her fanciest sunbonnet and slung her largest basket across her arm.

When she arrived at Marcy's front door, Sally noticed that Marcy had made beautiful dolls to place in the front yard for decoration. One doll was dressed in pink, one in yellow, and one in lavender.

"Oh, they're just wonderful," said Sally. "I must have one in pink for my yard." Sally knocked several times on Marcy's door, but no one answered. Finally, Sally decided to take the pink doll along with her and call Marcy later. So, Sally picked up the pink doll and plopped it in her basket as she went on to the grocery store.

Mr. Jackson was having a craft bazaar. The sign read, "Make your own craft basket, all supplies provided, just read and follow the posted directions."

"What a clever idea," said Sally. She looked at the directions posted. "Oh! that's much too complicated for me. I could never read all of that."

Sally picked up the example sitting next to the sign and spun the little yarn basket around and around in her hand. "What a darling little basket," Sally said again. "Well, I'll just take the example. After all, the supplies are free. Mr. Jackson is so talented that he can surely make another. I could never make one so fine." Sally placed the little yarn basket next to the pink doll and on she went to finish her shopping.

Next, Sally walked over to the flower shop. Mrs. Jones was teaching people how to make paper flowers. "Oh, I could never do that," said Sally.

"Of course you can," said Mrs. Jones. "This is actually a very simple flower to make. It only looks complicated. Once you know how to make a paper carnation, you'll be teaching others. Flower making is fun. Why don't you give it a try? You'll never know how much fun you can have till you try."

"Oh well, maybe just this once," said Sally. Sally gathered and pinched, just as Mrs. Jones instructed. Sally looked at her flower. It didn't look a thing like Mrs. Jones's example. Sally held her flower in her right hand and the example Mrs. Jones had made in her left hand. There was no question, the flower Mrs. Jones had made was definitely better. When no one was looking, Sally placed the flower she had made on the table where the example had been and dropped the flower Mrs. Jones had made into her basket.

With her nose tilted ever so slightly skyward, Sally started up the path to her home. There, right in front of Sally, was a little boy stealing apples from a cart parked at the side of the path. Sally immediately dashed over, caught the young boy by the collar, and said, "What do you think you are doing, young man? Don't you know that stealing is wrong? You should never take anything that does not belong to you."

Sally marched the small boy into the shop. "I caught this young man stealing from your cart," she said.

"James," the apple cart owner said in a stern sort of voice, "were you taking apples from my cart?"

The young boy looked at the ground very sadly and whispered, "Yes."

"Let this be a lesson to you, young man," said Miss Never-Thinks-of-Anyone-but-Herself, readjusting the basket on her arm as she turned to walk on home carrying the fancy pink doll from Marcy's yard, the little yarn basket from the craft table, and the beautiful paper carnation from the flower shop. "You must never take anything that doesn't belong to you," said Sally, feeling very satisfied with herself for having stopped the young man from stealing the apples.

Workstations

Workstation 1: Call to Worship

> INSTRUCTION SIGN
>
> Sometimes we think a lie is not a lie or stealing is not stealing if what we lie about or what we steal seems unimportant. Jesus said that we should not be concerned about what someone else is doing until we are certain that we are doing what is required of us. Read Matthew 13:31-32 and 7:3 and remember that little problems grow into big problems when you're not telling the truth. If you did not finish all of your scales last week, finish cutting and gluing scales on your fish.
>
> STEP 1: Trace and cut 2 mouths and eyes for fish.
>
> STEP 2: Once all scales are finished, glue mouth in place. Mouth and eyes should match on each side. Do not cover up your Bible verse. You can trim mouth if needed.
>
> STEP 3: Trace and cut side fin. Cut thin slashes in fin. Glue in place as indicated on fish pattern. Take to worship.

Workstation 2: Affirmation of Faith

INSTRUCTION SIGN

The mustard seed was one of the smallest seeds in Palestine. From one of the tiniest of seeds would grow a 7' to 12' tree with branches strong enough for birds to sit and rest. Mustard trees were planted out in the fields instead of in the garden because they grew so large. Read Mark 4:30-32. Jesus said that if we had faith even as small as the mustard seed (Matthew 17:20), we would be able to accomplish great things in our lives for God because our faith would grow. The great things Jesus talked about were not fancy cars, expensive clothes, or big houses. Jesus meant that we could do great deeds for God by being kind, helping those in need, and loving our neighbors. Finish your church booklet and remember what it means to be a follower of Jesus. It's not easy to follow the teachings of Jesus.

STEP 1: Cut a yellow and brown piece of paper using the pew pattern. Set brown paper aside.

STEP 2: This is the only step that is a little hard, but if you read the directions carefully, you'll do fine. Fold the yellow piece of paper in half as shown in the example and cut the pews and altar rail, following the lines on the pattern. Fold on dotted lines. Cut on solid lines. Repeat for each side.

STEP 3: Fold pews on dotted line, creasing tightly to hold pews in open chair position.

STEP 4: Glue edges of brown pew-shaped paper to back of yellow pews for support. Staple booklet together at left edge. Place church booklet on worship table for today's service.

Workstation 3: Offering or Carpenter Shop

INSTRUCTION SIGN

Jesus warns us that you cannot worship both God and money. If money is more important in your life, God and love will be lacking. Read Matthew 6:19-21, 24. Finish peace rocket.

STEP 1: Attach paper to pop-bottle rocket. First, tape one side to pop bottle. Then, wrap paper around bottle covering tape. Glue edge overlapping tape. You do not want any tape to show. Glue makes a nicer finished edge than tape.

STEP 2: Glue yellow, red, or orange streamers to bottom of rocket. Streamers will fly in the wind as you carry your peace rocket along. Place rockets near the worship table for service.

Workstation 4: *Sermon or Bible Study*

GETTING READY

You may need to schedule extra rehearsals for the musical. If so, announce times and places when choirs, readers, and actors will meet. Publicize upcoming musical to congregation.

INSTRUCTION SIGN

Sometimes we read about the conversion of Paul on the road to Damascus and we think that everyone must have some dramatic event happen in their life to become a Christian. Jesus reminds us with the parable of the mustard seed that your conversion may be a gradual process. Read Matthew 13:31-32. We become Christians step-by-step as we learn to follow the teachings of Jesus. Learning a new craft project is a step-by-step process too. You can't skip a step or leave a step out. Learning to be kind to others is one of the first steps for a Christian to learn. Think of a way you could show kindness to others today.

Practice the "Sermon" and "Witness" sections of the musical today. Make sure everyone knows their parts in the musical. Practice and help those who are having trouble.

Workstation 5: *Witness to Faith*

GETTING READY

Once the children have learned how to make the large pop-bottle puppet, make supplies available for those who wish to make a tall pop-bottle puppet to take home.

INSTRUCTION SIGN

Do not be overly proud, self-righteous, or certain that you are better than someone else. The rudeness you show to others will come back to you. The kindness you give to others will grow and not only make you happy but others as well. Kindness is like the mustard seed: A little bit makes a lot of happiness. Read Luke 6:37-38 and 13:18-19. Finish pop-bottle puppet today.

STEP 1: Cut fabric large enough to wrap around pop bottles for blouse. Turn under edges of cloth so that unraveling edges do not show. Glue to pop bottle for blouse. Tuck blouse underneath paper-plate face and completely cover top of pop bottle. Hold cloth in place till dry. Use straight sewing pins or tacks to help hold cloth in place. Push pins into pop bottle.

STEP 2: Cut matching fabric and make arms. Roll and glue cloth to form sleeve. Pin in place till dry. Roll scrap of old stocking into a ball and glue in end of each sleeve for hands.

STEP 3: While sleeve is drying, cut a piece of cloth large enough to wrap around pop bottles and box being used for a stand to make skirt for puppet. Use heavy fabric. You want the skirt to be full and completely cover box.

Place bottom of skirt on selvage or fabric edge that will not unravel. Glue and pin skirt onto pop bottles over bottom of blouse. Gather skirt fabric around pop bottle evenly to form waist. Use glue and straight pins to hold skirt in place. Make sure that raveling edges, cardboard box, or pop bottle DO NOT SHOW. Skirt should touch floor. Tie ribbon around waist.

STEP 4: Glue and pin sleeve to pop bottle to form shoulder. Use lace or other trims to cover over shoulder or edges that are exposed. Make puppet look pretty. Work together as a team to finish puppet today. Take finished puppet to worship today.

Workstation 6: Prayer and Sewing Center

INSTRUCTION SIGN

Everyone is important to God, and everyone is included in God's church. There is always room for everyone. Read Luke 13:18-19 and remember that God does not choose favorites. We all make mistakes, but God forgives us all for God is love. Our job now is to love one another as God loves us, to be forgiving, to be generous and kind, to be understanding, and to show that we care.

Continue sewing today. See how many flowers you can finish. Take the banner to worship today. Display the banner for the musical.

Workstation 7: Benediction

INSTRUCTION SIGN

Jesus calls us to do more than just say that we love God. Jesus calls us to demonstrate our love for God and our willingness to follow him by how we treat other people. Even a simple "Hello!" or a smile can make a difference. Even something as simple as walking around with a smile instead of a frown or saying something nice, instead of something grumpy or selfish, helps kindness to grow within us and with others. Read Matthew 13:31-32. One of our jobs as followers of Jesus is to share God's love with everyone we meet (Mark 16:15).

Finish your art booklet today by drawing a picture of a church. In your picture, show how your church helps others and shares God's love. Take your art booklet to worship today.

The Worship Celebration

SIGN-UP SHEET FOR TODAY'S WORSHIP
CELEBRATION

Sermon and Witness portions of musical:
Lead the Lord's Prayer in sign language

ITEMS TO GO HOME TODAY: CRAFTS
MAY BE TAKEN HOME OR KEPT TO BE
DISPLAYED FOR MUSICAL TODAY.

Session 43
A Children's Musical:
The Life and
Teachings of Jesus

GETTING READY

This week's session is scheduled as a dress rehearsal. All of your children should be involved as singers in the choir, actors in the play, or as stagehands with props and sets. Plan for a longer than usual session so that you can rehearse as a total group.

Time Needed: Approximately 1 hour (Time of musical will vary depending on the length and number of songs you include.)

PROPS AND SETS NEEDED

This musical can be presented with an elaborate set or as a chancel drama with no set at all. First, decide on the date, time, and location. When and where you are staging the musical will partially determine the props and sets you want to use. You may wish to decorate the sanctuary with red helium balloons to represent the Holy Spirit or build an entire biblical village in your fellowship hall to enhance the story. You can also reuse many of the props and sets from the Christmas service in volume 1 and the Easter services earlier in this book.

The opening scene might use nothing more than hairbrushes, a mirror, and newspapers, or you may create a living room scene with chairs and such. The importance lies in what is being said about helping others, not in elaborate sets and props.

The puppet stage may be as simple as a cloth held up by children, with the pop-bottle puppet in front, or your Sunshine Share-a-Lot puppet stage. The puppet can be simply an offstage voice with a microphone, a member of the choir, a hand puppet, or the tall pop-bottle doll made at Workstation 5. If you use a hand puppet, make sure puppet is large enough to be seen easily.

The biblical scenes may use nothing more than children in biblical costumes or use trees, house, and gate from Easter play.

COSTUMES

Costumes for the musical can be very simple or elaborate. Your children's choir can dress in their Sunday best or in robes. The five actors with memorized lines are dressed for church on Sunday, which can include fancy Easter hats and gloves for girls and suits and ties for boys. The pantomime actors can use simple biblical costumes from Christmas and Easter.

CAST

Five actors (girls or boys) with memorized speaking parts
>   Erin:
>   Ashley:
>   Morgan:
>   Kyle:
>   Cory:

Pantomime actors (need at least 7 children for good Samaritan scene—acting with no speaking part):

Bible readers (may have as many as 22 different children reading from the Bible or just one or two):

Puppeteer:
Reader for puppet:

Script

Prelude

[The musical is a worship service. The prelude includes all young people who take music lessons and would like to play their instruments or have learned to make a "Joyful noise to the Lord!" It is important to include *all* children, because so often in school only a few with superior skills are chosen. In God's house, everyone should be welcome, even beginners.]

CALL TO WORSHIP

[Cory enters dressed for church pushing a box of newspapers; plops down in a big chair and starts to sort through the stack of newspapers, making a mess. Kyle and Erin enter arguing over the comics from the Sunday newspaper and move to center stage.]

KYLE:	It's mine. I had it first.
ERIN:	That's not fair. We're supposed to share.
KYLE:	You can read the comics when I'm finished.
ERIN:	You're supposed to divide the comics evenly. You read half and I read half, then we trade. [Erin grabs paper from Kyle. Paper tears in half. Erin and Kyle sit with their backs to each other reading half of the paper.]
CORY:	[loud disgusted voice] There's nothing in here!
ASHLEY:	[Enters reading the Bible; sits in chair across stage from Cory.] Maybe you should try reading something different. [Morgan enters in middle of stage and shakes head in disbelief as Erin and Kyle swap comic pages. Morgan continues combing her hair and getting ready for church.]
MORGAN:	Whatever are the two of you talking about?
CORY:	I have to find an article from the newspaper for Sunday school this morning that tells about something *good* happening in the world. Something that shows how Jesus is working in the lives of people right here in our community.
MORGAN:	What's so bad about that?
ASHLEY:	She can't find anything. [Continues reading Bible]
CORY:	All this newspaper talks about is people getting shot with guns, drug deals at the park, and a robbery at the all-night grocery. There's just page after page of awful things happening. There's not even one story about anything good in this entire newspaper. I don't know why Mrs. Johnson gave us this assignment anyway. It doesn't make any sense. Jesus lived a long time ago. How can we possibly still find any evidence of his work today?
ERIN:	You can borrow my half of the comics if you want.
CORY:	No thanks, I have to have a *real* story.
ASHLEY:	Maybe you should look in the Bible. There are lots of stories in the Bible.
CORY:	I have to have a *current* story; something that happened this week.
MORGAN:	Well, there's bound to be something good that happened somewhere to someone. You just have to look harder. We'll help. Come on! [Motions to others to come over and help. Everyone moves toward Cory and takes a section of paper. Music begins. Ashley stops and turns toward TV.]
ASHLEY:	Listen! My favorite TV show is coming on. Maybe, they'll tell something good that has happened lately. It can't hurt to listen. [Sits down in front of TV screen. Have TV sign visible from puppet stage.]
FIRST SONG:	[Use a lively song for your intro.] [Puppet appears at puppet stage as soon as song ends. Puppet reader wants to use a clear but very charismatic, enthusiastic voice for puppet. If it is a hand puppet, have puppeteer keep

puppet active and moving around. The pop-bottle doll can easily enter from behind the curtains of the puppet stage if you use the doll from Workstation 5. If you do not want to use a puppet, use an offstage voice or member of the choir.]

PUPPET TV
ANNOUNCER: Good morning and welcome on this fine Sunday morning. We have come together today to celebrate God's love. This is God's house and we have gathered together today to sing praise to the Lord.

Clap your hands, stomp your feet, and sing right along with the choir. Don't let there be any doubt in anyone's mind that you are a follower of Jesus and that you are happy to be here this morning.

If you had an argument with the person sitting next to you this morning, turn right now and tell them you are sorry. We don't want to have any anger, rude words, or arguments standing between us this morning. We've come to celebrate God's love and to sing praise to him.

We'd like to tell you a story; a story told through the words of a song. It's an old story, but a story that is still meaningful to us today. So come along with us and celebrate. Tell everyone you meet that God loves them. God loves you. God loves me. God loves everyone.

SECOND SONG:

Affirmation of Faith

NARRATOR: Jesus' life began in a small town about four miles from Jerusalem called Bethlehem in the year 7 B.C. Bethlehem lay nestled in the hills and was known as the "House of Bread" because of the many wheat fields that lay at the outskirts of town. This wheat was frequently used by the peasants to make their daily bread. Life was hard. Comforts were few. Most of the Jews had become discouraged because there had not been a prophet or religious leader among the people for almost four hundred years. Some wanted war and hoped for a king to lead them into battle against the Romans. Others waited and prayed in silence as they daily hoped for the Messiah to come and lead them to freedom.

BIBLE READER: [Luke 2:1-7]
[Mary and Joseph enter and arrive at manger during reading.]

THIRD SONG:

BIBLE READER: [Luke 2:8-12]
[Shepherds arrive at manger.]

FOURTH SONG:

BIBLE READER: [Matthew 2:1-2]
[Wise men enter and present gifts.]

FIFTH SONG:
[Nativity actors clear stage quietly.]

NARRATOR: Jesus grew up in the small town of Nazareth in northern Galilee. As the son of a carpenter, Jesus learned to build houses, furniture, plows or whatever was needed by the people of Nazareth. When Jesus was about thirty, he went one day to hear John the Baptist preach.

SIXTH SONG:

NARRATOR: At the age of thirty, Jesus began traveling on foot from town to town in Galilee preaching and teaching the common people about God's love. People came from everywhere to listen to Jesus preach and tell about the kingdom of God.

BIBLE READER: [Matthew 4:18-20]
[Pantomime actors with boat pretend to be fishing with fishing nets. Drop nets and slowly go off to follow Jesus as Bible verse is read.]

BIBLE READER: [Matthew 4:23]

BIBLE READER: [Mark 1:22]

SEVENTH SONG:
BIBLE LESSON FROM THE GOSPEL

[The Bible lesson is a series of Bible verses being pantomimed by 4 actors. The Bible verses are all from the teachings of Jesus, and the actors show how the verses apply to us today. Use a different reader for each verse or two alternating readers at different lecterns. You may also have children read without pantomiming words, but the pantomime is very effective.]

BIBLE READER,
Pantomime 1:   [Matthew 5:11-12]
                [Have pantomimist pretend to be accusing the Christian: Actor 1 walks out reading Bible. Actor 2 comes by and pretends to be accusing Actor 1 of something. Actor 3 enters scene and Actor 2 starts explaining to Actor 3 how badly Actor 1 has acted. Actors 2 and 3 finally leave stage in disgust at Actor 1.]
BIBLE READER, Pantomime 2: [Matthew 5:14-16]
                [The Christian being accused in Pantomime 1 walks over and lights a hand lamp, places it on a stand, and kneels to pray. Then, Actor 1 picks up hand lamp on the wall near well and pretends to hold the lamp up to read the Bible. Actor 4 comes out limping. Actor 1 puts lamp and Bible down on the floor and helps Actor 4 across stage. Then Actor 1 goes back to center stage to kneel and pray.]
BIBLE READER, Pantomime 3: [Matthew 6:24]
                [Actor 1 continues praying while Actors 2 and 3 return with big shopping bags and come across stage jingling coins and laughing. Actors 2 and 3 stop and laugh at Actor 1.]
BIBLE READER, Pantomime 4: [Matthew 7:1-2]
                [Actor 1 remains kneeling and praying. Actors 2 and 3 put on radio headsets or hold radios to ear from their shopping bags and pretend to dance around. Actors 2 and 3 tease Actor 1 for praying. Actors 2 and 3 laugh, imitate, and point at Actor 1.]
BIBLE READER, Pantomime 5: [John 8:31-32]
                [Everyone freezes in a natural but not strange position while Bible verse is read.]
BIBLE READER, Pantomime 6: [Matthew 6:5-9]
                [Actor 1 continues on knees, head bowed, hands folded in prayer. Actors 2 and 3 put on fancy hats from shopping bags and raise hands to make a big scene of praying to God with exaggerated hand and arm gestures.]
                [Everyone freezes during Lord's Prayer; clear stage after prayer.]
Congregational Prayer
NARRATOR: Will you join with us as our sign language interpreters lead us in praying together the words Jesus taught the disciples to say?
LORD'S
PRAYER: [Spoken and in sign language]
EIGHTH SONG:

Offering of Time and Help to Others in Need
BIBLE READER: [Luke 10:25-37]
                [Actors will act out the parable onstage as it is read.]
NINTH SONG:

Sermon
BIBLE READER: [Mark 11:1-10]
TENTH SONG:
BIBLE READER: [Matthew 26:17-19]

[If you are using a set with a biblical village, you can have your children enter carrying baskets and water jars. Speak to person at house and enter biblical house.]

BIBLE READERS: [Mark 14:22-24 and John 13:34-35]

ELEVENTH SONG:

BIBLE READER: [Mark 15:24]

INSTRUMENTAL MUSIC: [Use sad and sorrowful music. If you have children who play in a school orchestra, a string selection is excellent.]

Witness to Faith

[Have music playing softly as readers read in continuous sequence, 1 through 5, but growing louder near the end. Go immediately from last Bible reading to song of resurrection and joy.]

BIBLE READERS:

[1] Do not be worried and upset . . . Believe in God and believe also in me. There are many rooms in my Father's house, and I am going to prepare a place for you . . .

    If you love me, you will obey my commandments . . . My commandment is this: love one another, just as I love you.
[John 14:1-2, 15; 15:12 TEV]

[2] The greatest love a person can have for his friends is to give his life for them. [John 15:13 TEV]

[3] I am the light of the world . . . Whoever follows me will have the light of life and will never walk in darkness. [John 8:12 TEV]

[4] "I was hungry and you fed me, thirsty and you gave me a drink; I was a stranger and you received me in your homes, naked and you clothed me; I was sick and you took care of me, in prison and you visited me." The righteous will then answer him, "When, Lord, did we ever see you hungry and feed you, or thirsty and give you a drink? When did we ever see you a stranger and welcome you in our homes, or naked and clothe you? When did we ever see you sick or in prison, and visit you?" The king will reply, "I tell you, whenever you did this for one of the least important of these brothers of mine, you did it for me!" . . . Whenever you refused to help one of these least important ones, you refused to help me." [Matthew 25:35-40, 45 TEV]

[5] Go throughout the whole world and preach the gospel to all mankind. [Mark 16:15 TEV]

TWELFTH SONG: [Song of resurrection and joy]
    [Choirs exit, form circle around room. Music continues. Actors return to positions on stage as they were when TV show began.]

MORGAN: You're right, Ashley, that was a nice program. My favorite part was the music. [Begins to hum and dance around]

ASHLEY: I told you the Bible had lots of good stories.

CORY: Sure, it's great to hear the story of Jesus' life from the Bible, but how does that help solve my problem? Mom and Dad are going to be downstairs any minute saying it's time to get into the car and go to church, and I still don't have a current, up-to-date story. What am I going to do?

OFFSTAGE
FEMALE
VOICE: [Spoken loudly backstage] Are you dressed and ready for Sunday school? Leaving in five minutes!

EVERYONE: Yes! [Everyone scrambles around looking for shoes, straightens clothes, puts on hat, and gets ready to go.]

KYLE: My shoes! Where are my shoes?

CORY: Five minutes! [Turns frantically through newspaper] I'll never find a story in five minutes.

ASHLEY: Why don't you write your own?

CORY:	In five minutes, I'm supposed to write my own story?
ERIN:	You could publish your own newspaper: The *Good News Herald,* written and published by Cory Livington.
KYLE:	I'll be the business manager and handle the money.
CORY:	[Looks over top of paper] Very funny, this has to be a *true* story, something that actually happened.
ASHLEY:	It will be true, if you make it happen. Remember how they talked about going out and feeding the hungry on the TV show? Well, we could go around the neighborhood collecting food for those in need right here in our community.
MORGAN:	What a good idea!
ERIN:	We could use our old red wagon. We could make a big sign to put on the side: "Food for the Hungry."
KYLE:	No, the sign should say "Feed the Hungry." [Kyle and Erin start arguing over whether the sign should read "Food for the Hungry" or "Feed the Hungry."]
MORGAN:	Stop arguing before Mom and Dad hear you. It doesn't matter whether the sign says "Food for the Hungry" or "Feed the Hungry." The important thing is to help.
ASHLEY:	We could print up flyers and hand them out door-to-door on Wednesday. Then return on Saturday to collect.
ERIN:	That's a good idea.
CORY:	[Still looking through the newspapers] Why? So we don't end up with twenty-five cans of black olives that nobody wants.
KYLE:	I have often wondered how someone would manage to put together a meal from the strange assortment of canned goods turned in during food collection drives.
MORGAN:	We could tell everyone we're trying to collect breakfast, lunch, and dinner for a family in each grocery bag.
CORY:	[Very sarcastically] That's a great idea! Then, we would have black olives for breakfast, green olives for lunch, and olives with pimentos for dinner.
ASHLEY:	We're trying to help.
CORY:	How does a food collection help my story?
ASHLEY:	Jesus said that when you help anyone in need you help him, too, so we're helping tell others about God's love. What better story could you want?
MORGAN:	Remember the song we sing in church? [Choirs in circle around room. Congregation encouraged to join singing.]

CONGREGATIONAL SONG:

OFFSTAGE FEMALE VOICE:	Time to go. Everyone in the car, please. [Everyone gets up to leave.]
MORGAN:	Let's tell Mom and Dad.
CORY:	What am I going to tell Mrs. Johnson?
EVERYONE:	Tell her about the project.
MORGAN:	Telling about something that's going to happen is still news.
CORY:	I hope this works.
ASHLEY:	Who knows? Maybe your whole Sunday school class will want to get involved. [Everyone rushes offstage.]

CONGREGATIONAL SONG:

[All children sing holding hands in a circle around the room.]

Benediction

[Use a musical benediction that everyone can join.]

Postlude

[Instrumental music provided by children.]

PART SEVEN

....

DON'T CLOSE DOWN FOR THE SUMMER

15

. . . .

Building a Biblical Village

Building a biblical village is a fun way to teach children about the Bible. The village may be used for your summer children's worship program, for vacation Bible school, or for a summer Sunday school program for all ages.

There are still seven learning centers for the seven parts of the worship service. Each workstation represents a different place in a biblical village. You may build your village in one small room, a large room, in seven different rooms, or even outside.

Building a biblical village teaches children about daily activities during the life of Jesus. The Bible lessons are from the parables.

Regardless of whether you set up your village only during the summer or year-round, it can be a wonderful educational environment in which to teach the Bible to children. The centers are easy to set up, teach authentic biblical-type crafts, and provide accurate historical information. The idea is to help children understand how it would have been to live during New Testament times.

Session 44
A Biblical House

The Bible Lesson
The parable of patience (Mark 4:26-29) and the parable of the talents (Matthew 25:14-30)

What the Children Will Learn Today

Never give up; never quit.

Time Needed

5 minutes for story
20 minutes for workstations
10 minutes for closing worship service

Supplies Needed (by Workstation)

1. Laundry boxes, brown paper or bags, and craft supply basket
2. Empty 2-liter plastic pop bottles, papier-mâché, paintbrush, newsprint or scrap paper, large pan for papier-mâché, dry sand, craft supply basket, and cover-ups for clothing and tables
3. Tools, wood for boat, and diagram, pages 240-244

4. Skit, puppets, and video camera or cardboard TV camera

5. Hanging weaving loom, 36" cloth scraps, and 2 dowel rods

6. Small boxes, yarn, construction paper, paper bags or scrap paper, and yarn needles, cardboard juice cans, hole punch, yarn or pipe cleaners for handles, and craft supply basket

7. Construction paper supply basket, log and flame patterns

Children's Meditation

STORY

I Hate Homework

Linda, the oldest of the three children in the Gordon household, had always been a straight-A student. Linda was in high school this year and came home with mountains of homework every single night. Linda would grab a quick snack after school and then go straight to the books.

Daniel was the middle child. Daniel hated school. He thought school was a total waste of time. Daniel usually came home with B's and C's because he just didn't care about school. Daniel was always too busy playing computer games or watching TV to bother with his homework. "It's busywork," Daniel would say.

Suzanne was the baby of the family, and she much preferred reading to doing homework. Sometimes Suzanne would carry her book bag to her bedroom as if she were going to work, but when the door closed, she would flop on her bed with a library book and read till dinner.

The Gordons were shocked when test scores for each of the children were sent home from school. Suzanne actually had the highest IQ of the three children. Linda, much to everyone's surprise, had an average IQ but nothing super special. Daniel, on the other hand, had not even bothered to answer half the questions. No one was sure what his actual score should be.

The Gordons held a family discussion. Daniel broke into the discussion every few seconds with, "I hate homework!"

Suzanne chanted, "It's not fair." Linda was defensive because her scores weren't higher.

Mrs. Gordon reminded Linda that "a test measures your ability to take a test, not necessarily how much you know. You can still be extremely smart and not be good at taking tests."

Mr. Gordon added, "God has given each of us different abilities, and the true test of life is measured by how you use the skills you've been given. If you just sit around and don't try, and say "I can't" all the time, then you may eventually lose some of your talent. It's like playing the piano. If you don't practice, you'll forget how to play, and you won't improve.

"Linda," Mr. Gordon continued, "is obviously using the talents God gave her, working hard, and doing well. Suzanne, you're doing a little bit when you actually could be doing a lot.

"Daniel, you, on the other hand," Mr. Gordon said, "are like the man in the Bible who hid the talent he was given in the ground and didn't even try. The worst thing you can ever do is not try. You should always try.

"We may not all have the same abilities, but we can give the same effort. You should never quit trying" said Mr. Gordon, "until you can truthfully say to God, 'I have done my very best.' "

Workstations

Workstation 1: Call to Worship

INSTRUCTION SIGN

Except for the rich or wealthier merchants, most of the people of New Testament times lived as poor peasants in small, simple limestone mud-brick houses that were usually about 10 feet square in size. This summer, we are going to build a simple one-room house from cardboard boxes covered with brown paper.

STEP 1: Tightly wrap a box with brown paper, just as you would wrap a present. Do NOT use tape; glue paper instead.

STEP 2: Find a friend and begin to arrange the blocks to build a sturdy wall for our house. Read Matthew 25:14-30.

In the parable of the talents, Jesus reminds us that the greatest failure in life is when we give up and refuse to try. The servant decided it was unfair that he wasn't trusted with as much money so he didn't try.

Never say, "I can't." Always say, "I'll TRY to do my best."

Workstation 2: Affirmation of Faith

GETTING READY

Use cover-ups for people and table area. Mix papier-mâché.

INSTRUCTION SIGN

Potters in Bible times frequently had small shops in the marketplace. The potter might sell a collection of bowls, plates, water jars, and hand lamps. Houses did not have closets or cabinets for storage, so everything had to be stored in clay jars or woven baskets. Usually women carried water every day from the well in large clay jars. Read Mark 4:26-29. Put on a cover-up and make a water pitcher.

STEP 1: Cover the outside of a 2-liter plastic pop bottle with papier-mâché. Make sure that the entire bottle is covered except for the opening at the top.

Use foil or stiff cardboard to make the top of the pitcher. You may also add handles to your water pitcher. Cover the cardboard or foil with papier-mâché.

STEP 2: Put a wad of paper in the opening of pop bottle. Paint glue onto the outside of the jar and then sprinkle dry sand over the glue as you would glitter. Once your jar is completely covered with sand, set aside to dry.

Workstation 3: Offering or Carpenter Shop

INSTRUCTION SIGN

The carpenter's shop made and repaired farm tools, plows, sickle handles, wooden carts and wheels, furniture, boats, wooden beams for houses, and sometimes wooden toys for the children. Some carpenters had a small shop adjoining the house. Others worked in a large shop at the marketplace. Everything made of wood was usually made by a village carpenter.

Fishing was a major occupation on the Sea of Galilee, and many carpenters made fishing boats. We are going to build a fishing boat. Follow the directions on the sketch.

A biblical carpenter would have used a bow drill, hammers, mallets, and chisels. You will use a hammer, saw, scrap wood, and leftover nails. Work together to build a biblical fishing boat. Your most important tool is your willingness to share with your neighbor.

Read Mark 4:26-29 to learn why it is important to build one step at a time. Start at the beginning today. Report on the progress of the fishing boat at worship each week.

Guide Sheet for Building the Biblical Fishing Boat

Three general rules to follow: (1) Always measure a board twice to make sure you measured correctly, (2) ask an adult to check your work before you saw, and (3) lightly pencil on each board cut to tell where it belongs (for example, "side right").

Lumber Needed:

New housing projects are excellent sources of free lumber scraps.

a. Lumber, two 90-inch-long pieces of plywood, ¾" thickness. Each 90" piece should be 24" wide. These are for the sides of the boat.

b. Lumber, four 2" x 8" boards, 18 inches in length. These are used to add stability to the bottom of the wooden box. Wooden box is the base of the boat.

c. Lumber, one 2" x 2" board 72" long for mast.

d. Lumber, four 18" x 18" pieces of ¾" thick plywood to build an 18" x 18" wooden box.

e. Lumber, approximately ten 18" long 2" x 4" scraps for braces. New housing projects will often give you all the scrap wood you need.

f. A box of 1¼" nails. These are short so the points won't stick out of the boards.

g. A handful of long nails for base and wood glue.

h. 2 nuts and bolts to fasten boat sides to box.

i. 36" long dowel rod, ¾" thickness.

j. One 1" eye hook.

Sawing:

STEP 1: Measure and cut two 90-inch-long pieces of plywood for the sides of the boat. Each side is 24" high.

Next draw a cutting line on each end. The board should measure 90" across the top, 73" in the middle, and 62" across the bottom. Measure carefully. You are cutting a corner off to form the ends of the boat. Cut straight.

STEP 2: Next build a wooden box. Begin with the base. Measure and cut four 2" x 8" boards, 18 inches in length.

STEP 3: Measure and cut four 18" x 18" pieces of ¾" thick plywood for sides of box.

STEP 4: Cut a 72-inch-long 2" x 2" board if needed. Sometimes you are lucky enough to be able to purchase the exact length you need and won't even have to cut the 72" board.

Step 4: Measure and cut 2" x 4" braces for wooden box. You may use leftover scrap wood. Cut two 8-inch-long braces. Cut four 18-inch-long braces. Cut four 12-inch-long braces.

STEP 5: Cut dowel rod if needed. You will need someone to drill the holes for the eye hook and side bolts when assembling boat. Make sure an adult is in charge of drilling holes.

Save all wood scraps. You will use them for other projects. You have now finished cutting all of the boards needed to build your biblical fishing boat.

Sanding:

Sand all boards until they are smooth. Do not nail any boards together until they have been sanded.

Hammering:

STEP 6: Build the boat from the base up. You are building an 18" x 18" wooden box. Use the 2" x 8" boards for the base. Nail two 2" x 8" boards together to form a 4" x 8" wooden block. Simply nail one board on top of the other.

STEP 7: Attach eye hook to top of 72-inch-long 2" x 2" mast pole. Nail mast pole to center of 4" x 8" block. Measure twice. Add glue before you hammer. See diagram. Let dry.

STEP 8: Nail 2 remaining 2" x 8" boards together. When mast pole is dry slide two 4" x 8" blocks together. Wedge two 8-inch-long 2" x 4" boards in beside mast pole for a snug fit. Use wood glue generously before nailing top braces in place.

STEP 9: Then nail four 18-inch-long 2" x 4" braces across top. Two braces should go beside mast pole. Nail these first. Then add braces to ends of wood block. See diagram.

STEP 10: Hammer two 12-inch-long 2" x 4" braces to 18-inch-long plywood board. Drill hole for bolt. See diagram.

STEP 11: Repeat the same process for other side of box.

STEP 12: Hammer sides of box onto base. See diagram.

STEP 13: Add wood glue and hammer 18" x 18" plywood ends onto box. The center base for the boat is complete.

STEP 14: Drill matching holes in side of 90-inch-long plywood panels for boat. Measure carefully. Measure twice. Double-check placement of holes before you drill. Holes on side of boat must match holes in box. Make sure sides of boat will sit evenly on floor before drilling the holes for the bolts.

STEP 15: Attach side panels of boat with nuts and bolts. Tighten securely.

STEP 16: Run dowel rod through eye hook on top of mast pole. Have an adult attach cloth sail with tacks to dowel rod. Be generous with tacks because children will tug on sail. Strings may be tied to lower corners of sail so that children may secure sail to boat. Children may sit in open ends of boat. Small chairs or benches may be used if desired or simply have children sit on the floor. Fishing net may be stored in wooden center box when not in use.

Congratulations! You have finished the boat. You are ready to paint.

Workstation 4: Sermon or Bible Study

INSTRUCTION SIGN

Prophets, rabbis, and teachers told parables. There are parables in the Old Testament (2 Samuel 12:1-7) as well as the parables of Jesus in the New Testament. The Jewish people were continuously asking, "What must I do?" In each of his parables, Jesus implies an action. Read Matthew 25:14-30. Decide what action Jesus calls you to take today.

We will be using our "Key to Bible Times" (KTBT) make-believe TV network to help us interpret the parables. Each week, it will be your job to act out the interview with puppets or as actors. Remember to use the principles of speaking slowly and loudly so that everyone will understand the sermon. You need a camera operator, Sam the reporter, and Professor Jordan.

SKIT FOR SERMON

To Have a Talent

REPORTER SAM:	Good morning and welcome to KTBT's "Tell Me a Story." Today, we are at the Archaeology Archives office to learn more about the meaning of the word *talent*.
	In the parable of the talents from Matthew 25:14-30, Jesus tells a story about a master who gave three of his servants certain amounts of money to invest for him while he was away. Two of the servants went out and doubled their master's money while the third buried the money he was given for safekeeping.
	Let's meet Professor Jordan and learn more about this parable. [Sam turns to Professor Jordan and shakes hands.]
	Professor Jordan, thank you for agreeing to meet with us.
PROFESSOR JORDAN:	I'm always pleased to talk about the Bible.
SAM:	Professor Jordan, in some translations of the Bible, we have noticed that the word *talent* is written as a "coin" while in other translations a talent is referred to as a "bag of money." Can you explain this difference?
JORDAN:	Certainly. A "talent" was a measurement of weight that equaled approximately 125 pounds or a certain amount of money. For example, the value of a talent of silver was 400 pounds of silver coins or approximately $1,940 today.
	Paper currency didn't exist. All money exchanged in Palestine at the time was in the form of coins. If you gave someone a large sum of money, you would weigh it out in talents and present the person with bags of coins equivalent to the amount owed or to be entrusted.
SAM:	Then, how did we ever start talking about the parable of the talents as a lesson in using our skills and abilities?
JORDAN:	Jesus told parables, not just because he could tell an interesting story, but because every parable was a lesson. Jesus was a teacher, and he wanted to teach the people of his day what they must do to prepare themselves for the kingdom of heaven. Jesus used parables to show the people how they could change the way they acted.
SAM:	I get it! We come along today, read the same stories, and learn how we can change as well.
JORDAN:	Exactly! Jesus preached mostly to peasants and poor people who certainly would not have had such large sums of money. Yet, the people would have understood that only a servant who had proved himself trustworthy and good would be given so much money to invest. The poor had not been given money, but God had given every person a special skill or job to do. Jesus encouraged everyone, regardless of whether they were shepherds, carpenters, farmers, or

SAM: I should spend time each day working to develop the talent that God has given me. If I don't try, then I'm like the servant who hid his talent in the ground.

JORDAN: That's right.

SAM: Thanks, Professor Jordan, for helping us to better understand the Bible. I'm going to go home and make a list of all my talents. Then, I'm going to put a check mark by the ones I've been working on and a circle around the talents that need work.

Let me see, there's math, playing the violin . . . I played the violin when I was a child, but I gave it up because I hated practicing.

JORDAN: Instead of giving up and saying, "I can't," or burying the talent because you're afraid of failure, Jesus encourages all of us to work at difficult tasks and never be afraid to *try*.

SAM: That's all from KTBT's "Tell Me a Story." Join us again next week for another interesting story from the Bible. In the meantime, why don't you make your own list of talents? Set a goal for yourself. You never know what you can do until you try.

Workstation 5: Witness to Faith

GETTING READY

Use the same loom from Session 8 in volume 1 or make a new loom. Yarn or string should be 36-inch-long and stretched tightly.

INSTRUCTION SIGN

Although the raised platform would have been the family living quarters, the roof was a favorite place for the family in this hot, dry region for drying laundry, sleeping, grinding wheat, making the daily bread, weaving, praying, and for other household chores. The roof was usually much cooler than the inside of the house, so people would eat and even sleep on the roof.

Today, we are weaving a floor mat to be used in our house. Both women and men of biblical times were experienced weavers. They would have used thin thread or reeds to weave a mat. Since we are just learning to weave, we will continue to use braided strips of cloth to make sleeping mats. Read Mark 4:26-29 and help make sleeping mats for our new house this summer.

STEP 1: Rulers and measuring tapes were not used in biblical times; a piece of cloth or thread would have been used as a yardstick. Make a "measuring string." Cut three 36" x 2" strips of cloth using measuring string.

When you have cut 3 long pieces of cloth, tape the cloth down on the table or have a friend hold the end. Pull tightly and begin to braid. You want your braids to be tight so they will hold together. Your finished braid must be longer than the width of the weaving loom so each braid can be tied into place.

STEP 2: You are now ready to weave. Weave from bottom of loom to top. Weave as you would weave paper. Weave braid over and under the strands of yarn. Don't forget to alternate over-and-under weaving pattern with each braid added; otherwise, the mat will not stay together.

STEP 3: Tie loose ends to sides.

Workstation 6: Prayer and Sewing Center

INSTRUCTION SIGN

Shepherds and other nomads lived in tents. Since the shepherds moved a lot, their dwellings were simple. A tent was made from a 6-foot-wide piece of goat's-hair cloth woven on a ground loom. The cloth was dark and long. The family's food and possessions were stored in baskets.

Make a basket to take home today. There are both a simple and a harder basket to make. Sometimes we give up before we even TRY. Read Matthew 25:14-30. Then, make a basket.

Simple Basket

STEP 1: Cut construction paper to fit can being used.

STEP 2: Fold paper and cut slashes FROM THE FOLDED SIDE. Do not cut all the way through the ends.

STEP 3: Cut paper strips for weaving.

STEP 4: Weave over and under. Then, wrap the weaving around a juice can, glue into place, and make a handle.

STEP 5: Punch holes in the side of your can and add a string, pipe cleaner, or braided yarn for a handle.

Harder Basket

STEP 1: Select a small box or make one. Cover with paper. Cut 5 slashes on each side panel as shown on pattern.

STEP 2: Tie a knot in yarn. Tape yarn to the outside bottom of basket with knot right where you want to start weaving.

STEP 3: Begin to weave yarn over and under each strip, pulling the sides of the basket up into place.

STEP 4: Continue basket weaving until you are about 1 inch from top. Stop. Bend cardboard down. Tape flap down.

STEP 5: Make a handle by braiding yarn. Sew handle inside. Place baskets on the worship table for today's service.

Workstation 7: Benediction

INSTRUCTION SIGN

The inside walls of a simple biblical house were plain, with niches and shelves carved out of the limestone blocks. A raised platform about 18 inches high at one end of the house served as the living quarters for the family. These simple houses had no separate bedrooms, kitchens, chairs, or beds. The family wrapped their cloaks around themselves at night and slept spread out across the hard stone floor on simple flat, woven mats around a fire pit dug into the floor. A small fire and lamp burned all night. Read the parable of the growing seed in Mark 4:26-29.

Make a paper biblical house to take home. Use pattern. Cut on solid lines and fold on dotted lines. Be creative. Add sheep, a well, or a tree to your house. See picture.

Then, build a paper fire for our village house.

STEP 1: Cut ten 8-inch-long logs from brown paper. Trace pattern. Use scrap paper. Roll paper on pencil to make log.

STEP 2: Glue the log and hold till set.

STEP 3: Glue logs together. Add a fire by tracing the flame pattern.

Leave log fire burning at our house, the tent, or in the village oven. Take your miniature house home to remind you of the house we are building in our village.

The Worship Celebration

SIGN-UP SHEET FOR TODAY'S WORSHIP CELEBRATION

Call to Worship (read Matthew 25:23):
Offering (report progress on boat):
Sermon ("To Have a Talent"):
Benediction (lead the Lord's Prayer):

ITEMS TO GO HOME TODAY: SMALL PAPER BIBLICAL HOUSES

125

Session 45
Daily Life in the Time of Jesus

The Bible Lesson

The parable of the good Samaritan (Luke 10:25-37)

What the Children Will Learn Today

Children learn today's parable is a Christian call to action.

Time Needed

5 minutes for story
20 minutes for workstations
10 minutes for closing worship service

Supplies Needed (by Workstation)

1. Brown tempera paint, sand, paintbrushes, cardboard oven, and cover-ups
2. Paper bags, scrap paper, pop bottles, stapler, and pattern for fish from Session 40
3. Boatbuilding supplies
4. Skit for sermon, 4 puppets (including Sunshine), and puppet stage
5. Tissue holders (2 per child), string, felt, stapler, scraps of cardboard and paper, hole punch, and craft supply basket
6. Felt or Aida cloth, patterns, embroidery thread and needles
7. Construction paper supply basket and patterns

Children's Meditation

STORY

The Dress-Right Crowd

Janie hated school, not because of her teachers, but because of the girls in her class. Janie wasn't very popular.

To be one of the "popular girls," you had to wear a certain brand of blue jeans with a T-shirt or sweatshirt. Near the end of school when it started getting warm, the popular girls only wore blue-jean shorts with a rolled-up cuff. Anything else was totally unacceptable.

Janie's mother was a seamstress and made all of Janie's clothes. The other girls teased Janie and said that she must be too poor to buy any decent clothes. Janie's family didn't have bundles of money, but they weren't poor.

Janie knew that her mother liked sewing for her and actually, Janie liked a lot of the clothes her mother made. But more than anything Janie wanted to be accepted by the popular girls. Janie knew that she would never be accepted in handmade skirts and blouses.

Janie begged and pleaded, cried, and acted as if her world were coming to an end every time she and her mother went shopping. Janie was certain that if she could just dress like everyone else, then all the girls in her class would like her.

One day a new girl moved into Janie's neighborhood. The new girl was the same age as Janie and would be in Janie's class in the fall. The new girl's name was Megan. Janie decided to go with her mother to welcome Megan's family to the neighborhood. Megan invited Janie to her room and the two girls played for hours. Janie really liked Megan. The girls spent most of the summer together and by fall had become great friends.

As the first day of school grew closer, Janie worried that Megan would no longer like her once she met all of the other girls at school, but throughout the first week of school Janie and Megan were inseparable as usual. When the popular girls started teasing Janie, Megan came over to find out why.

Janie said, "No one likes me because of the way I dress. They make fun of me. Now you'll probably even stop liking me."

"That's ridiculous." Megan laughed. "I can't even see. Why should it make any difference to me how you look? I like being with you because you're kind. You don't make fun of other people and you don't treat me differently just because I'm blind."

"As for the prissy crowd, they wouldn't like you even if your clothes came from the exact same store, same rack, even the same hanger. They're only interested in themselves. If someone really likes you and wants to be your friend, they'll like you no matter what you're wearing. The way you like me.

"Even though I'm blind, I can tell you're my friend by how you talk to me and how you treat me. No one worth bothering with picks their friends by what clothes they wear. So come on, let's go have some fun and not worry about the 'dress-right crowd.' "

Workstations

Workstation 1: Call to Worship

GETTING READY

Make cardboard oven before session. Use a rectangular cardboard box that is taller than it is wide and that opens with flaps on top. See picture and tape flaps with duct tape to make a cone-shaped top for oven. Cut rounded opening in front. Mix brown liquid tempera paint with plain dry sand to paint oven. Use cover-ups for floor, table, and people.

INSTRUCTION SIGN

The road between Jericho and Jerusalem is steep and full of twists and turns. Jerusalem sits high on a hill about 2,300 feet above sea level while Jericho, near the Dead Sea, is 1,300 feet below sea level. The road is twenty miles long. Travelers have to make a steep climb from Jericho to Jerusalem. The road's also notorious for robbers. The scene described by Jesus was a common occurrence. Read Luke 10:25-37.

Paint a biblical oven for our village. Paint the oven with the brown paint provided. The paint has been mixed with sand to give it a grainy texture much like a clay or sandstone oven would have had during biblical times. Paint the inside and outside of the oven, then clean up your workspace.

Workstation 2: Affirmation of Faith

INSTRUCTION SIGN

In biblical times, people rarely traveled the road from Jericho to Jerusalem alone. They traveled in groups for protection from robbers, but in the parable of the good Samaritan Jesus tells of several people walking alone. Each person who passes by the injured traveler must decide whether to help, just as we must often decide how we can help.

Do we stop and take time from our busy schedule to help those around us? The early Christians made helping others a requirement for being a follower of Jesus. Read Acts 2:44-47. Then make a fish to remind you to follow the teachings of Jesus.

STEP 1: Use the pattern and make 2 copies of paper fish.
STEP 2: Take bottle cap off to make opening for mouth of fish. Tape and glue the mouth of the fish around the mouth of an empty 2-liter pop bottle. Staple top sides of paper fish together. Do not staple underneath side yet.
STEP 3: Gently stuff inside of fish around pop bottle with newspapers, scrap paper, or leftover plastic bags. Staple shut.
STEP 4: Use pattern and cut cardboard fins. Glue and tape in place. You are ready to papier-mâché next week.

Workstation 3: Offering or Carpenter Shop

INSTRUCTION SIGN

A boat typical of the type used by Jesus' disciples and fishermen of the time was discovered buried in the mud on the bottom of the Sea of Galilee. The boat, often referred to as the "Kinneret Boat," was discovered in January 1986 by two brothers when the Sea of Galilee was at its lowest level after a severe drought. The boat is 27' long and 7'7" wide.

Our boat will not be as large. Read Luke 10:25-37 and continue working. Remember to work carefully with your neighbor.

Workstation 4: Sermon or Bible Study

INSTRUCTION SIGN

The Samaritans lived north of Judea and were hated by the Jews. "Samaritan" was used as a slang term to mean you were worthless. Read Luke 10:25-37.

Jesus made the hero of the story a Samaritan to show that everyone is equal before God. God loves everyone the same. The "teacher of the law" who was trying to trap Jesus would have been outraged that the Samaritan was the hero of the story.

You are in charge of the entire service today. You need 5 readers and 4 puppeteers. One reader will read the parable at the beginning of the service. Work on reading slowly and clearly so that everyone can hear.

PUPPET PLAY FOR SERMON

Who Is My Neighbor?

JUDY:	Did you read the Bible verse this morning?
JIM:	It's too long.
LINDA:	It's one of my favorite parables. It tells you to help anyone in need.
JIM:	Even if helping someone could get you in trouble?
LINDA:	I don't know. I never thought of it like that.
JUDY:	Hi, Sunshine. Am I glad you're here! We have a question.
SUNSHINE:	Sunshine Share-a-Lot at your service. What's your question?
JIM:	At the workstations today, we're reading the parable of the good Samaritan.
JUDY:	We understand that the parable means that we're to help, but does that also mean to help someone even if helping might cause you to get hurt or in trouble?
SUNSHINE:	Helping doesn't always have to mean that you actually bandage someone's wounds as the Samaritan did. Helping can also mean that you seek help from a parent, a doctor, a paramedic, a teacher, a police officer, or someone who is qualified to help safely. What the parable means is that you should not simply walk on by and not bother.
LINDA:	That's what happened when Carey, my best friend, got hurt on the playground. She fell off the climbing bars and hit the back of her head. She couldn't get up. The playground supervisor said not to move her, even though she was crying. One of the boys ran to the office, and the secretary called 911. The paramedics came and had to put Carey on a special backboard before they could pick her up. They said that if we had moved her or helped her up off of the ground we might have caused serious damage to her spine.
JIM:	My friend and I tried to break up a fight once and ended up getting in trouble along with the guys who were fighting. It wasn't fair.
SUNSHINE:	Did you stop the fight?

JIM:	No, they were bigger than we were. I just got a black eye and had to stay after school the next day.
SUNSHINE:	Maybe if you had gone to get a teacher, you'd have helped more. Going and telling a teacher or parent when something is wrong is the best thing to do, even if it means that your friends will be angry with you later.
JUDY:	Then everyone will say that you're a "tattletale."
SUNSHINE:	Jesus said that what others think of us should never keep us from helping. Jesus included the priest in the parable to remind us that we should always do what we know is right even if it means someone else will call us names or be mad.
LINDA:	I didn't understand that part about the priest. Why didn't he help?
SUNSHINE:	In biblical times, there were so many Jewish priests at the Temple that each priest was assigned a separate day to be responsible for leading the religious service. This was a very high honor, and there were all sorts of rules. The priest wasn't willing to risk losing his turn in order to help the traveler. Jesus said that we should help someone even if we don't know the person, even if it means we will be teased or called names, and even if the person in need is our worst enemy or someone we don't like. Jesus said to help everyone in need.
JIM:	The next time I see a fight, I'll go to get help.
LINDA:	The next time I see someone hurt, I'll go to get help.
SUNSHINE:	That's right, there are many ways to help.
JUDY:	Thanks for helping today, Sunshine.
SUNSHINE:	You can help too. Remember the parable of the good Samaritan and help whenever you are needed.

Workstation 5: Witness to Faith

INSTRUCTION SIGN

How you act toward others is more important than status or job titles. Read Luke 10:25-37.
Work with your neighbor and make a string puppet. You can make your puppet a disciple,
Jesus, a woman gleaning in the fields, a merchant, farmer, carpenter, or anyone from the Bible.

STEP 1: Use 2 tissue-roll holders to make the body. Flatten 1 tissue roll and cut it in half. Use a hole punch and punch a hole in the middle of cut half. Run a string through the hole and tie a big knot. Tape string so that knot cannot be pulled back through hole. Set aside till later.

STEP 2: Trace sleeve, hand, leg, and sandal patterns. Make 2 of each. Felt works nicely because you don't have to hem fabric. Roll felt to make arms and legs. Stitch hands and arms and legs and sandals together. Staple arms to top of remaining tissue holder. Staple legs to bottom. Arms will hang down from the sides. Legs will dangle at bottom of holder.

STEP 3: Make cardboard sandals. Glue to bottom of felt.

STEP 4: Put glue inside top of tissue holder. Stuff top of body with scrap paper. Flatten tissue holder with string to top of body for shoulders. MAKE SURE STRING IS ON TOP. Let dry.

Workstation 6: Prayer and Sewing Center

INSTRUCTION SIGN

The priests and Levites came from the tribe of Levi (Exodus 6:14-19). The Levites and priests would have considered their job at the Temple much more important than the needs of an unknown traveler. Jesus said that if we truly love our neighbor, then we will always want what is best for our neighbor. Read Luke 10:25-37. Then, work on a Bible bookmark.

STEP 1: Trace pattern on felt or Aida cloth and cut out.
STEP 2: Trace letter stencils for LOVE on bookmark.
STEP 3: Embroider letters. Use cross-stitch or a simple backstitch to outline letters. Place bookmark on worship table.

Workstation 7: Benediction

INSTRUCTION SIGN

The synagogue served as the school and the place of worship for the Jewish residents of a small village. There were no books. The only written words Jesus would have seen as a boy would have been on a scroll. If a village was lucky, they would have scrolls containing the first 5 books of the Bible.

We are going to make a scroll. Instead of the Old Testament, our scroll will have a picture of a sunset and a biblical house.

STEP 1: Roll a piece of brown construction paper or brown paper bag to resemble a scroll. Curl the ends around a pencil.
STEP 2: Color house picture and glue in center of scroll. Read Luke 10:25-37 and write Bible verse on scroll.
STEP 3: Color sunset and first star in sky to depict the start of the Sabbath. Sabbath begins at sundown on Friday and continues until the first 3 stars after sunset on Saturday. Sabbath is the Jewish day of worship. Take scrolls to worship.

The Worship Celebration

SIGN-UP SHEET FOR TODAY'S WORSHIP CELEBRATION

Call to Worship (read Luke 10:25-37):
Sermon (5 readers and 4 puppeteers for "Who Is My Neighbor?"):
Person to lead prayer written at affirmation station:

ITEMS TO GO HOME TODAY: SCROLLS

Session 46
A Typical Day at the Marketplace

The Bible Lesson

The parable of the unforgiving servant (Matthew 18:21-35)

What the Children Will Learn Today

The children will be learning about forgiveness today.

Time Needed

5 minutes for story
20 minutes for workstations
10 minutes for closing worship service

Supplies Needed (by Workstation)

1. Medium-sized tall box for well, enough small boxes to cover outside of tall box, brown paper, scissors, and glue
2. Pop-bottle fish from last week and papier-mâché
3. Boatbuilding supplies
4. Skit, KTBT TV camera, biblical house, and actors
5. Puppet from last week, clothing patterns, and cloth
6. Brown felt, bookmarks (last week), and scroll pattern   7. Construction paper supply basket and scrap paper

Children's Meditation

STORY

Please Forgive Me

The cafeteria at school was noisy, and it was hard to find a place to sit. Children were always saying, "That's saved" because they didn't want a particular person to sit beside them.

The boys had two tables. You either sat with the athletes or the nonathletes. The girls were divided among three tables.

The first group could have been called "Competition Plus." The second group was the "We're Better than You" group. The third group was the "Forgiving Four."

Sally moseyed over to sit with the Forgiving Four at lunch because she and Gail had got in an argument. Sally was a little bossy, but the Forgiving Four tried to be kind and include Sally in their conversation. Finally, Sally got mad, stood up with her hands on her hips, and said, "Jenny, you're impossible; Joan, you're conceited; Nancy, you're a snob; and Kathy, you're so self-centered that you can't think of anyone but yourself." Sally scooped up her lunch and stormed out of the cafeteria.

Two weeks later, Sally returned without a hint of apology. Everything was going smoothly, when out of nowhere Sally went into another rage. The next day, Sally returned and again it wasn't long before Sally went storming off in a huff.

"I've had it with her," said Kathy. "Who does she think she is anyway?"

"Maybe she's just lonely and hurt," said Jenny.

"We've given her three chances and that's enough," insisted Kathy.

"Jesus said that we must judge others the same way we want God to judge us," continued Jenny. "I wouldn't want God to give me three chances and then say, 'That's enough.' "

"She's impossible," said Kathy.

"No one is easy to get along with. Everyone needs something different from a friendship. If we focus on the things we like about Sally, then maybe we can overlook actions we don't like," said Joan.

"The Lord's Prayer says to forgive us as we have forgiven others," remarked Nancy.

"It's not easy," grumbled Kathy.

"Forgiveness never is," said Jenny, "but as followers of Jesus, it's our job to be forgiving and forgiving and forgiving and never stop forgiving."

"I'll try," said Kathy as the four went to look for Sally.

Workstations

Workstation 1: Call to Worship

INSTRUCTION SIGN

Water had to be carried in clay jars from the well every morning. The oldest girls in the family carried the heavy water jars home from the well balanced on their shoulders or hips.

Read Matthew 18:21-35. We should be as considerate, kind, and forgiving with others as we expect them to be with us. Think of someone you've been angry with and then go and tell them you're sorry.

STEP 1: Wrap small boxes with brown paper (paper bags), as if you were wrapping a package. Use glue, not tape.

STEP 2: Glue the wrapped small boxes to outside of large box. Start at bottom. Completely cover the well. Display at worship.

Workstation 2: Affirmation of Faith

INSTRUCTION SIGN

At the marketplace, a person could buy oil hand lamps, pottery, cloth, fish, vegetables, and other foods. Bread had to be baked fresh every day or it would spoil. Fish had to be salted, dried, smoked, or pickled. Read Matthew 18:21-35. Then, continue working on your pop-bottle fish from last week. If you did not make a fish, start at the beginning. Read instructions.

Once your fish is complete, put on a cover-up and papier-mâché your fish. Sign up to read Bible verse for service today.

Workstation 3: Offering or Carpenter Shop

INSTRUCTION SIGN

Ancient shipbuilders used a method called "shell-first construction" to build fishing boats. The carpenters first built the keel (the main timber that runs the length of the boat) and posts (curved end pieces), then they built the sides or "planking" directly onto the keel by means of "pegged mortise-and-tenon joints" (no nails). That means they chiseled out a small hole in one plank and made a post on the opposite plank to fit into the hole so that the planks would hold together. Once the sides were finished, then the carpenter would add the ribs and frame to the inside, but the frame of the boat would not be connected to the keel.

Modern shipbuilders use a totally different method to build wooden boats. They attach stem and sternpost to keel, then add the frame or ribs to form a skeleton for the boat. The "side hull planks," or sides of the boat, are then nailed onto the frame.

We're using a modified technique for building our boat. Our boat, thank goodness, doesn't have to float. Read Matthew 18:21-35 and remember to be forgiving with those you work with.

Workstation 4: Sermon or Bible Study

INSTRUCTION SIGN

In the larger villages, a carpenter might have a shop in the marketplace. Often the stone-mason's shop was across the street from the carpenter. The stonemason and the carpenter might work together to build a house. Work would begin at daybreak and continue till the evening meal. Read Matthew 18:21-35 to remind us that we should not demand things of others that we are not prepared to give ourselves. If we wish for others to be forgiving with us, we must forgive FIRST. If you want someone to treat you nicely, you should treat others nicely FIRST.

Practice for today's service. Use puppets or actors. Use the TV camera. Use the biblical house in the village for worship today. You need a reporter and a merchant for the sermon.

SKIT FOR SERMON

Buying a House

[Have the worship service in village today. Use biblical house.]

REPORTER: Good morning and welcome to KTBT's "Visit from the Bible" program. This morning, we are traveling back in time to Nazareth to see what life would have been like when Jesus was a boy growing up. Let me get my costume on [Reporter puts on biblical costume], and then if you're ready, let's go.

REPORTER: [Walks over toward house and speaks very softly] We're here to see a merchant from the marketplace about a house. Let's see if he's home. [Knocks on door. Merchant answers.]

MERCHANT: Peace be with you!

REPORTER: Good morning! I'm _____ [fill in name] from KTBT News. We're here today to buy a house.

MERCHANT: Well, you have come to the right place, for this house just happens to be for sale.

REPORTER: [Reporter looks inside.] It sure is small.

MERCHANT: The raised platform has more than enough room for fifteen to sleep elbow to elbow. How many are in your family?

REPORTER: Oh, just myself. [Merchant looks puzzled.] Do all of the houses have dirt floors? And where's the furniture?

MERCHANT: Of course the floors are dirt. What were you expecting? There's a carpenter at the market-place who can build furniture, and the stonemason directly across from the carpenter can even help you add an upper room on the roof.

REPORTER: Speaking of the roof, it looks a little muddy up there. Does the roof leak?

MERCHANT: Not very much! It rained two days ago, and as you can see, it's not too wet inside. You'll need to hire a day laborer at the marketplace to roll the roof smooth and seal out the rain, but many are in search of work these days.

REPORTER: Where do you buy food around here?

MERCHANT: Bread is baked fresh every day at the village oven. Salted fish is brought in from the Sea of Galilee, and some of the farmers have stands with grains and fruits. You may also purchase clay jars, bowls, and baskets at the marketplace.

REPORTER: I don't seem to see the kitchen, the light switch, or water faucet.

MERCHANT: I don't know what this 'kitchen,' 'switch,' or 'faucet' means. Are you from around here?

REPORTER: No, no, I'm from . . . [points off in other direction]

MERCHANT: I didn't think so. There are water jars for carrying water from the well. As for light, you may

133

buy hand lamps, oil, or wicks in the marketplace at the potter's shop.

REPORTER: I don't mean to be rude, but do you have any houses for sale with more windows and doors?

MERCHANT: Why would you want more windows and doors? It is not safe to have windows and doors. The robbers will come and beat you up and steal everything you own. What are you thinking of, man? Where did you say you were from?

REPORTER: Well, thank you for your time and information. I think I must be going now.

MERCHANT: Going! I thought you wanted to buy a house.

REPORTER: I think I've changed my mind. I think I'll just go home and appreciate what I have, but thank you for your time.

[Reaches to shake hands. Merchant throws up hands in disgust and returns inside house. Reporter returns to starting place and takes off costume.]

I don't know about you, but I don't think I would have found biblical times very comfortable. I think I'm going to start appreciating all the easy comforts I have in life a lot more after today. This is _____ [reporter's name], reporting for KTBT's "Visit from the Bible." See you next time.

Workstation 5: Witness to Faith

INSTRUCTION SIGN

The roof was made from branches woven together and covered with sun-dried limestone soil. The limestone turned to mud in heavy rain. After each rain the mud surface of the roof had to be smoothed again before it hardened. Around the edge of the roof was a wall, about 18 inches high, called a "parapet."

Work on your string puppet from last week as you continue to take turns weaving the mat on the weaving loom or weaving on the wooden loom.

Read Matthew 18:21-35 and remember to treat others as you want to be treated.

STEP 1: Use same cloth as last week for arms and legs. Trace clothing patterns and glue clothing to tissue-roll body made last week. Hang puppet where it can dry.

STEP 2: Stuff an old skin-colored sock or stocking with scrap fabric. Shape into a round 3" ball for head of puppet. If your sock or stocking is thin and scraps show through, cover with additional socks or stocking for face of puppet. Tie a knot in last sock or stocking to tightly hold round shape.

STEP 3: Sew eyes, nose, and mouth on puppet. Use buttons or sequins if you wish. Knot in stocking goes on bottom of head to form neck and attach to body of puppet.

STEP 4: Add yarn for hair and cloth covering for head. Glue cloth covering to head but also sew in place. Add string or yarn for headband.

STEP 5: Tie heavy string tightly around knot at neck of head. Tie string from head to string of body. Get help from adult if needed. Strings must be tied tightly and closely so that neck fits right inside body of puppet.

STEP 6: Tie sticks together with yarn. Make secure X by crisscrossing yarn in center. Sew strings to arms, legs, and top of head. Tie strings to sticks. Take puppet to worship.

Workstation 6: Prayer and Sewing Center

INSTRUCTION SIGN

A limestone block or raised platform would be up about 18 inches off the ground at one end of the house. This would be the living quarters for the family. There were no separate bedrooms or kitchens. The family wrapped their cloaks around themselves for warmth and spread out across the hard stone floor on simple flat woven mats around a fire pit that had been dug in the floor.

Trace pattern and cut scroll from brown felt for Bible bookmark. Roll ends of felt and stitch together. Sew scroll to top of bookmark. Sign up and write a prayer for our service.

Workstation 7: Benediction

GETTING READY

Young children may want to simply make merchant.

INSTRUCTION SIGN

Food could be bought daily in the marketplace. Farmers would set up stands to sell their crops. Traveling traders also would put up stands. A stand might consist of a table with an awning over it to keep off the sun. Carpenters, potters, weavers, or stonemasons might also have shops in the marketplace. The village oven was usually located near the market. If the town had a baker, fresh bread could be bought at the marketplace. If the village was near the Sea of Galilee, fresh fish would be available; otherwise, salted or dried fish would be sold. Day laborers would go to the marketplace to seek work.

Make a paper merchant's stand. Add as many stands to your marketplace as desired by merely stapling pages together.

STEP 1: Trace pattern and cut marketplace stand as shown on pattern. Place paper on table like a tent. Push cut sections through to inside. Fold and crease all seams.

STEP 2: Trace and cut awning covers using patterns. Staple in place as marked on pattern.

STEP 3: Draw foods or items to sell and place on table.

STEP 4: Trace and color merchant. Cut out and glue behind the table. Place marketplace on worship table for service today.

The Worship Celebration

SIGN-UP SHEET FOR TODAY'S WORSHIP CELEBRATION

Call to Worship (read Matthew 18:21-35):
Sermon (skit "Buying a House"):
Benediction (person to write and lead prayer from Workstation 6):

ITEMS TO GO HOME TODAY:
MARKETPLACES; STRING PUPPETS

Session 47
The Fishermen and Their Fishing Boat

The Bible Lesson

The parable of the net (Matthew 13:47-48)

What the Children Will Learn Today

To look for the good that others do and to forgive the bad.

Time Needed

5 minutes for story
20 minutes for workstations
10 minutes for closing worship service

Supplies Needed (by Workstation)

1. 2-liter pop bottles, tissue rolls, string, scrap paper, plastic bags, newspapers, thin cardboard, and masking tape
2. Paint, brushes, cover-ups, and pop-bottle fish   3. Boatbuilding supplies
4. Skit, puppets or actors, KTBT-TV camera, paper or cloth fish, plates, and table
5. Salt dough mixture and cardboard box for tabletop biblical house
6. Sequins, thread, needles, felt bookmarks from last week with finished felt scrolls, fish pattern, or fabric glue
7. Construction paper supply basket and boat patterns

Children's Meditation

STORY

Alone Without a Friend

Leon didn't have many friends. It wasn't that Leon didn't want friends. Leon desperately wanted others to like him. It was just that Leon was somehow different, and no one would bother to take the time to get to know him.

If Leon felt that someone cared and actually wanted to hear what he had to say, Leon would talk nonstop for hours. As fate would have it, though, most people are usually more interested in what they want, so Leon kept quiet.

At school, there was a boy named Joey. Joey was always one of the first players picked when teams were chosen in gym class, and everyone wanted to sit with Joey at lunch.

Leon often tagged along with Joey and his friends. Leon even started dressing like Joey.

On Tuesday, Leon was the first person through the lunch line, so he went over to Joey's table and sat down. When Joey arrived, Joey said, "That's my seat. Go bother someone else today. We're tired of you following us around."

Leon was crushed. Leon hadn't done anything wrong, so why was Joey being so mean? Joey didn't need to be mean to Leon, but being mean to Leon made Joey feel important.

Two days later, without explanation, Joey's popularity suddenly vanished. No one wanted to sit with Joey or even be seen walking down the hall talking to him, except for Leon.

Leon continued to sit with Joey at lunch and to tag along after school. Joey began to care about Leon's feelings. Leon wasn't as afraid, and Joey wasn't as cocky. As Leon explained, "There's good and bad in all people; you just have to look for the good and learn to forgive the bad."

God forgives us each and every day for the wrong things we do. He wants us to forgive those around us and to look for the good in others. If we learn to focus on what's good rather than on petty differences or traits we don't like, we, too, can be more forgiving.

Workstations

Workstation 1: Call to Worship

INSTRUCTION SIGN

The Sea of Galilee is actually not a sea; it's a freshwater lake. In biblical times the lake was most likely called "Kinneret" or "Yam Kinneret." The towns around the lake were known for fishing and agriculture. The residents kept sheep, cows, and goats.

STEP 1:   Start working on a lamb today. Place a wad of plastic inside a plastic bag to form the head or smash and shape newspapers for the head. Attach head to NECK of pop bottle with a rubber band. Do not use tape or head will fall off when wet.

STEP 2:   Punch holes at the end of 4 tissue holders. Run string through holes. Stuff tissue rolls with plastic.

STEP 3:   Tie tissue-roll holders around pop bottle for legs.

STEP 4:   Trace ears and tail. GLUE and tape in place.

Sign up to lead the Call to Worship: Read Matthew 13:47-48.

Workstation 2: Affirmation of Faith

INSTRUCTION SIGN

In February or March, the "month of Adar," each Jewish male was required to pay a half-shekel or didrachma for a Temple tax. Read Matthew 17:24-27. Peter found a stater, which was the same as two didrachmas, to pay the tax for both Peter and Jesus. The fish caught by Peter was most likely a "binet" or type of barbel. Put on a cover-up and paint your fish.

Workstation 3: Offering or Carpenter Shop

INSTRUCTION SIGN

In 1986, an archaeology team led by Shelley Wachsmann excavated an ancient fishing boat near Migdal from the bottom of the Sea of Galilee. The boat is 26 feet long and similar to the seine-net fishing boats of Jesus' day.

The boat is about 4 feet high from the center beam to the decks. It has decks built on each end to hold the heavy seine net. The middle is open for cargo. The boat carried a crew of 5 to 15 men. Read Mark 1:16-20. Then, continue working on our boat.

Workstation 4: Sermon or Bible Study

INSTRUCTION SIGN

The Gospels have about 45 references to boats and fishing. Jesus was familiar with fishing techniques and often traveled by boat on the Sea of Galilee. Fishing was done with spears, hook and line, a wicker trap, seine, throw nets, trammels, and even fish ponds. A seine net brings in all kinds of fish.

Jesus used the seine net as an example of how the kingdom of God includes everyone. God's church should include everyone too. Read Matthew 13:47-48. Then prepare today's sermon. You may do the KTBT skit with puppets or actors. You need a reporter, waiter, and professor today. If you use actors, set up a table.

SKIT FOR SERMON

St. Peter's Fish

REPORTER: Good morning! This is _____[name] with KTBT, your Key to Bible Times network for news from the Bible. We are at a restaurant on the banks of the Sea of Galilee this morning. We have come to talk to Professor Longtime about the history of the lake. We have also ordered St. Peter's fish for lunch. Here's Professor Longtime now. [Professor joins reporter.]
    Welcome, Professor! It's nice of you to join us today. PROFESSOR: Thank you, I'm very happy to be here.

REPORTER: I ordered lunch, so why don't we talk while we wait.

PROFESSOR: Excellent!

REPORTER: Why does the Sea of Galilee or Lake Galilee have so many names, and why does everyone call it "Kinneret"?

PROFESSOR: First, the Sea of Galilee is not a sea or part of the ocean. It's a freshwater lake that gets its water from the Jordan River and underground springs. It's 13 miles long, 7.5 miles wide, 150 feet deep, and covers 40,000 acres. It's called a sea because the word *yam* means "lake" or "sea" in Hebrew. When the Bible was translated the word *yam* was sometimes written as "sea" and sometimes as "lake" in the Scriptures.

REPORTER: Isn't it confusing for the lake to have so many names?

PROFESSOR: Not really. [Waiter arrives carrying fish.]

REPORTER: I ordered St. Peter's fish for lunch. Can you tell us anything about the St. Peter's fish we are eating?

PROFESSOR: The fish we are now eating is called a nurse fish and is served at most local restaurants as St. Peter's fish, but it is most likely not the same kind of fish.

REPORTER: [Shocked] This isn't St. Peter's fish? But I ordered St. Peter's fish.

PROFESSOR: The present-day "St. Peter's fish" feed on plankton and can only be caught with a net. Since in the Bible it tells us that Peter used a hook and line, the fish he caught would have been a type of carp. A sardine was probably used for bait.

REPORTER: Why the switch?

PROFESSOR: Tradition says that the true St. Peter's fish does not fry well and is therefore inconvenient to cook and quickly serve to tourists; therefore, in the fourth century, the nurse fish was substituted. Local residents figure that the tourists won't know the difference.

REPORTER: You're certain this is not St. Peter's fish?

PROFESSOR: This is a musht. Musht can only be caught with a net, usually a seine net or what we call a drag-net.

REPORTER: Like the net Jesus talked about in the parable?

PROFESSOR: Yes, exactly! In the parable of the net, Jesus uses a seine net to illustrate that everyone will be gathered together in the kingdom of heaven.

REPORTER: What's a seine net?

PROFESSOR: A seine net can be up to 1,000 feet long and 12 feet high in the center. It was used to form a net wall in the lake. The lower edge would drag across the bottom of the lake. Two to seven men would stay on shore. The rest of the crew would paddle the boat out about 300 feet into the lake. The seine net surrounds schools of fish and pulls everything in its path to shore. Men usually pulled the net in full of fish while standing on shore.

REPORTER: Well, even if this wasn't St. Peter fish, it was tasty.

PROFESSOR: Yes, it was, and thank you for lunch.

REPORTER: My pleasure! Thank you for joining us today. That's all from the Sea of Galilee, Lake Galilee, the Sea of Gennesaret, the Lake of Tiberias, or Lake Kinneret.

Workstation 5: Witness to Faith

GETTING READY

Cut top off, a small door, and a window in box beforehand. We will work on the house for several weeks.

INSTRUCTION SIGN

The town of Migdal Nunia was the home of Mary Magdalene, or "Mary of Migdal." Read Luke 8:1-3. In biblical times, it was possibly the center of the fishing industry in Palestine. "Migdal" means "tower"; therefore, Migdal Nunia is translated as "tower of fish". The city was also called "Magdala-Taricheae," meaning "place of smoked fish."

In John 6:1, 16-17, and 23-24, the Bible indicates that Jesus may have traveled from Capernaum to Migdal often.

Fisherman sometimes lived in family groups, with several brothers and their families all living together in one big house. Make a salt dough house. Cover the outside of the cardboard box with salt dough. You want the salt dough to be as thin and smooth as possible.

Workstation 6: Prayer and Sewing Center

INSTRUCTION SIGN

There were three nets used in the Sea of Galilee in biblical times: a seine or drag-net, the trammel, and the throw net. In Mark 1:16-18, the fishermen are using a throw net, a circular net thrown by one person like a parachute and pulled to shore.

Sew a fish in the center of the scroll from last week as a reminder of the teachings of Jesus. Trace fish pattern on scroll.

STEP 1: Glue or sew sequins on outline of fish. Tie a knot in a double thread to sew on sequins. Have a knot underneath the cloth and tie a knot on top of each sequin to hold sequin tight.

STEP 2: Knot thread for each sequin.

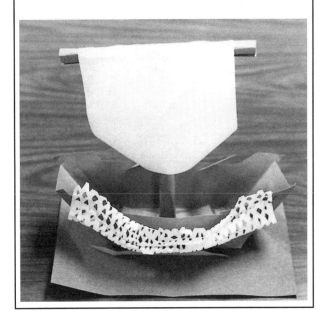

139

Workstation 7: Benediction

INSTRUCTION SIGN

In Luke 5:1-7, the fishermen were probably catching musht at night along the shore with a 115-foot-long trammel net. These nets are still used today. Make a fishing boat for worship.

Simple Boat
STEP 1: Select a blue piece of paper. Fold in half. Then, fold in half again. Cut slit as indicated on pattern.
STEP 2: Trace and cut boat pattern using brown paper. Place tabs on boat in slits on blue page. Glue in place.

More Challenging Boat

STEP 1: Start as described for simple boat above.
STEP 2: Cut slits for oars as marked on pattern. Cut 5.
STEP 3: Cut fore and aft decks. Use brown paper and pattern. Fold on dotted lines and glue in place.
STEP 4: Cut sail and mast poles. Use patterns. Cut slits in center mast pole. Roll both poles on a pencil and glue together. Staple the "horizontal yard" pole to the "mast" pole.

Fold square sail to form triangles as shown on pattern. Glue to "horizontal yard" pole. Pole is intentionally shorter than sail. Curl ends of sail on a pencil. Glue mast in place. Spread out slits as shown to stabilize mast.

STEP 5: Cut fishing net using pattern. Cut tiny triangles on folded net as you would to make a paper snowflake. Cut all edges. Unfold. Glue edge of net to aft deck and inside of boat. Let net hang over side of boat. Place boat on worship table.

The Worship Celebration

SIGN-UP SHEET FOR TODAY'S WORSHIP CELEBRATION

Call to Worship (read Matthew 13:47-48):
Sermon (skit "St. Peter's Fish"):
Benediction (lead the Lord's Prayer):

ITEMS TO GO HOME TODAY: POP-BOTTLE FISH; FISHING BOATS

Session 48
The Farmers at Harvest

The Bible Lesson

The parable of the wheat and the tares (Matthew 13:24-30)

What the Children Will Learn Today

To not judge others because we cannot tell good from bad.

Time Needed

5 minutes for story
20 minutes for workstations
10 minutes for closing worship service

Supplies Needed (by Workstation)

1. Pop-bottle lambs from last week, papier-mâché mixture, scrap newspaper, and leftover scrap white office paper
2. Yarn and masking tape
3. Boatbuilding supplies
4. Skit and puppets or actors
5. Salt dough, piece of plywood to fit as flat roof on salt dough house, scrap wood, sandpaper, sand or cornmeal, newspaper, papier-mâché mixture, and craft supply basket
6. Black or white felt, needles, bookmarks, and thread
7. Construction paper supply basket

Children's Meditation

STORY

A Friend Has Done This

Katy was a happy child. She played well with others and had lots of friends. She had just finished kindergarten and would be starting first grade in the fall. Katy was excited because two of her best friends would be in her class. Cory and Katy had been friends since they were three years old. Cory and Katy did everything together, especially at church on Sunday. They went to Sunday school together, they sang in the children's choir, and they worked at the same workstation in children's worship every single Sunday. After church, the girls either went to Cory's or Katy's house and played together all afternoon. It would be so much fun to be in school together. Katy could hardly wait.

Cindy was in the same class. Cory and Cindy didn't know each other, so on the first day of school Katy introduced Cindy and Cory and suggested that they all go off and play together.

Things went well for a while, but after a couple of weeks the three girls started to argue. Each girl felt jealous of the other. "You're spending more time with her," Cory would say. "You like her better than me," Cindy would say. Katy felt caught in the middle. Katy liked both girls, but the three couldn't get along together.

One day, Cory and Cindy went off to play, and left Katy sitting all alone. Katy felt rejected and started to cry. Her two best friends didn't need her anymore. Cory and Katy still played together on Sunday, but on Monday, Cory pretended that she didn't even know Katy. Instead, Cory went off with Cindy.

"It's not fair," said Katy. "You always want me to play with you on Sunday, Cory, but at school you won't even talk to me."

The bickering and fighting went on for months, each girl thinking of harsher and harsher things to say to the other. First grade ended with the girls still fighting. Katy didn't see Cindy at all during the summer. Cory and Katy still went to the same church and by the end of the summer had started playing together regularly on Sunday afternoons again.

At the start of second grade, the old feud resumed. "It's not fair," Katy said to Cindy. "We were friends once, but since I introduced you to Cory you want nothing to do with me and you won't let Cory and me be friends. It's not fair."

Unfortunately, the feud between the three girls went on from first grade through high school. Katy and Cory were still friendly toward each other when they were away from school, but never spoke at school. Cindy and Katy never spoke again, and Cindy and Cory remained casual but not close friends at school. The three girls had let their jealousy of one another destroy their friendship. It was never to be repaired. They could not separate their jealousy from their love, and jealousy destroyed would could have been a long lasting friendship.

Workstations

Workstation 1: Call to Worship

GETTING READY

Mix papier-mâché. Use pop-bottle lambs from last week.

INSTRUCTION SIGN

After the wheat harvest every year in June, the sheep were allowed to graze in the wheat fields. The sheep ate the lower part of the stalk and whatever was left from the harvest. The sheep were sheared after the summer grazing and in early spring.

Read Matthew 13:24-30. Remember that Jesus said we will be judged by God with the same standard that we use to judge others (Matthew 7:1-2). Be kind and understanding if you want others to be kind and understanding with you. Forgive others when they make a mistake if you want to be forgiven.

Papier-mâché your lamb. Completely cover the lamb with papier-mâché. For the last layer, cover lamb with white scrap paper so the lamb will not need painting. Let dry one week.

Sign up to lead the call to worship for our service today.

Workstation 2: Affirmation of Faith

GETTING READY

Use yarn in 3' lengths. Leftover 3' scraps work fine.

INSTRUCTION SIGN

Farmers often set up booths in the marketplace so that they could sell their crops. A farmer might trade grain from his field for other household items needed, such as a basket.

Farmers who needed help planting or harvesting their crops would go to the marketplace and hire workers. Workers were required by law to leave the corners of the field for the poor. The poor were also allowed to follow workers gathering the wheat or grain and "glean" (gather) anything that the workers missed.

Read Matthew 13:24-30. Work on being kind this week. We should be kind to everyone we meet, even people we don't like. Being kind is easy. Being mean takes thought and planning.

STEP 1:   Count off 9 pieces of yarn about 3 ft. long. With masking tape, tape yarn together in groups of 3 strands each.

STEP 2:   Braid strands into one long braid. Knot each end.

STEP 3:   If you finish before the end of the session, make extra braids and a smaller 12-inch-long braid for a handle.

Put your name on braid. Place braids on worship table as a symbol of your hard work. We'll make basket next week.

Workstation 3: Offering or Carpenter Shop

INSTRUCTION SIGN

Fishermen used boats for both seine-net fishing and trammel fishing. A trammel net is made of 3 different nets. The fish swam through the first net into the trap bag of the third net. Several trammel nets were often tied together to form a net fence along the bottom of the lake. Fishermen used the boat for carrying the heavy nets out into the lake. Fishermen then splashed the water with their oars to frighten and drive the fish into the net. The trammel is the only net that must be washed each day. The trammel net is heavy. It could not be handled by one person. Fishermen worked together in teams or families.

Read Luke 5:1-11 and work together as a team on our boat.

Workstation 4: Sermon or Bible Study

INSTRUCTION SIGN

The two most important grains grown in ancient Judea were wheat and barley. The farmer scattered seed from an open basket, then plowed it under with a wooden plow. The fields were kept free of weeds by constant hoeing from December to February. Tares were a kind of weed known as "bearded darnel," which looked exactly like wheat when growing. It was not until the wheat began to make a head that the farmer could tell the difference.

Read the parable of the wheat and the tares (Matthew 13:24-30). Prepare skit for puppets or actors. You need a reporter and a farmer. You may also use the KTBT camera.

SKIT FOR SERMON

An Enemy Has Done This

REPORTER: Good morning! We are traveling back in time today to Bethlehem to learn how farmers harvested wheat. Bethlehem is a good location because *Bethlehem* means "house of bread" and the town was so named because of the many fields surrounding the city. [Farmer or puppet comes running out.]

FARMER: Help! Help! An enemy has done this.

REPORTER: An enemy did what?

FARMER: An enemy has sown bearded darnel in my wheat.

REPORTER: Can you get it out?

FARMER: No! No! You don't understand. Bearded darnel looks just like wheat when it first starts to grow. By the time you figure it out, it's too late. To pull it out now would destroy my wheat crop.

REPORTER: What are you going to do then?

FARMER: They must be left together in the field until harvest time. Then, in the areas where the darnel weeds are not very thick, the weeds can be pulled and the harvest continued. In other areas, the wheat can be gathered over the top of the darnel because the wheat grows taller. It will be much harder and we must be patient, but we will get the harvest in.

REPORTER: Can you get rid of the weeds?

FARMER: Oh yes, we will set the field on fire and burn the weeds down to the ground. The women must inspect the wheat grains one by one, because even one slate-gray or black darnel grain can be poisonous. It make's you dizzy and sick. [Pause] An enemy has done this!

REPORTER: Well, I'm certainly sorry to hear about your problems. We came today to learn about farming but it seems we learned a lesson in not making snap decisions. At first glance, I would have said you had a great wheat field there. It was impossible to tell what was hidden down underneath the wheat.

FARMER:	It is often the same with people. You think someone is your friend. Then, up from nowhere this friend sows weeds in your field.
REPORTER:	We can't go around suspecting everyone, though. You have to be trusting and understanding. Just as we make mistakes, others make mistakes too.
FARMER:	I suppose you are correct. We must not judge others. Just as I can't tell the darnel weed from the wheat, we can't always tell good actions from bad actions. We must be patient and not judge others; otherwise, God will judge us in the same way that we judge others. [Farmer walks away saying, "My wheat! My wheat! My poor wheat!"]
REPORTER:	Well, I don't know about you, but instead of jumping to conclusions and accusing others when something goes wrong, I'm going to try to be more patient and forgiving. I wouldn't want God to accuse me of doing something I didn't do, so I won't accuse others. How about you?

Workstation 5: Witness to Faith

GETTING READY

Use plywood for roof. Cardboard bends too easily. Cardboard boxes or wood scraps can be used for raised platform.

INSTRUCTION SIGN

We often do not think of how easy it is to accuse someone of doing something they didn't do, but we each accuse someone falsely every day. It's a common mistake. Remember to forgive and give others a second chance. Tell someone you're sorry today for something that has happened in the past. Read Matthew 13:24-30 and continue working on our biblical house.

STEP 1: Spread salt dough on plywood. Make a smooth, thin layer on top of roof.

STEP 2: Use scrap wood or cardboard boxes to make a raised platform to fit in end of house. Cover platform with sandpaper. Glue sand or cornmeal in lower part of house for dirt floor.

Place biblical house on the worship table for service today.

Workstation 6: Prayer and Sewing Center

GETTING READY

Continue working on bookmarks from last week.

INSTRUCTION SIGN

Most clothing was made of wool, but flax was also grown in Palestine and harvested in March and April. Flax was used to make linen garments and sails for fishing boats.

Trace lamb pattern. Sew lamb to bottom of bookmark. Sew an eye for your lamb. We will finish bookmarks next week.

Read Matthew 13:24-30. Sign up to lead prayer.

Workstation 7: Benediction

The Worship Celebration

INSTRUCTION SIGN

Grain and straw were tossed in the air with a five-pronged winnowing fork. The wind would blow the straw aside. The heavier good grain fell back to the ground. The chaff (outside covering) was used for fuel for the fire, the leftover straw was given to the animals, and the grain was ground for bread.

We often have trouble separating what's important in life from what is not. We think being popular is the most important thing in life, and we are willing to do anything just to be popular. Read Matthew 13:24-30 and make a winnowing fork.

STEP 1: Trace patterns on brown paper. Cut 2. Glue 2 forks together for thickness. Roll handle on pencil and glue.

STEP 2: Staple handle to fork. Make yellow straw by cutting slivers of yellow scrap paper. Practice GENTLY.

SIGN-UP SHEET FOR TODAY'S WORSHIP CELEBRATION

Call to Worship (read Matthew 13:24-30):
Sermon (skit "A Friend Has Done This"):
Benediction (write a prayer):

ITEMS TO GO HOME TODAY:
WINNOWING FORKS

Session 49
Shepherds in the Field

The Bible Lesson

The parable of the lost sheep (Luke 15:1-7)

What the Children Will Learn Today

To think about consequences of our actions before we act.

Time Needed

  5 minutes for story
20 minutes for workstations
10 minutes for closing worship service

Supplies Needed (by Workstation)

1. Pop-bottle lambs, black paint and brushes or black paper
2. Yarn and yarn braids from last week
3. Boatbuilding supplies
4. Skit and puppets
5. Salt dough house, black paint, brushes, and salt dough
6. Bookmarks, polyester stuffing, pattern, and fabric glue
7. Black construction paper, pattern, and white chalk

Children's Meditation

STORY

Johnny Is Impossible

Everywhere Johnny goes, someone says, "Johnny is impossible." Johnny likes to do what he wants, when he wants, and exactly how he wants. Johnny's seven. He has to be first in line, takes five cookies when he's told to take two, and never listens.

Johnny's teachers are frustrated because Johnny constantly causes trouble from the minute he arrives till he leaves. Johnny's parents are worried. They've tried everything to make Johnny behave, but Johnny doesn't want to.

"Why is everyone always yelling at me?" complained Johnny.

"If you change the way you treat others then they'll change how they treat you. Absolutely no one can be number one or get to do exactly what they want one hundred percent of the time. You have to give to others if you want them to give back to you."

Johnny decided to try. Johnny started out by trying to say nice things to others and to take turns. It was amazing. Even by lunchtime, no one had yelled at him. But in the afternoon, Johnny wasn't selected to be the team captain, and he resumed yelling and screaming. The next day, Johnny was determined to try harder because he really did like it better when others were nice to him.

Johnny got angry once, but he didn't throw a tantrum. He made it through a whole day without screaming and yelling.

"Behaving sure is hard," Johnny told his brother.

"It get's easier with practice, and the rewards are worth the effort," said Rob.

A month later, Johnny was totally different. No, he wasn't perfect, and yes, Johnny still did lose his temper now and then.

Johnny had learned to care about the wants, needs, and feelings of others. No one likes to sit back and watch someone else always be chosen to be team captain. Everyone needs a turn to be special.

When Johnny stopped thinking just about what he wanted and began to think about how his actions affected others, Johnny became a much happier person. Johnny's life was no longer filled with just "me, me, me" or "I want" and "give me." Now, Johnny says, "May I help?" "Would you like?" "Here's one for you."

Johnny learned to control his temper and thereby control his own happiness. We can follow Johnny's example by asking ourselves, Do I think of the needs of others or just *myself*?

Workstations

Workstation 1: Call to Worship

GETTING READY

Use black paint or tear small pieces of black scrap paper and glue bits of black paper to lower leg and nose.

INSTRUCTION SIGN

During the winter, sheep were only allowed to graze a few miles from town during the daytime. At night, the sheep went back to the sheepfold, which was a low "arched building" with an enclosure or pen built of rocks and stones on one side. The sheep were kept inside the building or in the pen, depending on the weather. Read John 10:2-4.

Sheep often wander away and get lost. We, too, wander away from Christian principles. Jesus said to treat others as you want to be treated (Luke 10:27). Think of someone you could be nicer to. Go and be kind to that person today and every day.

Continue working on pop-bottle lamb. Paint just the lower part of feet and the face black today. Use cover-ups.

Sign up to read the Bible verse for the call to worship.

Workstation 2: Affirmation of Faith

GETTING READY

Use braids of yarn from last week.

INSTRUCTION SIGN

Merchants and wealthy people hired a shepherd to care for their flock of sheep and goats. The shepherd was responsible for replacing any animals that were lost or killed. In the spring and summer, the shepherd would take the flocks to higher pasture in the mountains. The shepherd would build a circular sheepfold of stones or find a cave. The shepherd would lay across the entrance to become the gate. Read John 10:7, 11-15.

Often when a project is hard, we want to give up and quit, but Jesus says we should never run away from the hard jobs we face in life (Matthew 5:6). We should keep trying until we can master the task. Use the braids from last week. Make a basket.

STEP 1: Tie 4 strands of yarn to knotted end of braid.

STEP 2: Place yarn on pattern and start to form a circle. Tie yarn around braid as you form circle. Tie knots twice.

STEP 3: Braid will begin to curl upward. Stack braided circles one on top of the other. Tie each braid as you go.

STEP 4: When braid is finished, tie handle in place. Take basket to worship to remind you not to be afraid to TRY.

Workstation 3: Offering or Carpenter Shop

INSTRUCTION SIGN

As Christians, we are called to think before we act. Read John 10:14-15. Everyone is included in God's church. Stop and think if your actions in the carpenter shop exclude others. Ask yourself if everyone has been given a turn. Are you supportive when others have trouble hammering a nail or do you laugh and tease? How many times do you give someone else a turn ahead of you?

Workstation 4: Sermon or Bible Study

INSTRUCTION SIGN

Sheep need constant protection and are totally helpless when it comes to finding good pasture and water. Therefore, the good shepherd takes care of his sheep. The phrase "Good Shepherd" is often used as a name for Jesus. Read Luke 15:1-7 and Matthew 5:1-11. In today's puppet play the reporter turns to talk to the audience and also turns and talks to the shepherd. Practice your puppeting skills for entering, exiting, and turning to speak directly to a specific puppet. Helpers from Workstation 6 are making sheep to be counted in the skit.

SKIT FOR SERMON

To Be a Shepherd

SHEPHERD: [Shepherd enters counting and makes a whistling noise. Show sheep on pencils from Workstation 6 as shepherd counts.] 156, 157, 158, 159—[whistle] Where's Nebo?

REPORTER: Excuse me, are you a shepherd?

SHEPHERD: Yes!

REPORTER: I thought so. I'm _____ [name] from KTBT news. Do you have a few minutes to teach us how to be a shepherd?

SHEPHERD: It would take you much longer than a few minutes to learn to be a shepherd. Look at the sky! It is almost nighttime, and I must account for the sheep I took to pasture. I have counted as they scooted under my rod into the sheepfold and one is missing. It is a young lamb named "Nebo." I named it after Mount Nebo, for this lamb wanders as aimlessly as Moses and his followers did.

REPORTER: Will the lamb find its way home?

SHEPHERD: No, I must go and look for Nebo.

REPORTER: What about the rest of the sheep?

SHEPHERD: My hired man will watch and care for them while I am gone. They will be safely bedded down for the night.

REPORTER: Where will you look?

SHEPHERD: In the high pasture where we were grazing today.

REPORTER: [Shepherd has stick.] Is that stick to fight off wild animals?

SHEPHERD: No, this is my staff. It is a walking stick. I can also use it to rescue Nebo if the lamb has fallen into a hole. I must go now and find Nebo. Nebo will be frightened.

REPORTER: [Shepherd leaves. Reporter shouts.] Thank you and good luck. [Turns back to audience.]
Being a shepherd is certainly a lot harder than I thought.
[Shouts of "Hooray!" are heard in background.]
I wonder what all of the noise is about?
[Shepherd returns.]
You're back!

SHEPHERD: Yes, I have found Nebo and there is much rejoicing.
REPORTER: That's fantastic! I never thought about each individual lamb or ewe being so important. I see now why they call Jesus the "Good Shepherd." Jesus leads us by showing us the safest path to take in life. If we read the parables and follow his teachings, we'll be listening to or heeding Jesus' call. Thanks for teaching us all about being a shepherd.
SHEPHERD: My pleasure, and peace be with you.
REPORTER: And peace with you.

Workstation 5: Witness to Faith

GETTING READY

Mix salt dough and have paint and cover-ups ready.

INSTRUCTION SIGN

Sheep and goats were kept in the same flock. The shepherd drove the goats to pasture ahead of him and called the sheep. Sheep followed the shepherd's voice and came when he called. Sheep were kept in a sheepfold at night. If the family kept a goat to provide milk, the goat was kept in the lower level of the house at night. Read John 10:16.

Houses made of sun-dried limestone bricks were dark inside. There was, of course, no electricity. The only source of light was one or more small oil hand lamps. The lamp was originally an open bowl filled with olive oil and a burning wick in the spout. These lamps frequently caught fire. When Jesus was a child, a method was developed to place a cover on the lamp so that the oil would not catch fire. The family might also use a small hole or pit dug in the floor for a cooking fire. Sometimes the fire would be kept burning all night for warmth and light. Most of the family's cooking though, was done at an oven. The smoke from the lamp and fire turned the ceiling black.

Paint the underneath side of the roof black today. Make a parapet or wall around the top edge of the roof and also make a tiny clay lamp to go inside the house.

Workstation 6: Prayer and Sewing Center

INSTRUCTION SIGN

Some people, even today, still live as nomadic shepherds in tents, moving their sheep from pasture to pasture. A nomad's life is hard. The entire family travels with the shepherd and helps tend the sheep. Read Psalm 23:1-6.

Finish your bookmark by gluing stuffing to your felt lamb. When dry, place your bookmark in your Bible at the Twenty-third Psalm.

If you did not made a bookmark, you can make a fuzzy lamb by tracing the lamb pattern and gluing stuffing onto paper lamb. Color nose and feet black. Tape your lamb to a pencil.

Sign up to help with the sermon. Practice with puppeteers.

Workstation 7: Benediction

INSTRUCTION SIGN

Each shepherd usually watched more than one hundred sheep. The shepherd had to keep all one hundred sheep safe from harm. Shepherds led their sheep to grass for grazing and to water by walking in front and calling with familiar vocal signals. Even if the sheep became mixed with another flock during grazing they would return to their shepherd's call. Read John 10:14 and 1 Peter 2:25.

Make a paper lamb today to take home as a reminder to follow the teachings of Jesus. Trace lamb pattern on black paper. Then, color with white chalk or crayon.

The Worship Celebration

SIGN-UP SHEET FOR TODAY'S WORSHIP CELEBRATION

Call to Worship (read John 10:2-4 and sing a song):

Sermon (skit "To Be a Shepherd"):

Benediction (lead the Lord's Prayer):

ITEMS TO GO HOME TODAY: PAPER LAMBS;
BIBLE BOOKMARKS; YARN BASKETS

Session 50
Education and Worship

The Bible Lesson

The parable of the unfruitful fig tree (Luke 13:6-9)

What the Children Will Learn Today

Worship customs during the life of Jesus

Time Needed

5 minutes for story
20 minutes for workstations
10 minutes for closing worship service

Supplies Needed (by Workstation)

1. Pop-bottle lambs, glue, and white polyester stuffing
2. 2-liter pop bottles, skin-tone felt, cloth, black or brown yarn or fake fur, buttons, scrap paper, and ribbon
3. Boatbuilding supplies
4. Skit, Bible, puppets, and puppet stage
5. Salt dough mixture and small box for upper room
6. Heavy cloth or felt for Bible cover
7. Construction paper supply basket

Children's Meditation

STORY

The Lazy Fig Tree

Fig trees were very valuable in biblical times. During the months of April and May, the fig trees were bare, but throughout the remainder of the year figs were plentiful. Figs were a sweet fruit eaten straight from the tree, dried or sometimes pressed into cakes for traveling. Most young, newly planted fig trees did not produce fruit for the first three years, so the farmer had to be patient.

In the parable of the unfruitful fig tree, Jesus told about a farmer who had planted a new fig tree in the best of all possible places—the vineyard. The farmer had given the fig tree the best of everything. At the end of the three years, the farmer visited the vineyard expecting to see fruit on the tree, but the tree had not even begun to do any work. The tree simply hadn't tried. At first, the farmer wanted to cut the tree down and plant something else in its place, but the worker who trimmed the grapevines pleaded for the chance to work around the tree and give it one more chance.

We are sometimes like the fig tree. We waste time and don't produce work. There was once a little boy named Mark who wasted all his time and talent.

Mark liked to play any game that kept him too busy to practice the piano. Everyone said that Mark showed great promise and talent on the piano, but Mark didn't like to practice. Mark complained terribly when his mother made him practice.

"It's not fair. I'll practice later. There's still plenty of time."

Of course, Mark always ran out of time and wasn't able to practice. Mark loved to enter piano contests, and he always expected to win.

At the end of the year, there was a piano contest. The prize was a scholarship to a special summer music camp for gifted piano students. Mark really wanted to go.

The first week, Mark practiced without fail. The second week, Mark practiced about half of the week. By the third week, Mark only practiced one or two days. The week before the contest, Mark didn't practice at all. Mark was too busy reading, riding his bike, and playing soccer.

On the day of the contest, Mark was confident and sure he would win, but he didn't. Another student played better. This student was normally not thought to be as talented as Mark, but had worked very hard to prepare for the contest.

151

The greatest failure we make in life is when we do not try to do our best. Like the fig tree in the parable, God has given us the best of everything, but we often fail because we do not try as hard as we should. Still, God is not harsh; he offers us another chance.

Think of a task that you could work on harder than you do at present. Make it your goal this week to try as hard as you can. You'll be surprised how much you'll improve if you *really* try.

Workstations

Workstation 1: Call to Worship

GETTING READY

You may purchase eyes for lambs or cut paper eyes.

INSTRUCTION SIGN

Jesus used the parable of the unfruitful fig tree to teach that laziness or not trying is wasting what God has given you. You have worked hard for several weeks. Read Luke 13:6-9 and finish your lamb today. Do not waste the polyester stuffing or use more than your share. Remember always to think of the needs of those around you.

STEP 1: Make eye from scrap paper. Glue in place.

STEP 2: Work with small areas at a time. Place glue on lamb. Cover glue lightly with stuffing. Take lamb to worship.

Workstation 2: Affirmation of Faith

INSTRUCTION SIGN

Jesus lived in a hot, dry region of the country and worked outside. He probably had rather tanned skin and dark hair. The Jews wore long, flowing robes with cloth coverings to protect their heads from the heat. Read Luke 4:16-21.

STEP 1: Wrap skin-colored felt around bottom of upside-down pop bottle for face. Decorate eyes, nose, and mouth with the supplies provided. Glue the face of your puppet onto the bottom of your pop bottle. The neck of the bottle will be the handle.

STEP 2: Add yarn or fake fur for hair and a beard. Men in biblical times often wore long beards. Add yarn only to the front, because the back of the head will be covered by the cloth that the Hebrew people wore over their heads.

STEP 3: Pick fabric to drape around the bottle for the loose-fitting robes. Make sure the cloth is longer than your bottle so it will cover your hand when you are holding your puppet. Glue cloth. Tie ribbon around waist for a belt. Add arms.

STEP 4: Cut a piece of cloth large enough to drape over head and down sides for head covering. Glue in place. Tie a ribbon around head to hold cloth securely in place.

Workstation 3: Offering or Carpenter Shop

INSTRUCTION SIGN

At the synagogue school, boys learned to trace the 22 letters of the Hebrew alphabet in the sand. When they were ready, they would be given wax tablets to write on. In the afternoon, the boys would return home to learn the trade of their fathers. Jesus learned to be a carpenter and Paul a tent-maker. We, too, learn from reading the Bible. Read Luke 13:6-9.

Continue working on fishing boat. Report on progress.

Workstation 4: Sermon or Bible Study

GETTING READY

Have the biblical string puppets from Session 44 available.

INSTRUCTION SIGN

At the age of 10, boys would go to more advanced classes for interpreting the law. Only the Torah was taught. Math, music, and art were not included. The teacher would raise a question or problem of everyday life. Students then recited law that applied. Jesus used a lesson from Isaiah when he taught in the synagogue in Nazareth. Read both Isaiah 61:1-2 and Luke 4:1-24.

The sermon today is a puppet play describing a synagogue service. You will need 4 puppets and 4 readers today. The puppets will be making several entrances and exits. You will need a Bible. The reporter will narrate and explain a synagogue service. Make any props or scenery desired. If you are using the Sunshine Share-a-Lot Puppet Theater, use hand puppet at top and biblical string puppets from Session 44 with the lower curtain.

SKIT FOR SERMON

A Synagogue Worship Service

REPORTER: Welcome to KTBT's time travel report from the Bible this morning. We have arrived in Nazareth, the childhood home of Jesus, early on Sabbath morning. The ram's horn was sounded to announce the Sabbath and the people are gathering this morning in the synagogue. The synagogue is a square stone building built so that the door and fourth wall face Jerusalem. The other three walls are lined with hard clay-brick benches.

There is a seven-branched lamp stand placed near a raised reading table or desk. Today's prayer leader, the man who sounded the ram's horn, will take his place behind the reading desk in a moment. There is not a priest in the synagogue, but the adult men take turns being the prayer leader.

It looks as if the service is about to start. We'll listen. [REPORTER moves to one side. PRAYER LEADER puppet enters. All puppeteers speak from background for response marked "ALL."]

PRAYER: Praise God with shouts of joy, all people! Sing to the glory of his name; offer him glorious praise! [Psalm 66:1-2 TEV]

ALL: Amen! [Spoken by all very loudly]

ALL: Hear, O Israel: The Lord our God is one Lord.

REPORTER: [In a whisper voice] At this point in the service, the "hazzan" or assistant brings in the ark or wooden chest. The ark contains the Torah. This act is symbolic of bringing in the word of God, similar to the tradition of carrying the Bible and placing it on the altar during the call to worship in many of our churches today. The hazzan will take the scroll out of the ark, unroll it, and place it on the reading desk.

PRAYER LEADER: The world and all that is in it belong to the Lord; the earth and all who live on it are his. [Psalm 24:1 TEV]

REPORTER: A member of the congregation is now being called up to read the Torah in Hebrew. He will read three lines, and then an interpreter will translate the Hebrew into Aramaic. The Torah is written in Hebrew, but most of the people of Jesus' day spoke Aramaic. Jesus may have spoken Hebrew, Aramaic, and Greek.

READER: [Puppet can pretend to hold scroll or just have a child read the Bible verse offstage. Read Deuteronomy 6:4-9.]

PRAYER LEADER: I will praise you, Lord, with all my heart; I will tell of all the wonderful things you have done. I will sing with joy because of you. I will sing praise to you, Almighty God. [Psalm 9:1-2 TEV]

REPORTER: The reading from the Torah is followed by an interpretation or sermon explaining the scripture. The sermon today explains that we should each ask, "What have I put into life?" Instead of being concerned with how much we have received, we should ask how much can I give.

At the close of the sermon, another member of the congregation is called upon to read from one of the books of the Prophets, as Jesus did when he read from the book of Isaiah.

READER: [Luke 4:18-19]

PRAYER LEADER: We give thanks to you, O God, we give thanks to you! We proclaim how great you are and tell of the wonderful things you have done. [Psalm 75:1 TEV]

REPORTER: As the service ends and the people walk out sharing greetings with their neighbors, we, too, must think how lucky we are. God has richly blessed us. We should use the talents that God has given us to praise him. We can praise God at home with our families. Instead of saying unkind words, we can work hard to make our home a happy place filled with love.

I'm going home right now and tell everyone at my house one reason they're special. I'm also going to remember to say, "I love you," each day and show that I mean it by how I treat each person in my family. How about you?

Workstation 5: Witness to Faith

GETTING READY

Small box should fit on end of roof. Cut door and window.

INSTRUCTION SIGN

We are adding an upper room to our biblical house. An upper room was often used for guests as well as a workroom for the women. Read Acts 9:36-37. Cover box for upper room with salt dough. Keep as smooth and as thin as possible. Let upper room dry before placing it on the roof of the salt dough house.

Workstation 6: Prayer and Sewing Center

INSTRUCTION SIGN

Daily life was filled with prayer. Before each meal, the father said a "blessing" for the bread. The blessing was followed with a prayer of thanksgiving and praise to God.

Girls did not attend the synagogue school but were educated at home by their mothers. Girls learned the dietary laws from the Torah, home rituals for the Sabbath and festivals, and how to follow the law in the family's daily life. Girls also learned cooking, sewing, weaving, the use of herbal medicines to treat illnesses, caring for children, and singing or playing an instrument for religious festivities. Read Luke 13:6-9.

STEP 1: Cut a piece of cloth or felt that is 2" wider and longer (ALL SIDES) than your Bible to make a Bible cover.

STEP 2: Lay Bible in center of cloth. Mark fold lines. Fold fabric so that it will fit around Bible like a book jacket.

STEP 3: Stitch edges together that slide over end of book.

Workstation 7: Benediction

INSTRUCTION SIGN

When boys reached the age of 3, the father began to teach the Torah. At the age of 5 or 6, Jewish boys would go to the synagogue school or "house of the book." The boys sat on the floor in a half circle and memorized and recited verses from the Torah. Read Luke 13:6-9. Trace pattern. Make a card.

The Worship Celebration

SIGN-UP SHEET FOR TODAY'S WORSHIP CELEBRATION

The puppet skit is the entire service today.

ITEMS TO GO HOME TODAY: POP-BOTTLE LAMBS; PUPPETS; POP-OPEN CARD

Session 51
Clothing in Biblical Times

The Bible Lesson

The parable of the two sons (Matthew 21:28-32)

What the Children Will Learn Today

Our daily actions tell more about our faith than our words.

Time Needed

5 minutes for story
20 minutes for workstations
10 minutes for closing worship service

Supplies Needed (by Workstation)

1. Old light bulbs, Styrofoam cups, papier-mâché
2. Yarn, scraps of cloth, patterns, and a hardcover book
3. Boatbuilding supplies
4. Skit, puppets, 2 plastic bags, cloth scraps, and book
5. Salt dough, cereal box, Popsicle sticks, and pattern
6. Bible covers from last week, needles, and thread
7. Construction paper supply basket and paper doll patterns

Children's Meditation

STORY

She's a Snob

Mary Alice constantly found fault with everyone. "She's a snob," Mary Alice would announce. "Have you seen the way she walks? Can you imagine anyone wearing clothes like that? She and her friends are so conceited; they just think they're better than everyone else."

Mary Alice did not realize that in pointing out the faults of others, she was showing her own. She also could not see that everything she despised in others was true about herself.

If Mary Alice lost her temper, it was always someone else's fault because they provoked her. If Mary Alice didn't get her homework done, it was the teacher's fault for assigning boring work. If Mary Alice made a rude comment to another person, it was not her fault. The other person deserved it. Someone else was always to blame, according to Mary Alice.

"I'm afraid not," her mother said. "There's no one person better than another and no one's perfect. We each have faults, problems, and make mistakes every day. Children and adults alike.

"God forgives us and allows us to correct our mistakes. God also gives us a chance to change the way we act. It's one thing to say that you are a kind and understanding person. It's another to actually go out and be kind and forgiving with others even when they are not always kind to you.

"Each day is a new beginning. If you were rude to someone or made a mistake yesterday, as we all do, then say you are sorry and work hard to do better today. If you have grown accustomed to thinking that you're better than others or deserve to have everything go the way you desire, stop and remember the words of Jesus: 'Your heart will always be where your riches are' (Matthew 6:21 TEV). If you return rude comments when rude comments are made to you, you will become a rude and obnoxious person because you will spend all of your time trying to think of rude, sarcastic comments to say to others. If, on the other hand, you ignore rude comments and try to continue to think and say kind words, kindness will rule your heart.

"The nice thing about being a child of God," continued Mary Alice's mother, "is that we can begin to change immediately. We can go to bed after a disastrous day, get up the next morning, decide to change, and then proceed to do so. Change is not always easy, but if you really want to change, you can. If you focus your life on loving others instead of being angry or getting even, then others will act more kindly toward you. No, not at first, and not always, and not everyone. There will always be people in the world who think they are better than everyone else; there will always be people in the world who are rude and obnoxious and do and say things just to make others angry, and there will always be people in the world who *try* to be kind and loving to each person they meet. The question is: What kind of person will you be?"

Workstations

Workstation 1: Call to Worship

GETTING READY

Have papier-mâché ready before session.

INSTRUCTION SIGN

Throughout his three-year ministry, Jesus continually asked people to change the way they lived their lives and treated one another. Instead of being rude when others are rude to you, Jesus said to be kind to those who are rude to you. Say kind words and think kind thoughts about those who hurt your feelings. Read Matthew 21:28-32 and Luke 6:27-28. How would you respond?

The people of ancient Palestine were often identified by the clothes they wore. A Christian is identified through words and actions. Make a puppet to remind you to be a follower of Jesus.

STEP 1: Place a lightbulb into an upside-down cup.

STEP 2: Put on a cover-up. Then cover the lightbulb with papier-mâché. Dip pieces of newsprint in the glue mixture. Press the paper around the lightbulb and cup. Completely cover the lightbulb with THREE layers of thick papier-mâché—inside and out. Make sure every single speck of the lightbulb is covered with at least 3 layers of paper. Then set aside to dry.

Sign up to read Luke 6:27-28 for the call to worship today.

Workstation 2: Affirmation of Faith

> ### INSTRUCTION SIGN
>
> Early Christians were said to be followers of the "Way" (Acts 9:2). You were said to be a follower of Jesus not because you belonged to a group and recited certain creeds. It was the way you lived your life that made you a follower of Jesus. Being kind, helping those in need, sharing what you had with others, and speaking nicely to one another were only a few of the requirements. In the parable of the two sons, Jesus reminds us that saying you will do something and doing it are often two different things. Read Matthew 21:28-32. Sign up to read today's parable for the service. Then make a biblical person from yarn to remind you to follow the Way of Jesus.
>
> STEP 1: Wrap 130 strands of yarn around the middle of a book or encyclopedia. Put a pencil underneath your first wrap to work as a spacer and make the yarn easier to slip off later.
>
> STEP 2: Tie yarn together at top. This will hold your yarn in place. Slide yarn off book.
>
> STEP 3: Tie yarn about one-third of the way down for head.
>
> STEP 4: Tie again two-thirds of the way down for waist.
>
> STEP 5: Cut the bottom of the yarn off evenly.
>
> STEP 6: Wrap 25 strands of yarn around hand to make arms. Tie at each end for hands. Cut ends even. Stuff into body.
>
> STEP 7: Use the felt or cloth scraps for a biblical tunic. Trace pattern. Wrap yarn around tunic at waist to hold in place.
>
> STEP 8: Sew or glue sequins or beads on for face (eyes, nose, mouth). Glue cloth covering on top of head.

Workstation 3: Offering or Carpenter Shop

> ### INSTRUCTION SIGN
>
> Jesus told many parables reminding us to be humble rather than boastful. Jesus was also very concerned that we learn to make commitments and keep our word. Read Matthew 21:28-32.
>
> Finish boat today. Be ready to paint next week.

Workstation 4: Sermon or Bible Study

> ### INSTRUCTION SIGN
>
> It is one thing to say that we are Christians and that we follow the teachings of Jesus; it is another to actually do so. Read Matthew 21:28-32. Which will you be: (1) a person who says "Yes, I will," but does not, or (2) a person who says "Yes" and then actually tries to follow the teachings of Jesus?
>
> You will need 4 puppeteers and 4 readers today. Include the puppet you use for Sunshine Share-a-Lot. For props, you need 2 plastic bags, cloth scraps for clothes or make some from paper, and a book for Fran to read. Practice making entrances and exits. Use a pause between scene changes.

SKIT FOR SERMON

The Unkept Promise

SCENE I:	[Mother and children enter at center of puppet stage.]
MOTHER:	Cleaning time! I'd like you to clean your closets, underneath the bed, and your chest of drawers. Here's a bag for trash, and this bag is for clothes and toys you've outgrown. The church is collecting food, clothing, and toys for families in need. While we are cleaning, we'll help others.
MARK:	Do we have to? We just cleaned last week. All we do is clean. It's supposed to be summer vacation. I'm watching TV. I don't want to clean. I like my room messy. I can't find things when I clean.
FRAN:	What a good idea. Sure, I'll be glad to clean. It will be fun to sort through my closet. Thanks, Mom.
	[Children take plastic bags. All puppets exit.]
SCENE II:	*Fran's Room*
FRAN:	I don't know what Mom was thinking. This room is not a mess. I'm certainly not going to waste my day cleaning. I want to finish that new book I started reading. I'll clean later *if* I get around to it. I certainly don't have anything I want to donate anyway. [Fran takes a book and exits to read.]
SCENE III:	*Mark's Room* [Have puppet start at center stage where he is watching TV. Exit down and come back up at side for his room.]
MARK:	I guess Mom's right; I really should clean my room.
	There's not much to watch on TV anyway. [Make clicking noise for TV's OFF switch or snap fingers.] The sooner I get started the sooner I finish. [Puppet throws cloth scraps or paper clothes out over puppet stage. Absolutely nothing hard may be thrown.] She did say to sort through everything in the closet, so I guess that means this pile of clothing on the floor.
SCENE IV:	*Fran's Room* [Fran appears reading a book. Sunshine arrives.]
SUNSHINE:	Hi, Fran! What are you doing?
FRAN:	Hi, Sunshine! I'm reading a great book. Sit down and I'll tell you all about it.
SUNSHINE:	Didn't you promise your mom you'd clean?
FRAN:	I hate cleaning. Besides, I like my room messy. It gives the room character.
SUNSHINE:	What about keeping your promise to your mom? When you tell someone you'll do something, you should do it. Otherwise, people learn that you can't be trusted to do what you say you'll do. If you tell someone you will do something and then intentionally don't do it, you're telling a lie.
FRAN:	It's just cleaning, Sunshine. It's not like it's something important. No one cares about cleaning.
SUNSHINE:	Everyone has to learn to clean. If we never clean, the world would be a mess. Learning to keep your room neat and tidy is a good place to begin. Come on, I'll help.
FRAN:	Not now, I want to finish this book. The room can wait. Go visit Mark, he's watching TV. [Sunshine and Fran exit.]
SCENE V:	*Mark's Room*
MARK:	Hey, there's the sweatshirt I've been looking for. I wonder how it got in the bottom of my closet. It's supposed to be in my chest of drawers. Oh well!
SUNSHINE:	Hi, Mark! I see you're cleaning.
MARK:	Hi, Sunshine! I found my sweatshirt, my art pad, and my football.
SUNSHINE:	Your mom will be pleased. She was really upset when you said you wouldn't clean.
MARK:	I know, I'll go apologize when I finish.
SUNSHINE:	Would you like some help?
MARK:	Sure, dive in anywhere. I think I could use a little help. [More clothes go flying over puppet stage.]

Workstation 5: Witness to Faith

GETTING READY

An adult must cut Popsicle sticks with sharp craft shears.

INSTRUCTION SIGN

A mezuzah, or a box containing words from the Torah, was placed on the doorposts of the house. Guests and family members touched the box upon entering the house to remind them that God was always to be the center or most important factor in their life. Make a mezuzah for our salt dough house and a ladder or stairs. Make stairs from cardboard and cover with salt dough. Have an adult help you cut Popsicle sticks for ladder and mezuzah. Read Deuteronomy 6:5-9 and Luke 10:25-28.

Write and sign up to lead a prayer for our worship service.

Workstation 6: Prayer and Sewing Center

INSTRUCTION SIGN

The parable of the two sons in Matthew 21:28-32 reminds us that there have always been people who say they will do something but do not. Jesus tells us to be the kind of person who says, "Yes, I will," and then goes to work. Read the parable, finish your Bible cover from last week, and write a prayer for worship.

STEP 1: Tape edges of Bible cover with masking tape to prevent raveling. Embroider your initials on the front of cover.

STEP 2: Fold Bible cover as indicated on pattern and stitch edges together to make a slip-on Bible cover. Take to worship.

Workstation 7: Benediction

INSTRUCTION SIGN

People in biblical times did not have closets full of clothes. There were no blue jeans or T-shirts. Men, women, and children wore tunics. Many poor people had only one set of clothing. Others were able to afford a tunic to wear to work and a nice tunic to be worn only for the Sabbath and festivals. The rich also wore the tunic, cloak, and coat, but their clothing was much fancier and made of finer cloth. Men often wore stripes and their tunics would range in length from their knees to their ankles. Women wore light blue tunics with embroidery around the v-neck opening. A woman's tunic always covered her ankles. Children dressed similar to adults. The cloak was worn over the tunic for warmth. A coat or cloak with large sleeves might also be worn if a person could afford one. Sandals were the only kind of footwear. Men wore a skullcap with a piece of fabric folded around the edge to make a kind of turban. Women wore a piece of cloth folded to shield the eyes and allowed to fall over the shoulders. Shepherds and workers in the fields wore long cloths on their heads instead of turbans to protect their neck and shoulders from the sun.

Make biblical paper dolls. Trace patterns and make several items of clothing. Read Luke 6:37-38 and write the Bible verse on the back of your paper doll as a reminder to help others.

Sign up to read the Bible verse for the benediction today.

The Worship Celebration

SIGN-UP SHEET FOR TODAY'S WORSHIP CELEBRATION

Call to Worship (read Luke 6:27-28):
Affirmation (read Matthew 21:28-32):
Sermon (skit "She's a Snob"):
Person to lead the prayer written at Workstation 5:
Benediction (read Luke 6:37-38):

ITEMS TO GO HOME TODAY: YARN PEOPLE; BIBLE COVERS; PAPER DOLLS

Session 52
Learning a Trade

The Bible Lesson

Jesus stressed putting God's work first and the work of the world second (Luke 14:15-24;18:1-5 and Matthew 4:18-22).

What the Children Will Learn Today

Workstations emphasize work people did in biblical times.

Time Needed

5 minutes for story
20 minutes for workstations
10 minutes for closing worship service

Supplies Needed (by Workstation)

1. Lightbulb puppets from last week, cloth, and paint
2. Any kind of string or cord to use for fishing net
3. Paint, brushes, fishing boat, and cover-ups
4. Skit, puppets, or props for acting
5. Construction paper, unbleached coffee filters, white tissue paper, craft supply basket, and patterns
6. Salt dough
7. Construction paper supply basket and turban patterns

Children's Meditation

STORY

Too Many Excuses

Andrew sat wiggling in the pew as the minister talked about people making excuses. The minister said, "Everyone is called by God, but it is up to us to answer the call." Andrew thought to himself, *God's never called me. Maybe God only calls adults.*

It was sort of interesting to think of adults making excuses to God. Andrew was always getting in trouble for making excuses.

If he didn't have all of his homework done on time, Andrew's teachers made him stay in during recess and sometimes even after school. Andrew always had a good excuse too. Andrew would say, "I did my homework but somehow I lost it on the way to school."

If Andrew didn't clean his room, his parents would lecture him about being responsible and say, "No TV till that room is clean." For some reason, Andrew's parents never believed him when he said, "I cleaned my room. It got messy again when I wasn't in there."

"God calls everyone, even children," the minister said. "If you haven't been working for God today, you need to reexamine your schedule and discover the special job God needs you to do."

What could God possibly want me to do? thought Andrew. *I don't have any money, and I go to Sunday school.*

Andrew thought about his daily schedule as the minister suggested. Let's see, he got up this morning and argued with his sister at the breakfast table. He and two other boys got in trouble in Sunday school for flying paper airplanes. Now, he was sitting in church squirming and feeling totally bored. This afternoon after lunch, his family was going to the church picnic.

Andrew hoped he'd get a chance to play on the softball team. Even though he wasn't very good, Andrew enjoyed playing on the church team. People didn't criticize you if you couldn't hit the ball. At school, no one wanted Andrew to be on their team.

Andrew didn't see anything in his daily schedule that God could possibly be interested in. Do you? Think about Andrew's schedule for a minute. What could Andrew do for God?

[Pause and give the children time to answer. Encourage the children to think about: (1) sharing and taking turns working on the fishing boat, (2) encouraging other players who might be having trouble during the softball game, (3) telling his Sunday school teacher he was sorry for misbehaving, or (4) trying really hard not to have another argument with his sister.]

Working for God doesn't have to be a big event like going to the hospital as a clown minister, collecting food, or sending health kits to a missionary. Working for God can be as simple as saying a kind word, helping your mom or dad, playing a game fairly without cheating, or just thinking of ways to act kindly to other people. When you plan out your daily schedule, make sure you include God. What are you doing for God today?

Workstations

Workstation 1: Call to Worship

INSTRUCTION SIGN

A stonemason used iron tools to cut and carefully fit stones together to make buildings, walls, and aqueducts, cisterns, or pools for collecting water. In areas where stone could not be dug from the ground, such as the area near Jericho, the workers made mud bricks by filling a hole with water, then mixing the thick mud with straw and treading or squishing it together with their feet. The mud-and-straw mixture was packed in wooden molds, dried in the sun, and later hardened and fired in a kiln (oven) to make them stronger. The stonemason also made baked-clay roof tiles. The roof tiles did not get soggy and muddy like a regular roof. Clay roofs had to be rolled smooth after each rain or they would leak. Read Luke 14:15-24.

Make a lightbulb puppet into a carpenter, stonemason, or a woman baking bread. If your lightbulb is not completely covered with papiermâché from last week, stop and recover lightbulb.

STEP 1: Paint face a skin-tone color. Let dry.

STEP 2: Select cloth. Cloth should completely cover cup. From extra cloth, make two matching sleeves. Roll sleeve on pencil. Glue and pin sleeve to make arm. Roll and glue small ball of old stocking into end of sleeves for hands.

Sign up to read Luke 14:15-24 for worship today.

Workstation 2: Affirmation of Faith

INSTRUCTION SIGN

Fishing was a family business. Often a family owned a boat and brothers and fathers would work together. At least two men, usually four, were needed to row the boat. Seine nets were about 8' wide and hundreds of feet long. They were often suspended between two boats. The net was dragged between the two boats into a tight circle. Then, the fish were hauled into the boats. The fishermen worked in pairs to sort the good fish from the bad.

You're going to work in pairs today to make a seine fishing net for our boat. Read Matthew 4:18-22. You need 4 people to make the net. Each person needs six 3' lengths of cord.

STEP 1: Tie 2 ropes together. Tie end to doorknob. Label end of each rope with masking tape: 1, 2, 3, 4, 5, and 6.

STEP 2: Tie 2 and 3 together, making a knot. Then, tie 4 and 5 together, making a knot.

STEP 3: Tie 1 and 2 together. Tie 3 and 4. Tie 5 and 6.

STEP 4: Return and tie 2 and 3 again. Tie 5 and 6 again.

STEP 5: Then, tie 1 and 2 again. Tie 3 and 4. Tie 5 and 6.

STEP 6: Repeat pattern until you are out of rope. Tie your net to your partner's net. Make net as long and as wide as desired by following the same instructions. Take net to worship.

Workstation 3: Offering or Carpenter Shop

INSTRUCTION SIGN

The work of a carpenter was very hard and required a lot of physical strength. Carpenters had to cut down trees by hand. Read Luke 18:1-5. Put on a cover-up and paint the boat.

Workstation 4: Sermon or Bible Study

INSTRUCTION SIGN

As you work, remember that it is easy to criticize others and to make excuses for our own mistakes. We are always quick to notice when someone is being selfish and not sharing, but how often do we admit when we are being selfish and not sharing?

We also frequently find ourselves making excuses for our actions. Just as in the parable of the great feast, our excuses sound important. Read Luke 14:15-24. Jesus used this parable to remind the people of his day that they must not let the problems and needs of everyday life interfere with serving God. Practice. Check for props. You need 4 actors or puppeteers.

SKIT FOR SERMON

Do You Take Your Bible on Vacation?

REPORTER: Good morning, I'm_____[name] with KTBT News, and we are taking a survey this morning to see how many people plan to take their Bible with them on vacation this summer. Let's find out if this young lady on her way to the beach plans to read her Bible this summer. [Turns to vacationer walking by.]

Good morning, are you taking your Bible along on vacation?

VACATIONER: [with big sunglasses, beach towel over the shoulder, and a beach ball] No way! We're spending the summer at the beach. You can't build sand castles or swim in the ocean with a Bible tucked under your arm. [Exits bouncing ball]

REPORTER: I suppose that is a point. You don't see many people sitting under beach umbrellas reading a Bible. Let's ask someone else. Surely, someone plans to read their Bible.

Excuse me! I'm with KTBT News. We're taking a survey to see how many people are taking their Bible on vacation this summer.

LADY: [with children carrying grocery bags] Bible! Does it look like I have time to sit down and read the Bible?

I have five children, a stack of laundry almost taller than me to wash and fold every day, three meals to prepare for an ungrateful, complaining family who always wants something other than what I made for dinner, floors to mop and vacuum, a sink full of dishes that, of course, can only be washed by me with my many years of experience, furniture to dust, ten billion toys to pick up and put away, and a never-ending sea of spiderwebs to sweep down off the light fixtures and ceiling. Now, just exactly where in my daily schedule do you think I have time to sit down, prop up my feet, and read the Bible?

REPORTER: Well, you do seem a tad busy.

LADY WITH
GROCERIES: Busy is right, and if I don't get these groceries home, I'll have ice cream dripping all over the sidewalk. [Lady stomps off.]

REPORTER: Let's ask this gentleman. [Man with nose buried in the newspaper] He seems like an avid reader. Good morning, sir. Are you planning to read your Bible this summer?

MAN ON
HIS WAY
TO WORK: No, I have enough trouble just keeping up with the news. I don't have much free time for reading the Bible. [Man hurries away.]

REPORTER: So far we haven't found anyone who even plans to open the cover of the Bible this summer. It seems people are much too busy to give any thought to reading the Bible this summer, but wait, here comes a lady who might be able to answer our question. Excuse me, we're doing a survey for KTBT News. Are you planning to read your Bible this summer?

LADY WITH
FANCY HAT: Oh my . . . well . . . you see . . . uh . . . not really. But I do go to church on Sunday, except for the two weeks we are on vacation.

REPORTER: Do you take your Bible along on vacation?

LADY WITH
HAT: Why would I take my Bible along on vacation? No one takes a Bible on vacation. I attend church regularly; I go to church every Sunday or at least most Sundays. And I'm in an excellent Sunday school class. Our teacher reads from the Bible every Sunday.

REPORTER: Fantastic! We finally found someone who reads or listens to someone read from the Bible during summer vacation.

LADY WITH
HAT: Oh, our Sunday school class doesn't meet during the summer. We take the summer off. Doesn't everyone?

REPORTER: Well, there you have it. We couldn't find even one person who was planning to read the Bible this summer, much less anyone planning to take it along on vacation. I suppose people don't give much thought to reading the Bible while they are having so much fun. [pause] Are you taking your Bible on vacation with you this summer?

Workstation 5: Witness to Faith

> INSTRUCTION SIGN
>
> All clothing in Jesus' time had to be made by hand. Both men and women wore long tunics. Men wore stripes or dark colors. Women wore light colors and embroidered designs around the neck. Read Luke 14:15-24. Make biblical family for house.
>
> STEP 1: Crumble old white tissue paper into a hard 1-1/2" round ball. Glue unbleached brown coffee filter over tissue ball for face. Keep one side free of wrinkles. Leave stem for neck.
>
> STEP 2: Cut tunic using pattern. Glue tunic together at tabs. Glue stem or neck of head into tunic neck opening.
>
> STEP 3: Cut 2 sleeves. Roll on pencil making cylinders. Glue and hold together till set. Use pattern and cut hands from coffee filters. Shape hands around pencil top. Glue inside the end of sleeve. Glue sleeves at neck of tunic.
>
> STEP 4: Cut cloak using pattern. Fit cloak over head and around neck. Glue cloak ONLY around neck and shoulders.
>
> STEP 5: Both men and women wore long hair. Glue thin strips of paper across top of head for hair. Back of head will be covered by paper head covering. Decorate face.
>
> STEP 6: Trace pattern to make head covering and headband.

Workstation 6: Prayer and Sewing Center

> INSTRUCTION SIGN
>
> In biblical days, women would not go to the jeweler and buy a necklace. The women made necklaces from leftover dough from making pottery. They would bake the beads in the clay oven. The clay was not always easy to work with. Read Luke 18:1-5.
>
> Put on a cover-up and make beads today. Shape and roll the dough into small round balls. Place your beads on a piece of foil with your name on it to be baked. Use a toothpick to make a hole in the center of each of your beads.

Workstation 7: Benediction

INSTRUCTION SIGN

Most of the village houses in Nazareth had a very low doorway with a wooden door hanging on leather hinges. Most men had to duck to walk into their own house. There was usually one small window with bars across the opening to keep out burglars, and a dirt floor that turned to mud if you spilled water on it. It was easy to lose small objects on a dirt floor as was the case with the lost coin. Read Luke 15:8-10. It was the custom that a woman was given a gift of coins at her wedding. These coins were attached to the woman's headdress. Some of the coins were given by her prospective husband and others as a marriage gift from her father. The coins became a symbol like the wedding ring.

Men often wore a kind of turban. Make a paper coin headdress or turban to wear to worship today.

Headdress of Coins
STEP 1:   Cut a 1-inch-wide strip of paper to fit around your head. If your paper is not long enough, tape 2 pieces of paper together. Punch holes with a hole punch along the front.
STEP 2:   Trace a quarter for coins. Write a letter of your name on each coin. Punch hole in top of coin to attach to band.
STEP 3:   Cut thin strips and make paper chains to attach coins to head band. Coins should dangle on forehead.

Turban
STEP 1:   Trace skullcap pattern. Glue at tabs.
STEP 2:   Cut band. Use pattern. Fold in half. Write name on band. Staple to skullcap. It will curl and stand up.

The Worship Celebration

SIGN-UP SHEET FOR TODAY'S WORSHIP CELEBRATION

Call to Worship (read Luke 14:15-24):
Sermon (skit "Do You Take Your Bible on Vacation?"):
Benediction (lead the Lord's Prayer):

ITEMS TO GO HOME TODAY: COIN HEADDRESSES; TURBANS

Session 53
Festivals

The Bible Lesson

Today's lesson combines the parable of the Pharisee and the tax collector (Luke 18:9-14) with the advice in Luke 6:32-38.

What the Children Will Learn Today

To love even your enemies.

Time Needed

5 minutes for story
20 minutes for workstations
10 minutes for closing worship service

Supplies Needed (by Workstation)

1. Lightbulb puppet from last week, and cloth
2. Foam egg cartons, permanent marker, and beans or pebbles
3. Cloth to be used as sail and fishing net
4. Puppets and skit
5. Salt dough house, salt dough, Popsicle sticks, paper, and craft supply basket with items to use for making furniture for house
6. Embroidery cloth, thread, and needles
7. Construction paper supply basket and patterns

Children's Meditation

GETTING READY

Give each person a penny at the end of the story.

STORY

I Won't Share

"I don't want Hannah Catherine to have a friend over. I want her to play with me," said Megan. "If Jenny comes over, Hannah Catherine will ignore me and play with Jenny. Why can't Jenny stay home? Hannah Catherine's mine."

"Learning to share can be hard," said Megan's mother. "Sharing our toys is one thing. Sharing someone we love is another.

"Instead of being mad because Hannah Catherine is spending time with a friend, use that time to do something you really want to do. Work on a project. Read a book. Jesus said that we should always treat others the way we want them to treat us. You don't want Hannah Catherine to be jealous and mean to you, so don't be jealous or mean to her.

"If you've decided to follow Jesus, then you'll wake up each day saying, What can I do to help others? What do I have that I can share? What can I do today that will help my family get along better? How can I go and make amends for what I did yesterday?

"In the parable of the Pharisee and the tax collector, Jesus pointed out that if we think only of ourselves, then we will most likely end up being lonely and unhappy. On the other hand, if we start and end each day asking how we could make life better for those around us, then we'll be happier and make those around us happier. By bringing happiness to others, you'll bring happiness to yourself," Megan's mother said.

She concluded, "Here, I have a penny for you. This is not just any old penny; it's a special penny."

"It doesn't look any different," Megan said.

"It's what you do with the penny that makes it special. You're special, too, and you show how special you are by how you share love with others. Take this penny and go out and share God's love with everyone you meet."

Workstations

Workstation 1: Call to Worship

> **INSTRUCTION SIGN**
>
> Purim is one of the children's favorite celebrations because it tells of Queen Esther's victory over the evil Haman (Esther 9:20-26). Read Luke 18:9-14. Then, finish your biblical person today to get ready for the festival.
>
> STEP 1: Glue cloth for tunic to cup. Glue arms in place.
>
> STEP 2: Glue yarn across top of lightbulb for hair. Both men and women wore their hair long. Glue cloth covering to top of head. Add headband if desired.
>
> STEP 3: Draw a face with markers or cut pieces of construction paper and add eyes, nose, and mouth. Sequin or buttons may also be used. Place on worship table for service.

Workstation 2: Affirmation of Faith

> **INSTRUCTION SIGN**
>
> Hanukkah is often called the Festival of Lights and is a happy celebration (2 Maccabaeus 10:6). Go to Workstation 7 and help make cards to send to a nursing home and hospital.

Workstation 3: Offering or Carpenter Shop

> **INSTRUCTION SIGN**
>
> Passover (Festival of Unleavened Bread, Exodus 12) is the festival Jesus went to Jerusalem to celebrate with his disciples. Read Luke 6:32-36. Add sail and net to boat.

Workstation 4: Sermon or Bible Study

> **INSTRUCTION SIGN**
>
> Seven weeks after Passover is the one day "Shavuot" or Pentecost celebration (also called the Festival of Weeks or Harvest Festival, Deuteronomy 16:9-12). In Jesus' time, Pentecost was celebrated at the end of the barley harvest and in the middle of the wheat harvest. The story of Ruth is often read.
>
> Read Luke 18:9-14 and 6:32-38. You need 4 puppeteers plus Sunshine and 5 readers. You need a strong reader for Sunshine.

SKIT FOR SERMON

Work! Share! Love! And Pray!

LYDIA: Lucy Jones thinks she's so smart. I can't stand her.

REBECCA: She's also the teacher's pet.

MICHAEL: Who cares about Lucy? We've got a game this afternoon, and we've got to win. We're going to grind the Tigers into the dirt. We're the best!

PETER: I just got a new race car model. It had forty-six tiny pieces, and I put it together all by myself. Look!

SUNSHINE: When I was little, my dad told me a story about life. He said that when we go to heaven, we'll enter this gigantic room, like a movie theater in the round. All around us will be showing a movie about our life. Everyone and everything we've ever done will be showing on the movie screen. We'll hear the thoughts and feelings, the pain, the joy of those we've encountered in life. Just like in the movies, my dad said we'd feel the pain we had caused others, the times we rejected someone, the times we cheated, the times we lied, but most of all, my dad said, we'd feel the sorrow others had felt as they dealt with us throughout our life.

PETER: Wow! Is that real? Is that really what happens?

SUNSHINE: It's just a story my dad told me to make me think about how I was treating people, and I admit it really made me think. From that day on, I started asking: How do others feel when I talk? Do I make others happy or am I too busy cutting everyone down to size with my sassy, rude comments? Am I nice to everyone or just the people who are nice to me first? If someone is rude to me, do I smile and ignore it, or do I make sure the other person pays for what they said to me? Which matters more, the time I was nice to someone I didn't like or the time I really told someone off? That's when I became known as "Sunshine Share-a-Lot," and I made it my job each and every day to work for Jesus.

                   Every day, I *work* hard to *share* with someone I don't like, I never let the day end without telling those in my family that I *love* them, and I stop at least once sometime during the day to *pray* to God for guidance and most of all, forgiveness.

REBECCA: I like that: Work, share, love, and pray. It's easy to remember.

SUNSHINE: Jesus said that if your life is filled with love, then your actions and words also will be filled with love. If we truly "love our neighbor as ourselves" then we want the same good things that we wish for to be true for others too.

MICHAEL: Except when we're playing baseball, then I want to win.

SUNSHINE: There's nothing wrong with wanting to do your best, but if you truly love your neighbor as yourself, then you want the other team to win just as much as you want to win. A home run is exciting, even if it's for the other team.

MICHAEL: No way! Can you imagine our team cheering for the Tigers? Never!

SUNSHINE: Jesus meant for us to love our neighbors all the time, not just when it's convenient. You should be just as excited about the home run made by the other team as you are when you make a home run. It doesn't take anything away from you when you're nice to others. The love and kindness you give away will always be returned to you. Maybe not at that exact moment, but kindness when given away always comes home.

MICHAEL: I'd be laughed off of the baseball team if I cheered for the Tigers. Maybe at church, but you can't do that sort of stuff at a baseball game.

SUNSHINE: Many people laughed at Jesus for his actions too.

PETER: That's a lot to ask, Sunshine. I'm not sure I'm brave enough to go over and tell the other team they played a great game when I lose, especially not when I wanted to win.

REBECCA: I'd have a hard time telling someone who just won first place how fantastic they did if I won second place.

MICHAEL: My teammates wouldn't talk to me for years.

LYDIA: Work, share, love, and pray! It sounds good, but I have a feeling it's going to be a lot harder to do than to say.

SUNSHINE: Following Jesus has never been easy, but if we actually follow his teachings, instead of just saying we do, we can't stop trying.

I may never succeed, but I'll never stop *trying*. *Try* is a positive word with Jesus. When I make a mistake and I'm rude or selfish, I ask God to forgive me and I try again.

We must all make a decision in life. We must decide how we want to live our lives, how we want to treat others, and how we can best serve God.

If we truly follow Jesus, we won't be going around finding fault with others (Luke 6:37); instead, we'll be busy working hard to be nice to others. It isn't hard to say the words of Luke 10:27: "'Love the Lord your God with all your heart, with all your soul, with all your strength, and with all your mind'; and 'Love your neighbor as you love yourself,' " but it sure is hard to live it.

Workstation 5: Witness to Faith

INSTRUCTION SIGN

Rosh Hashanah lasts for 10 days and ends with Yom Kippur, a day of prayer and asking for forgiveness. Many people leave the Yom Kippur service to go home and build their "sukkah" or booth. When the Jews escaped from Egypt and slavery with Moses they wandered for 40 years before arriving at their new home. Because they were traveling they had to build temporary huts for shelter. Families in Jesus' time and today often build a booth next to their house to remember the escape from Egypt and to celebrate the end of the harvest. "Sukkoth" is usually held in the fall (Deuteronomy 16:13-17). On the ninth day of the festival, the last chapters from the book of Deuteronomy are read and then the Torah is rerolled to the beginning. The first chapter of Genesis is read to start the year's reading again. It will take an entire year to read through the Torah. Read Luke 6:37-38.

Make simple furnishings for our salt dough house: water jars, sleeping mats, small table, or whatever the house needs.

Make a booth to fit on the roof of the salt dough biblical house. Make a wooden shelter with sticks provided. Decorate with paper flowers, fruits, and tree branches. Take to worship.

Workstation 6: Prayer and Sewing Center

INSTRUCTION SIGN

"Sabbath" means "to cease or rest from" in Hebrew. Sabbath begins at sundown on Friday and continues until the first three stars can be seen after sunset on Saturday. Sabbath is the Hebrew day of worship. In biblical times, no work or travel was allowed, not even cooking. All of the cooking had to be done before sundown. Families enjoy a special meal on Friday evening with two loaves of "challah" bread. Each loaf of bread is braided from six strands of dough for the twelve tribes of Israel and covered with a special cloth. Use markers, crayons, or embroidery thread and make a "challah cover," writing or sewing the word "shabbath" in Hebrew. The word "bread" is also used in the Bible to mean that Jesus is the Bread of Life, the necessary ingredient that makes our lives special. Read John 6:35 and Luke 6:37-38.

Use markers, crayons, or embroidery thread and make a "challah cover," writing or sewing the word "shabbath" in Hebrew:

שבה

Take bread cover to worship. Sign up to lead the Lord's Prayer.

Workstation 7: Benediction

The Worship Celebration

INSTRUCTION SIGN

Rosh Hashanah is the Jewish New Year and is usually celebrated in September or October. It is a time to ask for forgiveness. Rosh Hashanah lasts for 10 days and ends with Yom Kippur, a day of prayer and forgiveness (Leviticus 23:23-27).

On the evening the ceremony begins, families gather to eat challah bread and to dip apples in honey to wish for a sweet and happy new year. Jewish children today make Happy New Year cards to share with friends and family. Trace patterns. Make a plain basket or weave a basket. Read Galatians 5:22-26.

You may write *"Leshanah Tovah Tikateuv"* (Happy New Year) or "Have a Nice Day" and the Bible verse on a card to send to a shut-in or a nursing home. Place cards on the worship table.

SIGN-UP SHEET FOR TODAY'S WORSHIP CELEBRATION

Sermon is entire service today.

ITEMS TO GO HOME TODAY: CARDS; BREAD COVERS; DREIDELS; PUPPETS

APPENDIX

Frequently Used Recipes
Salt Dough

1 cup table salt
2 cups flour
1 cup water

Mix well. Knead by hand to make smooth. Do NOT add more water. Sprinkle flour on hands if dough is a little sticky.

Papier-Mâché

1 cup white school glue
2 cups water

Mix in washable tub or bowl. Stir slowly till mixed.

There are many recipes for papier-mâché that you may use. I use simple glue and water because it washes out of children's clothing easier than the traditional flour-and-water paste.

How to Use the Patterns

It's a proven fact that children learn best through action. Yet, if you peek into a Sunday school classroom on Sunday morning, you still see most children parked around a table listening to a lecture, completing worksheets, dot-to-dot activity pages, and, if they're lucky, an occasional craft project. It's time for a change.

Come, Follow Me! presents a wonderful new approach in Christian education that's packed with hands-on activities. Each session has been designed and tested with Sunday school teachers and children on Sunday mornings. All you need to do to take advantage of this program is to prepare yourself for a new way of thinking.

Children no longer sit around tables. Children stand up, move around the room, and go from learning center to learning center.

Teachers do not need to spend hours preparing lectures. There are no lectures.

The classroom can even be totally void of chairs. There's no need for them. No one will be sitting down.

Tables are helpful, though, especially tables that are the appropriate height for the ages of children in your class. Teens obviously need a taller table than five-year-olds, but, overall, it's easier for tall people to work at a lower table than for young children to stretch to reach a tall table. The children must be able to trace patterns, draw, write, and cut at the tables. Try to offer variety, something for everyone.

The key to successfully directing this hands-on program lies in how you organize supplies and use the patterns contained in this book. All you need to do is follow three easy steps: (1) check the "Supplies Needed" list before class to see if you need anything special, (2) photocopy the "Instruction Signs" each week, and (3) photocopy the patterns for each session. Remember that some holiday sessions use special supplies not contained in the supply closet, so check the list each week.

If you're a teacher who only teaches once a month, be sure you check the supply closet the week before you teach unless your church has a designated supply person who restocks the cabinet for you. Easy, ready-to-use patterns are useless if you don't have the necessary supplies. You must have the correct supplies in the quantity needed, the "Instruction Signs," and the patterns for each workstation in order for the program to work correctly.

There are fifty-three sessions, an entire year's worth of programming. Each session has a five-minute story, seven learning centers called workstations, and a ten-minute worship service that usually includes a puppet skit that can be used for the sermon.

The children work for twenty minutes at the workstations, reading the Bible, making a craft project that reinforces the Bible lesson, and preparing to lead a portion of that day's worship service.

Come, Follow Me! is designed to accommodate churches that have different people teaching each week. Photocopy the session you're leading the week before, take it home, look it over, then simply walk in and pass out the instructions and patterns to those who are helping at each workstation.

I have actually tested the program with teachers who never glanced at the book before class.

They simply walked in with the children after the children's story and taught the class successfully.

The essential ingredient is to read the "Instruction Sign" out loud to the children before you start, look up the Bible verse, and then work together on the craft project. The "Instruction Sign" is your teaching tool. The ready-to-use patterns enable you to teach the children about the Bible and to have fun at the same time.

The patterns and craft projects in this book can help you challenge and motivate your children to use their creative, inventive power. The church should be one place where we encourage children's imagination to soar.

Photocopy the patterns. Do not cut patterns from the book. Save the originals and use photocopies instead. Have the children cut copies, take special note to notice any instructions written beside the pattern.

Most patterns ask children to place one edge of the pattern on the fold. This may be a new concept for children. Placing patterns on the fold allows younger children to cut two equal halves, reduces tracing time, and enables more people to work at a workstation. If you have a large group or if you think a particular project might be overly popular with your class, photocopy several copies of the pattern so that more than one child can trace a pattern at a time.

Being patient, tracing patterns, striving for accuracy, following step-by-step instructions, working together in a group, cooperating, taking turns, and thinking about the needs of others are all benefits of working with learning centers, and these are life-long skills that everyone needs to learn. If we can teach these skills at church, we will have mastered the first step in helping children learn to become followers of Jesus.

If you are using the entire year-long program, then start with Session 1. If you are searching for craft projects to supplement your regular Sunday morning curriculum, then turn to the table of contents. Select a theme that fits with your planned lesson. Photocopy the session you have chosen, the whole session. Make sure you have the workstation "Instruction Signs" and the pattern for that particular session. Check supplies needed. Then you're ready to begin.

New Terms to Learn. There are a few basic concepts that are used throughout the book. "Place on fold" means to have children fold paper in half, matching side of pattern marked "place on fold" with fold on paper.

"Fold on dotted line; sold on solid line" is another expression frequently used throughout the book. Any time a pattern has a dotted line or series of dashes, this always means to fold. You only cut on solid lines.

Sometimes the "Instruction Sign" directions or the pattern will say to use scrap paper. Children are encouraged to keep a scrap paper basket and to use it whenever they only need a small piece, rather than cutting a tiny circle out of the center of a new piece of construction paper. Conserving and recycling are requirements. We must teach children at an early age not to waste resources, even something as simple as construction paper.

Keep Your Class Active. Make sure you use all seven workstations each week, unless you have a tiny class of five or six, in which case you may want to only set up a couple of workstations. Children need the freedom to choose between projects.

If you run out of time each week, analyze how you spend your time. Are you spending 10 minutes taking attendance? Do the children get right to work when they arrive? Each workstation is designed to keep the appropriate age level busy for twenty minutes. I intentionally do not plan goof-off time into the workstations. Free time turns into trouble. My class has an average of fifty-six children each week. Therefore, I keep everyone busy.

If any children have trouble, encourage them to start with an easier project next week. Workstation 7, the Benediction, is a good place to begin. This workstation has paper and glue projects that are simple but interesting. Help the children to work to a more challenging workstation. If you have extra youth helpers, assign a youth helper to give individual help to a child who has difficulty.

The ready-to-use-patterns and "Instruction Signs" make it easy for you to teach without hours and hours of preparation time. Cleanup is easy when you teach the children to be responsible for putting unused supplies back where they belong.

Save patterns. Don't throw patterns away even though they're just copies. Start a file.

Keep the pattern file in the classroom or storage closet used for supplies. If someone didn't finish or was absent during a long term project, they may simply go to the file, retrieve the pattern, and get right to work.

You're Ready to Begin. All you need now is a room or space for your class to meet, a group of energetic, fabulous children, an itty bit of patience, and bunches of love. *Come, Follow Me!* will do the rest.

Help, What Do We Do Next Year?

Don't panic! If you successfully completed the year, even if you used all fifty-three sessions, you still have plenty of material to work with. There are seven different workstations each week. It is highly unlikely that your children were able to do every project, unless you have an extremely large group. Repeat favorite projects. You may even repeat the entire program if you have substantial turnover in children attending each year.

I rerun favorite workstations, stories, or puppet skits. It's like reruns on TV, everyone has favorites.

Sometimes I even conduct an entire special request month, and call it "By Request Only." The children submit the names of favorite stories, puppet skits, and workstations that they would like to do again.

The children in my classes always beg to repeat the seasonal programs and projects. Children find comfort in repeating the traditions of Christmas and Easter.

I also have a group of children who insist on building the paper fold-up church from Chapter 6 every year. Sometimes it's the same children, sometimes not. Often younger children will decide that they are now ready to tackle the church. Or a child who only completed the outside structure of the church last year will decide to build the inside as well this year. Some of the more creative children have added Sunday school classroom wings onto the church, designed their own stained glass windows, and made tiny bricks to glue over the entire outside exterior of the church. It's wonderful to see what children can create when given an opportunity.

If your children had trouble finishing the church in the allotted eight weeks, this time around allow more time. As long as the children are enjoying the project, there's nothing wrong with spending more time building a church.

Another frequently requested repeat project is the paper biblical village. Some children want to make a fancier village than they made last time. This is an open ended project that encourages creativity and individuality so it's easy to repeat.

As you repeat favorite workstations, you may also supplement with new projects to offer variety. Not everyone wants to work on the same project.

While one child may work for three months on nothing but her masterpiece church complete with an attached Sunday school wing, designer windows, and brick exterior, another child may need the stimulation of a different project each week. Never have just one workstation for everyone. Keep seven workstations going even when doing reruns.

Use the Evaluation Questionnaire found in the Appendix. What are some of the children's favorite projects? Which projects did the children not get a chance to do? Are there projects that the children would like to repeat?

The Bible verses used each week throughout *Come, Follow Me!* are universal and never grow old. The children may choose to write their own puppet skits for the sermon or find a parable that teaches the same lesson and act out the parable.

Parables can be used for your children's story and sermon. Read or tell the parable during the children's meditation. Then for the sermon have the children practice how they would act out the parable, write a modern day version of the parable, or plan a puppet skit using the parable. Many of the children's favorite craft projects fit nicely with the teachings of the parables.

It's true that we do not have as much learning center Christian curriculum available as we need, but you can make do. One possible source of multiple age curriculum available is *One Room Sunday School*. It is graded for ages three through middle school and is available from Abingdon Press. The lessons can be easily adapted to the seven workstation format used in *Come, Follow Me!* There are activities and projects for younger children as well as challenging material for older ones. This is a quarterly publication, so it can be an ongoing source of new material for you.

Another source for children's worship curriculum is my previous book *No Experience Necessary!* (Meriwether, 1992). This, too, is a complete, year-long children's worship curriculum with seven learning centers or workstations each week. The highlight of *No Experience Necessary!* is building a wooden classroom-size children's church and having the children write their own sanctuary worship service.

Outreach Ministry. If your students are not interested in reruns and don't wish to repeat projects, you may want to develop a new program. Service projects may be your answer.

You may decide to organize your entire next year's program around outreach ministry projects. If so, remember that children need action. Select a project that is truly hands-on. Something that children can become involved in personally. Children's don't usually get excited about a canned food drive, but they love cooking Thanksgiving dinner for a needy family. Some of the organizations that deliver hot meals to shut-ins do not serve meals on weekends or holidays. Those who are dependent upon others for a hot meal would certainly appreciate having your group deliver a steaming hot dinner from your kitchen to their table.

The children in my class still talk about delivering Thanksgiving dinner straight from the oven to the table last year from a single mom with two small children. The mom had just been released from the hospital and was unable to stand, much less cook. As the children sat Thanksgiving dinner down on the table in front of a two and three year old, they realized how special their hard work had been.

Some items can be prepared ahead of time. Others will need to be done at the last minute. Your children's worship class may spend weeks or months planning such a project, assigning jobs to be done, planning the menu, or even going after church one Sunday to do the shopping.

The Appendix lists twenty service projects that have been tested and proven to work with children's worship programs. Add your own favorite projects and build a weekly curriculum based on outreach ministry.

Making Get-Well Cards. Many of the craft projects in *Come, Follow Me!* may be used as get-well cards for nursing homes and hospitals. The God's eye weaving, the huge paper bag fish, pop-up cards, and flowers are just a few suggestions. Each year, when we visit the nursing home, many of the residents rush to show us that they still have the God's eyes we made for them several years ago hanging on their well where they can look at them each day. God's eyes made on cinnamon sticks make a nice gift for seniors.

Pop-up cards are very popular with children and can actually be simple to make. They also make excellent gifts for sick children in the hospital. Remember not to place anything on a card going to a child that could be taken off and swallowed.

You can cut pictures from Christmas cards or any kind of greeting card, out-of-date curriculum, or even religious coloring books. If the paper is too thin to stand erect, have children glue a piece of construction paper behind it. Then make simple pop-up cards from the pictures.

Review the techniques taught in Session 26

for making a Father's Day card. You can make the same kind of tab that was used for the tree. With this one technique, you can make an entire picture pop up. Make the tab larger or wider depending upon the size of the picture.

You may also cut a picture into puzzle sections, stagger the tabs placed behind each section of the picture, and make a picture pop up in segments. Use the three simple techniques taught for making the Father's Day card in volume 1, and you'll be able to make dozens of pop-up cards. Children of all ages love pop-up cards.

A get-well card doesn't have to be in the shape of a folded card. Think of projects from both volumes that can be converted into a greeting card—fish, flowers, or even houses.

We undertook a gigantic project one year. We decided to make fifty of the large paper bag fish from Session 40 to pass out at the nursing home and hospital.

Instead of just decorating one side of the fish as described in Session 40. We completely covered both sides of the fish with scales.

Every workstation had a job. It was like an assembly line.

The Call to Worship workstation traced and cut out the paper bag fish. The Affirmation workstation stuffed each fish with scrap paper and stapled the edges shut. The Offering workstation traced and cut out mouths and tail fins for each fish. The Sermon workstation cut thousands of scales. Each of these pieces were passed along to the Witness workstation where tail fins and scales were glued into place. The Prayer workstation traced and cut out eyes and side fins. The Benediction workstation added the finishing touches by gluing the mouth, eyes, and side fins in place. Everyone helped, even the youngest child. It took us months to complete fifty fish, but the children were genuinely pleased when they saw the expressions of surprise and gratitude pleased when they saw the expressions of surprise and gratitude on the faces of the children at the hospital and the seniors at the nursing home. The residents at the nursing home were just as proud of their fish as

the children at the hospital, so it was truly an excellent project for all ages. We hung two fish from the ceiling in our classroom to always remind us of the year we made fifty paper bag fish.

Spend Several Months on the Same Theme. Your group may want to plan a big Christmas or Easter project. My class loved it the year I announced: "Christmas in September." We spent the entire fall getting ready for Christmas. We put on a church-wide Christmas Pageant, decorated a Christmas tree and sold it to help raise money for the local Children's Hospital, delivered Christmas dinner and presents to a needy family, and went Christmas caroling at the nursing home. It would have been impossible to coordinate all of these projects within the span of the four weeks of Advent. We started in September and the excitement grew each week as we got closer to Christmas.

Each week the children had assigned duties at the workstations—decorations to make for the Christmas tree, Christmas cards to make for the nursing home. During our worship time we studied the Bible story and practiced for the Christmas Pageant. My series called *The Christmas Tree* (Meriwether, 1998) includes a play kit and two books of patterns with forty-two different Christmas Christian ornaments for children and youth.

The ornaments are graded by age appropriateness the same as the projects in this book. The patterns are easy to follow, and the ornaments are inexpensive to make.

The children enjoy hanging their finished ornaments on the tree each week as work progresses. Many businesses are willing to purchase a fully decorated tree so that they do not have to bother with decorations. So children can use their decorating skills to earn money to help others. Be sure and contact local businesses to see what kind of tree they would like before you start decorating. Have the business select a theme—world peace, save the rainforest, an old fashioned Christmas . . . The possibilities are endless.

Puppets are a Wonderful Teaching Aid.
Children love puppets. A puppet show is a natural way to teach children about the Bible. The parables of Jesus provide an excellent variety of material that can either be used alone or in combination with other curriculum.

Children can often write their own puppet plays based on a parable, or they can simply act out the parable. Each workstation can be assigned a different job. Some workstations can be designated to make scenery while others make the puppets needed. The sermon workstation could be in charge of writing the skit.

The parable of the Good Samaritan, for example, needs at least seven puppets. These puppets could be made from pop bottles and paper plates as taught in previous sessions of this book. The paper plate becomes the head, the plastic pop bottle the body. The neck of the pop bottle becomes a handle for the puppeteer. An entire session can be built around making puppets to tell a parable as was done in Session 10.

You can also use the patterns and instructions in Session 45 and make string puppets. The Sunshine-share-a-lot puppet stage was designed for use with both hand puppets and string puppets. The double curtain gives you a perfect backdrop.

With just a paper plate and a popsicle stick, you can make a little girl with long curly hair and glasses, Dad with a black fuzzy beard, a tree, a beautiful rainbow, flowers, all kinds of animals, a sunshine with a big smiley face, or people from the Bible.

Paper plates provide a simple and inexpensive way to make puppets and even simple scenery for a puppet play. Puppets can be made with all sorts of materials: long paper curls, springy legs, tall hats, braided yarn hair, fake fur beards, painted faces, glitter, sequins, and even button eyes. Use tan and brown paper plates for skin color. Plain white plates can also be painted, colored with crayons, or covered with paper to give the color you want for the puppet's skin.

You can also make animal puppets or make believe characters of any color. If you do not have construction paper, use old shopping bags, cloth, or crayons to make the colors you want.

Cur paper slashes for special effects. When you cut slashes for eyelashes, bangs, grass, and flowers, remember cut down to about ¼" of the edge. Stop before you cut all the way across so that your slashes do not fall apart. You need that uncut edge to glue the eyelash in place.

Fake fur or fuzzy fabrics are fun to work with. You may use fake fur to create a kitty, puppy, or even people with fuzzy hair and beards.

White cotton balls or polyester stuffing make great hair for Grandma. Don't forget the granny glasses.

Cars, houses, or even a boat puppet can be built onto a pop bottle. Use the pop bottle as a base to build upon. Then create whatever you like.

You can also cut cars and boats from stiff paper, punch holes, and attach a long string at the front and at the end. Cars can be made to bump up and down on a bumpy road and boats to toss and pitch with the rolling waves.

Felt hand puppets are another easy alternative. Puppets can be made with only felt and fabric glue. You can make people or animals with felt. You may do simple sewing or absolutely no sewing. For a special effect, you may add buttons, pom poms, fake fur, yarn, feathers, hats, flowers, fancy fabrics, and even sequins.

Old socks can be used to make simple puppets that open their mouths and talk. A circular piece of cardboard is glued into place to form the mouth. Then, you can turn your sock puppet into any person or animal you wish.

Paper tubes from wrapping paper or paper towel rolls can be turned into fabulous inexpensive puppets. Make paper clothes, a round circle for a race, arms, and legs if desired, and, of course, don't forget to add hair.

Make city skyscrapers or a simple country cottage, biblical houses or the gates of Jerusalem from empty cereal boxes. You can create an entire city just with different size boxes. Attach a string and you can lower houses into place and even make them move in case of earthquakes or sudden storms.

Paper coffee filters for drip coffee machines make wonderful little bugs and insects that creep into your puppet plays. Attach a string to your critters and have them slide down suddenly from the top of the Sunshine-Share-a-lot puppet stage.

The addition of bubbles can add excitement to any puppet play. The children in my class use bubbles for skits they perform when visiting children in the hospital. One particular favorite is when a puppet tries to count and naturally gets confused.

With the basic supplies suggested and your imagination, you can make the cast for any puppet play or story. You might even decide to become traveling missionaries and take your puppet shows out into the world to tell others about God's love. You can spend an entire year devoted to puppetry if you want to.

KTBT News. If your class enjoys the KTBT news crew, encourage them to write their own skits and stories. Older youth might write stories and puppet skits for younger children.

You may even want to expand the KTBT news concept. Use time traveling reporters to investigate the Bible. Create a news room and produce a news program every week on what's happening in the world today. Send investigative reporters back-in-time to report on happenings from New Testament times as they happen.

The children might write, act out, and video tape their stories each week. Then they could send the video tape to anyone from the group who was sick or unable to come that week.

If your class likes to write and act out stories, have the children produce a news program, a video tape. They might spend several months preparing a script on "What does it mean to be a Christian?" They could write modern day stories from a child's point-of-view. At school! In the home! Around the neighborhood!

Build a Biblical Village. If you have your own classroom or a corner of fellowship hall that no one will object to having you convert into a biblical village, you can spend the year building a village. You have more than enough ideas and props to get you started. The children will love it.

Look back through Chapters 12, 14, and 15. You have complete instructions, everything needed. You may even want to make costumes and have the children act out each week's Bible story in the village.

Expand the basic plan given in Chapter 15. Add extra houses by simply covering more boxes. It's easy.

Use an old table, cover with cloth, and set up a marketplace. A piece of cloth can be suspended from the ceiling for an awning. Make extra clay jars for the well and clay pottery for the potter. Don't forget to have a carpenter's shop.

You'll definitely want to make extra sheep for the sheepfold. The children love the fluffy sheep.

You can have a fun-filled, spiritually enriching year learning about the Bible as you build a village and act out Bible stories. Follow the guidelines in Chapter 15. Set up seven workstations throughout the village.

If your church doesn't meet during the summer, as some churches do not, don't forget to use the material in Chapter 15. There are ten sessions tailor-made to fit perfectly into your biblical village. Use these sessions to get started, then develop your own ideas. This is also a good chapter to repeat since many children are away part of the summer. So even if you haven't used Chapter 15, you may want to repeat portions of it.

Develop new ideas and projects for your children. Plan long term and weekly projects. Some children need the comfort of taking home a completed project each week.

Many curriculum craft projects can be adapted to the learning center concept. Write a list of step-by-step directions for children to follow. Make patterns.

Remember to check your local library. Many children's crafts can be modified to fit a religious theme.

Be creative; don't despair. The end of the year does not need to bring an end to your children's worship program. Quite the contrary, it's only the beginning.

Twenty Possible Service Projects That Have Been Tested and Used with Children

1. Adopt a family for Christmas or for the year. You can provide meals if family members are sick or elderly. Decorate and donate a Christmas tree. Plan birthday parties for children. Offer to do the grocery shopping. Our group played a musical Christmas concert for a family who couldn't get out to enjoy the music and festivities of the year. The possibilities are endless.

2. Decorate Christmas trees to sell and raise money. Check with businesses. Secure a potential buyer before you decide to decorate.

3. Cook meals for shut-ins or others who rely on organizations to deliver hot meals during the week. Many of these people are without a hot meal on weekends and holidays. You might want to adopt a specific family and make sure they receive a hot meal every weekend and especially for holidays.

4. You may also volunteer to help deliver food for Meals-on-wheels during the summer. Children are allowed to accompany an adult and visit with those who receive the meals. Your class can make cards to send with the meals.

5. Host a church-wide dinner to raise money for the homeless and hungry. Invite everyone to help. Children can help cook, make table decorations, or even plan and provide a program for the dinner. Families, the women's society, or possibly even an adult Sunday school class might volunteer to help. Some grocery stores will donate turkey or ham for a good cause.

6. Christmas caroling at a nursing home or hospital works well with children, particularly if you live in a part of the country where the weather is cold and wet at Christmas time.

7. Adopt a mission school or church in a financially challenged area. Have the children write letters to the children at the school. Prepare school supply kits or health kits for each child. If possible, encourage your children to becom e pen pals. Try to write letters, send holiday cards, and pictures back and forth between your group and the mission school or church. If you live within driving distance, you might plan an end-of-the-year picnic to bring both groups together.

8. Adopt a grandparent or shut-in from your church. Bake cookies. Send cards, Visit when possible, Plan a birthday party.

9. Clown ministry is a wonderful outreach to use with children. They are less inhibited as their clown personality. Visit hospitals, nursing homes, and use puppets. Puppets allow the children to teach stories of sharing and caring for others.

10. Don't forget the ever-popular bake sale. Children can bake cookies at home to bring and sell after church or bake during the children's worship time. Our group bakes homemade bread and sells it after church to raise money. Use the bread recipe listed for Thanksgiving. It's very popular.

11. Children love to raise money for farm animals or for specific villages in need. You can incorporate learning about the animals or country you are sending your donation to as part of your workstation activities. Many relief organizations will send you free information if you ask. Check with your minister for suggestions. Heifer Project International is one example. If you have a small group, you can buy portions or shares in an animal as well. Call Heifer Project, Int. at 1-800-422-0474.

12. Habitat for Humanity is another world wide organization that fits nicely into the learning center study format of this book. You can build houses out of paper, soap boxes, cereal boxes, or even milk cartons. Then raise money to buy nails, windows, doors, or just to help build a house. The nice thing about Habitat is that you may specify your donation to go toward a house being built in your area. Then, if desired, the children may bake cookies and deliver cookies to the volunteers building the house that the children helped to raise money for. Call 1-800-HABITAT.

13. Plan a game party for a nursing home. You'd be surprised how much residents enjoy playing children's board games and working big-piece children's puzzles. Our first game party was scheduled to last for an hour. It went for two straight hours because the residents didn't want it to end. Children can read game cards for residents who can't see well enough to read game pieces.

14. Decorate Easter eggs. You can seel the decorated eggs to members of your church to raise money for a good cause. There are plenty of suggestions in the Lenten section for making all kinds of eggs. You might also choose to deliver decorated eggs to children in the hospital or even plan a decorating party for the residents of a nursing home.

15. If you have students who take music lessons on the piano, violin, or suitable instru-ments, go to a nursing home or even a homeless shelter. Have children play songs they've learned during the dinner hour. Children who do not play instruments may pass out cards. Residents enjoy the music and appreciate the children taking the time to make them feel special.

16. Homeless shelters are always in need of help. Children might bring warm mittens, hats, or scarves to fill a basket. The children can also make small cards to attach to each item. Tell others you care is a wonderful way to learn to express God's love. When the basket is full, the mittens can be sent to the homeless shelter for distribution.

17. Our group planned a unique sort of project with one of our local homeless shelters. It's a small shelter that serves as home to those who need a chance to start over. My class filled grocery bags of nonperishable food for what we called "Feed a Family." The idea was to provide a balanced day's diet for each family's first day back out on their own in a new apartment or house. The children planned menus: breakfast, lunch, and dinner. They then went shopping with their parents and filled a grocery bag full of food to feed a family for a day. If you wish to involve your entire church in this project, announce the project in your church newsletter or bulletin. Then have the children take a wagon around during Sunday school to collect donated food. Afterwards, the children can sort and bag food according to the menus they've made. Staple the menu to each bag. Tuck a "Have a Nice Day" card inside.

18. Cooking Thanksgiving dinner is probably the most popular service project the children in my group have ever done. Everyone knows that we always cook the Sunday before Thanksgiving every year. I often have youth who have graduated from the program, show up, and volunteer to help. Many families and seniors in the church know about our project and often drop off bags of groceries.

19. Each year, the Salvation Army hosts a Christmas toy store. They often need volunteers to help dress or decorate stuffed animals and dolls. Your children can put ribbons on teddy bears or sew simple dresses for dolls. Check with your local Salvation Army. See what they need. They often provide the bears and the dolls.

20. Plant a "Sharing Tree." If your church has space, get permission to plant an evergreen tree. The children can then make pine cone bird feeders to hang on the tree in winter and early spring. If appropriate, decorate the tree with tiny clear lights at Christmas time to remind children to be gentle with animals and to care for all of God's creation. You might also plant flowers around the tree and encourage the children to care for their garden. Bulbs work nicely or start seeds inside and then move them outdoors when weather permits. Wonderful lessons can be learned from growing a flower garden.

Evaluation Questionnaire

What was your favorite craft project(s)? Would you enjoy doing it again?

What story would you enjoy hearing again?

Did you have a favorite puppet play? Did you get a chance to be in the skit? Would you like to?

Did you have a favorite Bible verse? Do you remember it?

Were there any projects that you didn't get a chance to work on that you would like to do?

What did you like best about the program?

What would you change about the program?

What did you learn this year in children's worship?

Do you plan to attend children's worship again next year?

Do you like having seven different workstations to choose from each week? What was your favorite workstation? Why?

Would you enjoy working on service projects—helping those in need? If so, tell two or three projects you would like to see our group do.

Do you like making puppets? Would you like to learn more about puppetry? Would you be interested in writing and presenting puppet plays to children at the hospital or residents at the nursing home?

Would you be willing to write a puppet play? A story? If so, what topic would you like to write on? What Bible verse would you use?

Would you be interested in having our class write its own worship service to present in the sanctuary? Would you be willing to help? What would you like to do?

Questions

Question 1. How do you handle ongoing projects with new children?

Answer. The church in Chapter 4 is an example of a project that children may get interested in starting after others are partially finished. Not a problem. Children can start on the church at any time. The church can be completed in stages. I have seen children who only make the outside of the church. Others will make the entire church, floor, pews, banners, balcony, and all. Some children like details. Other children only have the patience for the basic frame. Those who did not decide to start on the church till the fourth week can still complete the outside frame of the church and be very proud of their work.

Two third grade boys in my church's group started at the exact same time on a church. Each boy worked hard during every session. One boy finished every step, pews, banners, siding on the outside, and everything. The other boy worked just as hard but was only able to finish the basic church and windows. Yet, both boys went home beaming with pride.

Having a project that can be completed at several different levels allows children of different ability levels to work together in harmony. If you try to have all children work together at the same pace, some will be left behind while others are bored.

Make envelopes or packets for children to store their projects. Keep instructions for each week posted. This will allow children to work successfully at their own pace, even if they start late.

Question 2. If the Sunday school classes uses the same learning centers that we use in children's worship, won't the children be bored and uninterested by the time they come to the children's worship program?

Answer. No, because you have seven different learning centers every week. There is always something new and different for the children to work on. If the 4th grade Sunday school class worked at Workstation 2, the Affirmation during Sunday school and then many of those same children come the next hour to your children's worship program, just encourage them to work at a different station. You have more than enough material to keep you going for hours. Each workstation is timed to take 20 minutes, providing over 2 hours worth of material every week.

Question 3. We have lots of guests each week and also children who come regularly but on an every other week basis because of parent custody and visitation situations. What should we do when there are ongoing projects that take several weeks?

Answer. If you know that the children are just visiting Grandma and won't be back next week, encourage them to work at a station that can be completed in 20 minutes. The Benediction, for example, changes every week and needs only 20 minutes to complete. Older children who are just visiting may enjoy sewing on the prayer banner or working in the carpenter shop or helping with the sermon for the day.

If you have children who attend regularly but on an every-other-week basis, make envelopes or packets to hold their projects till they return. They will appreciate having their projects waiting for them.

If you know a child is just visiting, always send their project home with them even if it is not finished.

Question 4. Why are the patterns placed on a fold? Isn't that harder for young children?

Answer. No, actually working with paper on the fold is easier once you teach the children to trace and cut their projects on the fold. Even young children who do not always cut straight will be able to assemble their projects if they cut on the fold because both sides will turn out identical. Cutting on the fold also requires less time. If you are cutting two sides at the same time, it takes half the time to complete the project.

Question 5. Some of the projects at the Benediction workstation look too hard to 4- and 5-year olds. What if the children can't do the project?

Answer. Each workstation has been timed and tested with children and can be completed in twenty minutes by the age group listed. When a harder project is offered at the Benediction workstation to challenge the children, there is always a simple version offered as well. As adults, we often look at a project and tell children, "This project is too hard for you. You'll never be able to do this project." In truth, the children could do the project if we would take the time to help them. The child would also acquire a great deal of pride and motivation from doing a project that seems a little bit harder. Too often we think that 4 and 5 year olds can't do anything but color or glue pictures that we have cut out. Children do not learn unless we take the time to teach them.

Some children acquire skills faster than oth-

ers. If you have a child that has trouble each week, assign a youth helper to work specifically with that child. The child will appreciate having a buddy.

Question 6. Some of the projects look too hard. I can't even figure the project out, so how will the children figure out what to do?

Answer. Adults often have more trouble with the craft projects than children do. Children are willing to try something new or to give it a try before they decide it's impossible. Adults often walk in, look at the picture, and say, "O dear! that looks hard. I couldn't even do that."

I saw an adult helper one day go around and look at each project without reading the directions or even trying to make the project. Within two seconds, she told the children which projects were too hard for them and which ones they were allowed to try.

One of the primary lessons taught in *Come, Follow Me!* is not to give up before you try. The words "I can't" do not exist.

We are raising our children in a world of ready access, computers, video games, microwave snacks, and a school system based on worksheets. We have grown to expect everything to be easy and not require any effort. Yet, real life is not easy and young people must often grow up and go out and work in a world where they have to read the directions and figure out how to solve a problem or make something work.

Some of the projects in this book are very easy and some are a definite challenge, but each and every project is workable by children.

I work with two totally different groups of mixed age level children each week. One group consists of approximately three to eight children. The other group has over fifty children in attendance most Sundays.

I test each project. I also have other teachers test projects.

As you go through the year, watch the sense of accomplishment grow. Children will often depart for home and leave behind the simple workbook cut and glue project from Sunday school but rarely ever forget to take home a project they have spent twenty minutes constructing with their own two hands in children's worship. Our society needs to redevelop a sense of pride in our work. Help the children start today.

Question 7. What do I do with all of these tiny pattern pieces?

Answer. Since I use the program year after year, I save all pattern pieces in an expandable file. I place the patterns for each project in a separate envelope and place them in a pattern file arranged by session. When I need a particular pattern, I can just turn to the file and easily find what I need.

Question 8. We don't have enough time. There's too much to do at each workstation for twenty minutes. Can children really finish each project listed in twenty minutes?

Answer. Yes, children can and do finish in just twenty minutes, but not all children work at the same speed. Each workstation is designed to be fast-paced and keep children very busy for twenty minutes. To finish, the children will have to work and not waste time. When chldren have too much free time on their hands, trouble and mischief set in; therefore, I do pack each session with lots to do and intentionally design each workstation with the maximum amount of work possible. I find when children are busy, discipline is not a problem. If a child continuously works veryslowly, the child can start on easier projects and gradually work up to harder projects.

Question 9. Should I repeat special projects for those who missed it?

Answer. Ongoing projects are a good way to encourage attendance each week. For example,

on World Communion Sunday, I always have the children make bread to take home. The next Sunday, the children can't wait to tell me how delicious their bread was or how high it rose. New children or those who were not in attendance for the bread making session feel a little sad at first that they didn't get to make bread too, but I always cheerfully remind them that we make bread several different times throughout the year, so they will get a chance later on. Smiles immediately return and usually their attendance improves.

Keep the excitement going so that children do not want to miss. As one child told his parents, "We have to come each Sunday; otherwise, you never know what you'll miss."

Churches should be an exciting place for children to come. Children should look forward to coming to God's house for worship more than staying home watching TV or playing outside on Sunday morning. Your goal is to make each week's program so exciting that the children just can't wait to see what will happen next.

Question 10. I think children would be overwhelmed by so much moving around. As a teacher, I would feel more comfortable if children only had one activity to choose from. Do you think children really learn from this program?

Answer. I frequently check to make sure what the children in my program learned from the week before. I will ask periodically, "What was the Bible lesson last week?" Since the lessons are presented with child-oriented examples, the children can easily remember the main idea of the lesson.

One Sunday, I asked who remembered what last week's sermon and Bible lesson was about, and a little five year old boy raised his hand. If you had asked me before he answered, I would have said that he had no idea what last week's lesson was about because he didn't seem to be paying attention last week. Yet, he said, "the lesson was about saying your're sorry when you hurt someone's feelings and being kind to others if you want them to be kind to you." The lesson was from Luke 6:37-38.

We must remember that children do not learn the same way adults do. What might look like a well organized orderly program to an adult might look boring and totally uninteresting to a child.

Keep the lesson short and simple each week. Do not try to cover the entire Bible in only thirty minutes. Just take one small bit that Jesus taught and build an entire lesson around that one central idea. In this way, it is easier for children to remember the lesson and how it applies to their life today.

Each week's lesson is taught in nine different ways. The story, the workstations, and the puppet play sermon are all based on the same theme and same central Bible verse. The key is to get children and adults to read the workstation signs and related Bible verses.

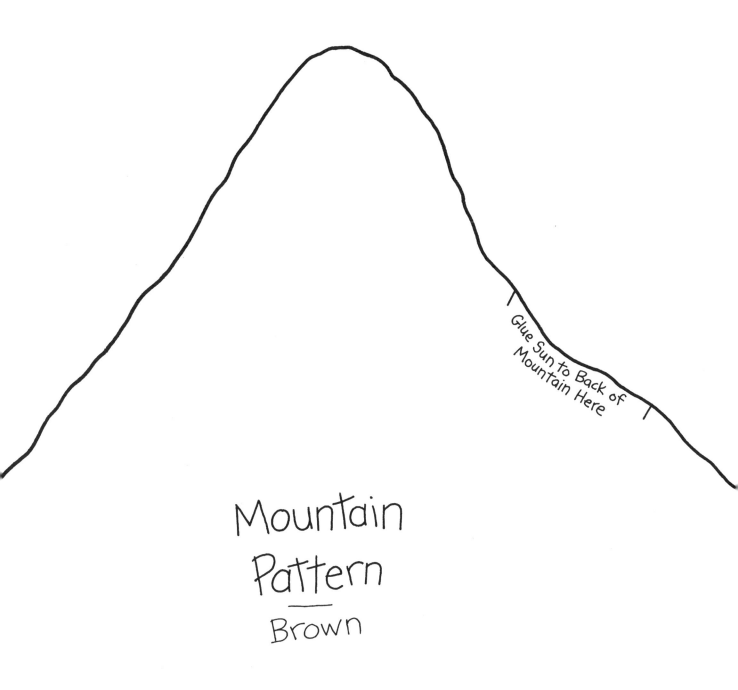

Glue Sun to Back of Mountain Here

Mountain
Pattern
—
Brown

Session 27
Workstation 4

Cut 1

Raindrop

Sun
Session 27
Workstation 4

Place Along Edge of Construction Paper

Ground
Pattern

Session 27
Workstation 5

Lake
Pattern

Session 27
Workstation 5

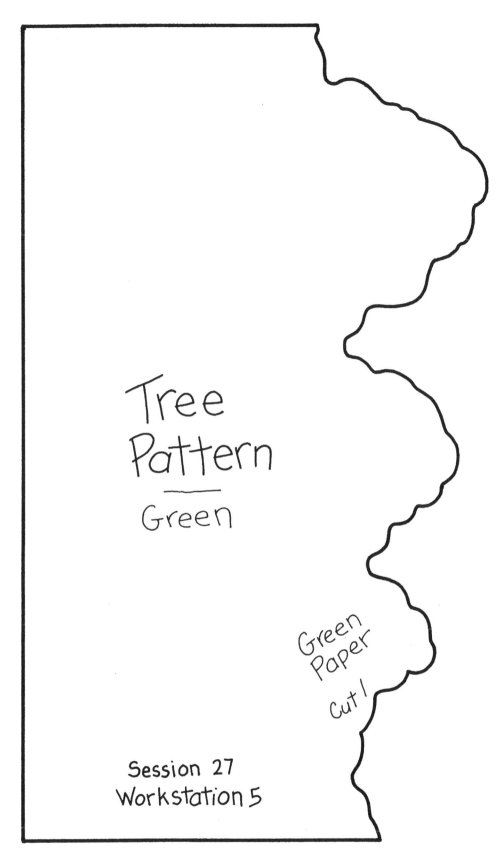

Tree
Pattern
—
Green

Green
Paper

Cut 1

Session 27
Workstation 5

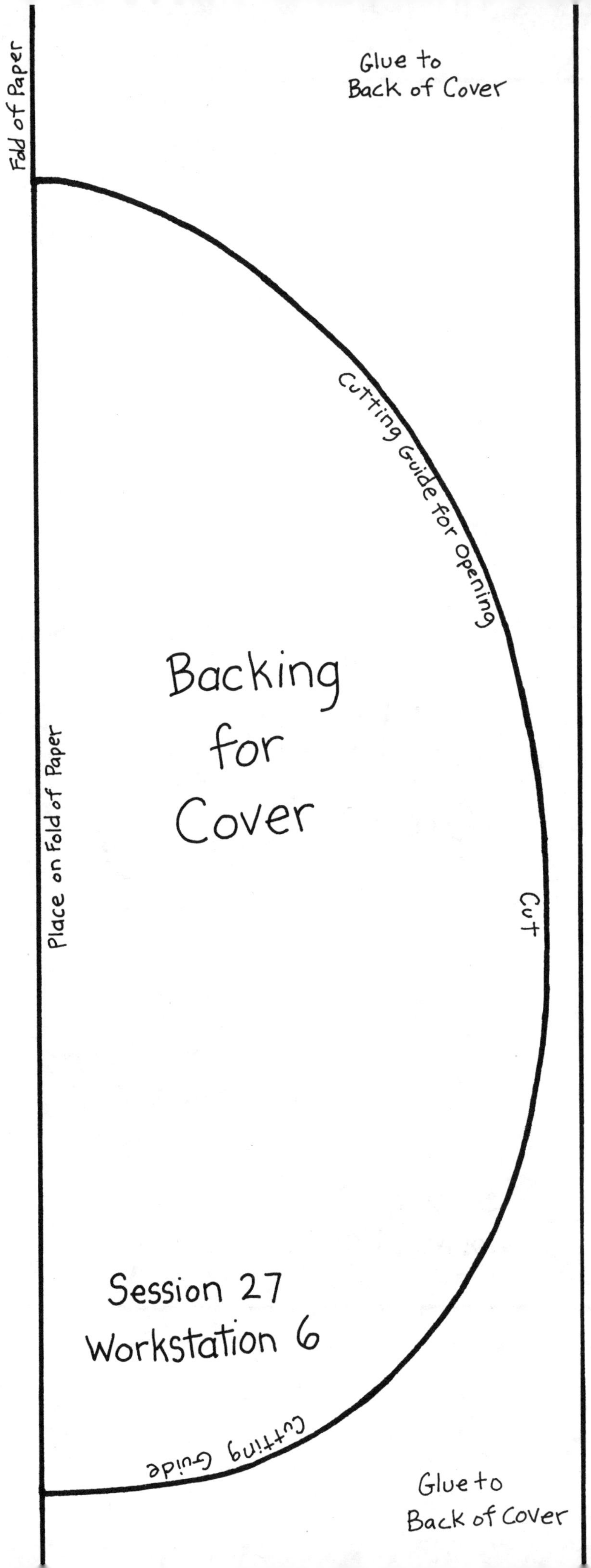

Fold of Paper

Glue to
Back of Cover

Cutting Guide for Opening

Place on Fold of Paper

Backing
for
Cover

Cut

Session 27
Workstation 6

Cutting Guide

Glue to
Back of Cover

3rd Rainbow
Pattern
—
Pink

Cut 1

Session 27
Workstation 7

Place on Fold

Place on Fold

Cut 1

2nd Rainbow
Pattern
—
Lavendar

Session 27
Workstation 7

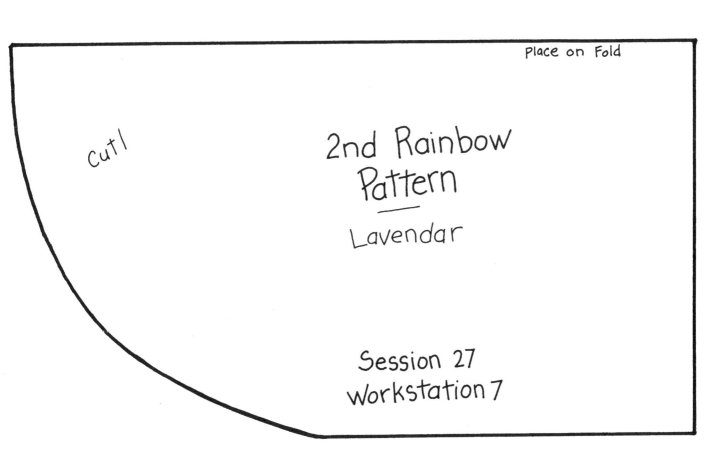

Session 27
Workstation 7

Place on Fold

1st
Rainbow
Pattern
—
Purple

Cut 1

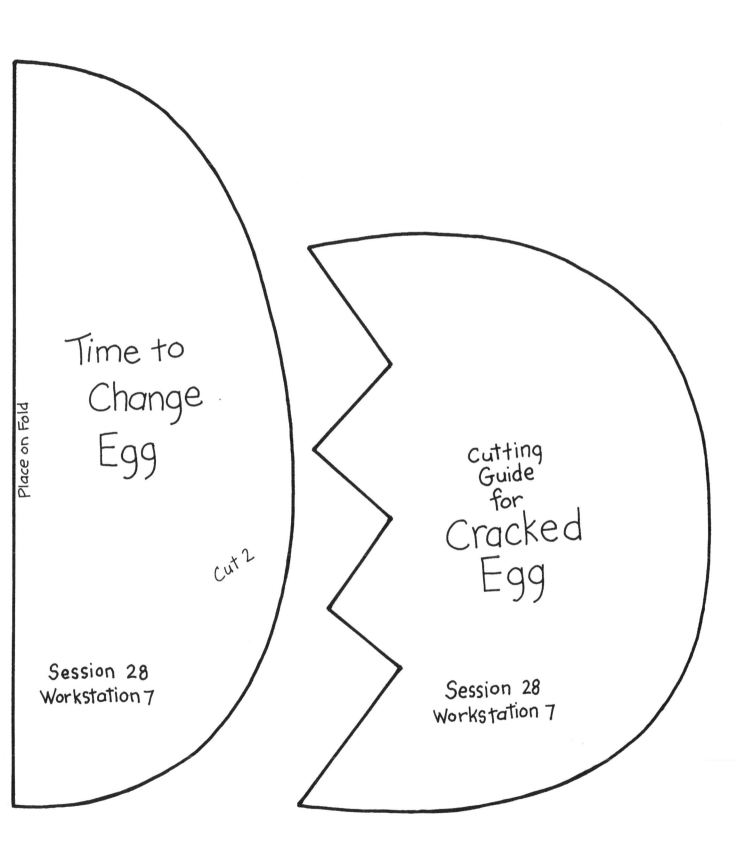

Place on Fold

Time to
Change
Egg

Cut 2

Session 28
Workstation 7

cutting
Guide
for
Cracked
Egg

Session 28
Workstation 7

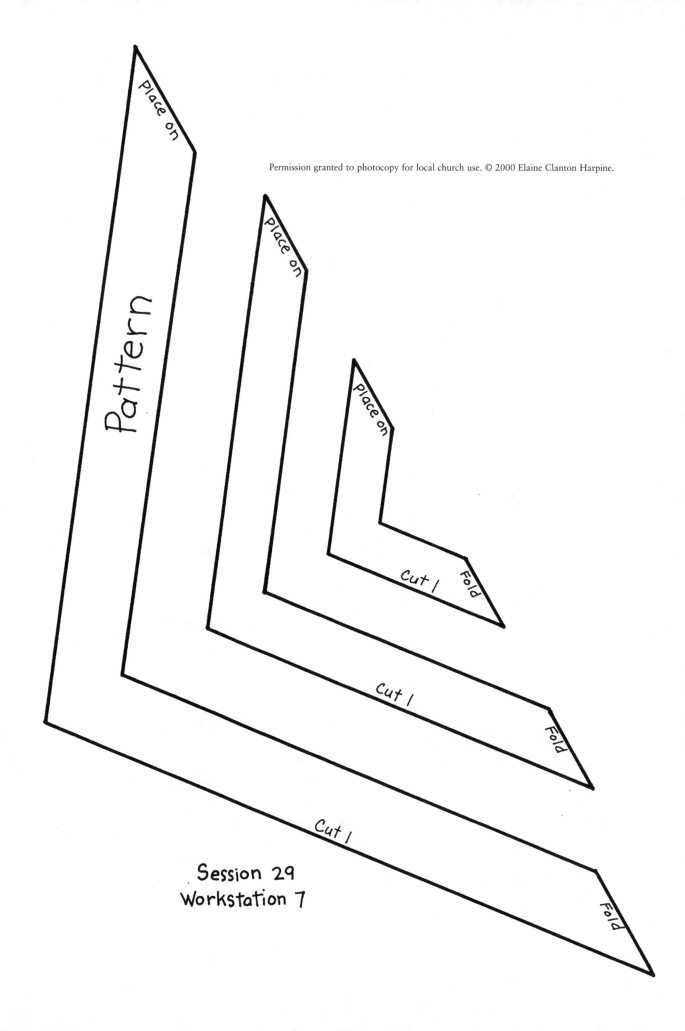

Pattern

Place on

Place on

Place on

Cut 1

Fold

Cut 1

Fold

Cut 1

Fold

Session 29
Workstation 7

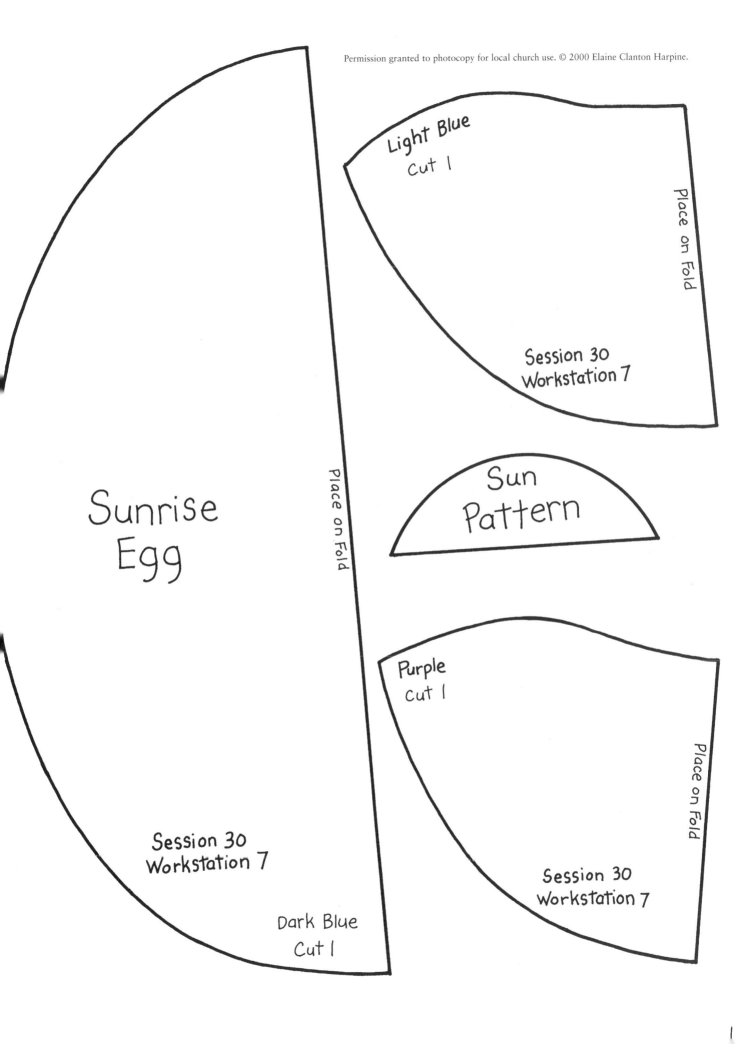

Permission granted to photocopy for local church use. © 2000 Elaine Clanton Harpine.

Light Blue
Cut 1

Place on Fold

Session 30
Workstation 7

Sun
Pattern

Sunrise
Egg

Place on Fold

Purple
Cut 1

Place on Fold

Session 30
Workstation 7

Session 30
Workstation 7

Dark Blue
Cut 1

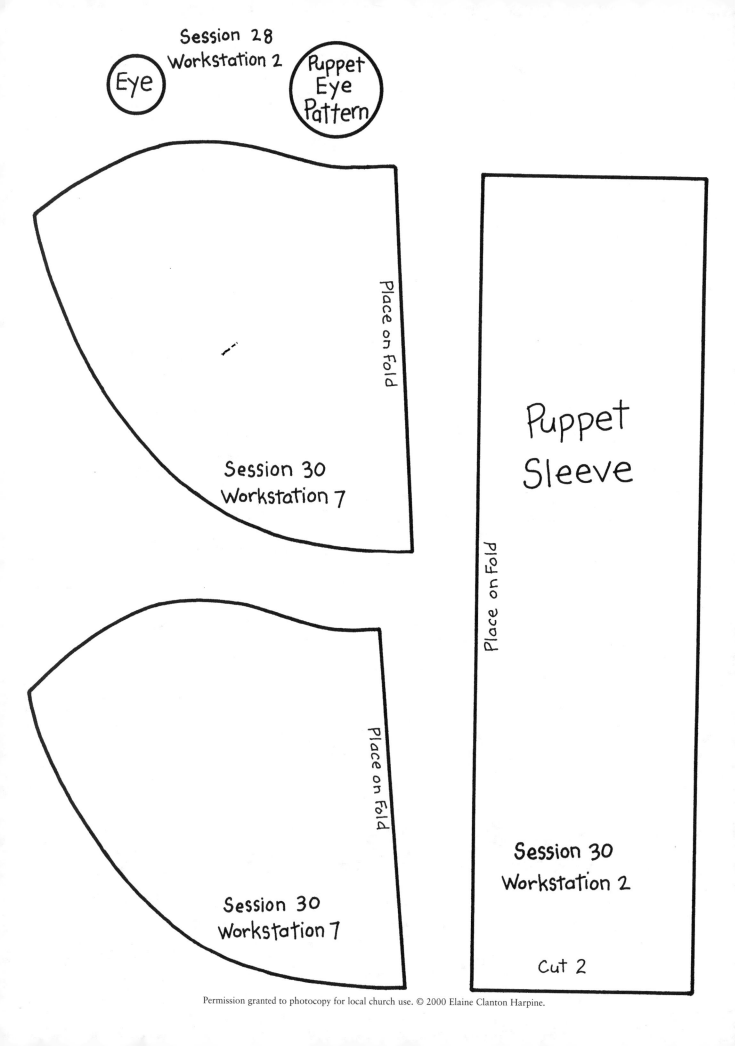

Session 28
Workstation 2

Eye

Puppet
Eye
Pattern

Place on fold

Session 30
Workstation 7

Puppet
Sleeve

Place on Fold

Place on fold

Session 30
Workstation 7

Session 30
Workstation 2

Cut 2

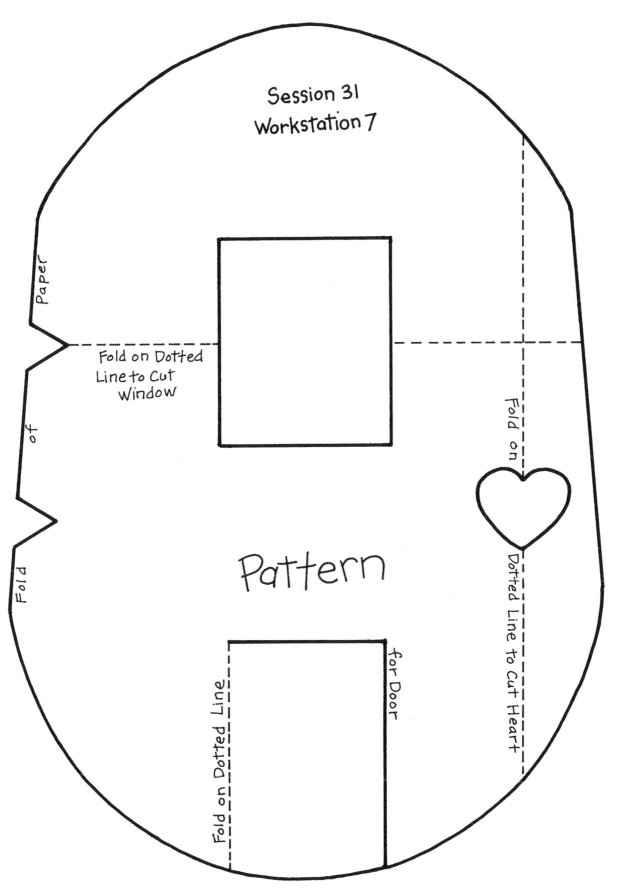

Session 31
Workstation 7

Paper

Fold on Dotted
Line to Cut
Window

of

Fold

Pattern

Fold on

Dotted Line to Cut Heart

Fold on Dotted Line

for Door

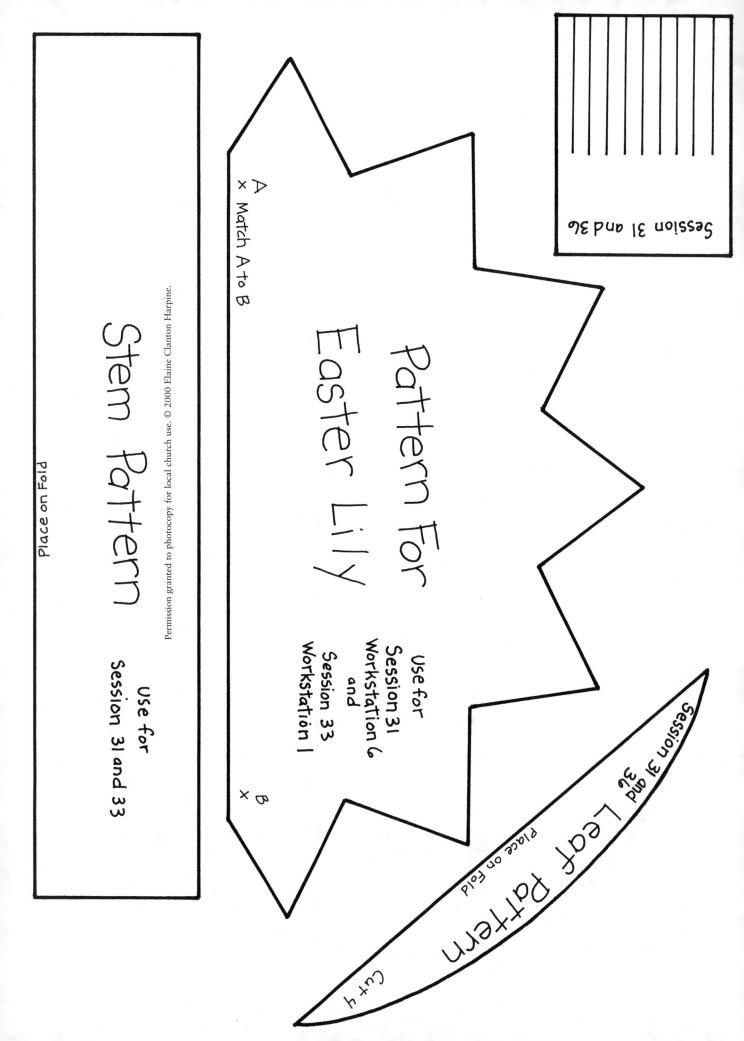

Place on Fold

Stem Pattern

Use for
Session 31 and 33

Permission granted to photocopy for local church use. © 2000 Elaine Clanton Harpine.

A
x Match A to B

Pattern For
Easter Lily

Use for
Session 31
Workstation 6
and
Session 33
Workstation 1

B
x

Session 31 and 36

Session 31 and 36 Leaf Pattern

Place on Fold

Cut 4

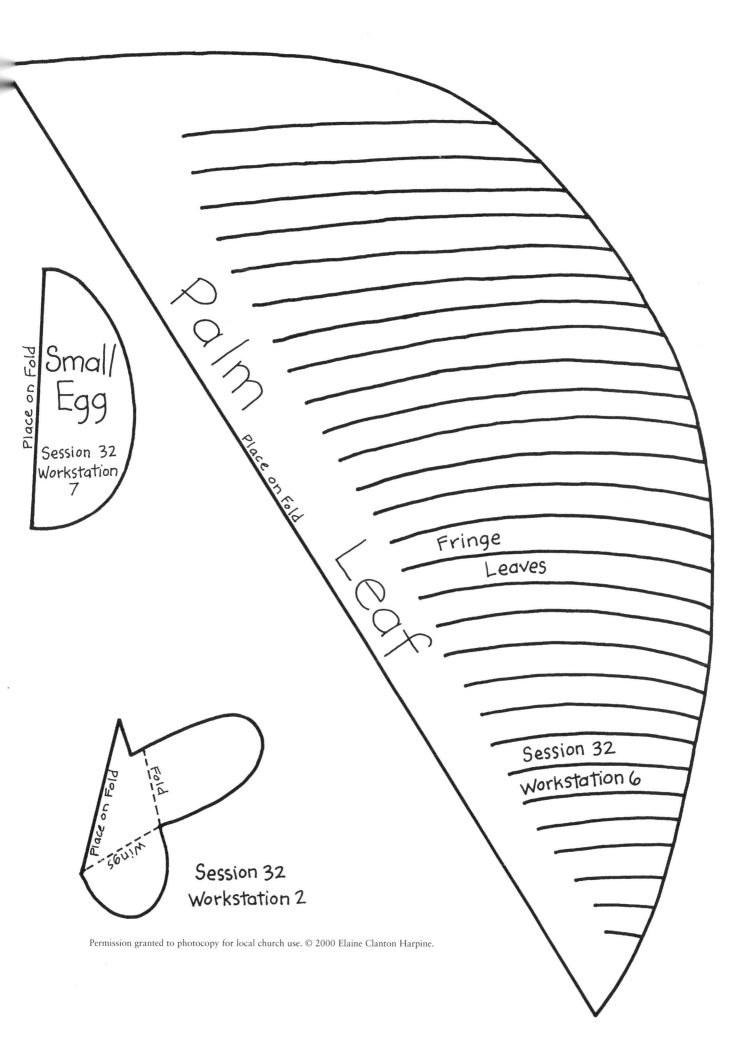

Palm Leaf

Place on Fold

Place on Fold

Small Egg

Session 32
Workstation 7

Place on Fold

Fringe

Leaves

Session 32

Workstation 6

Place on Fold

Fold

Wings

Session 32
Workstation 2

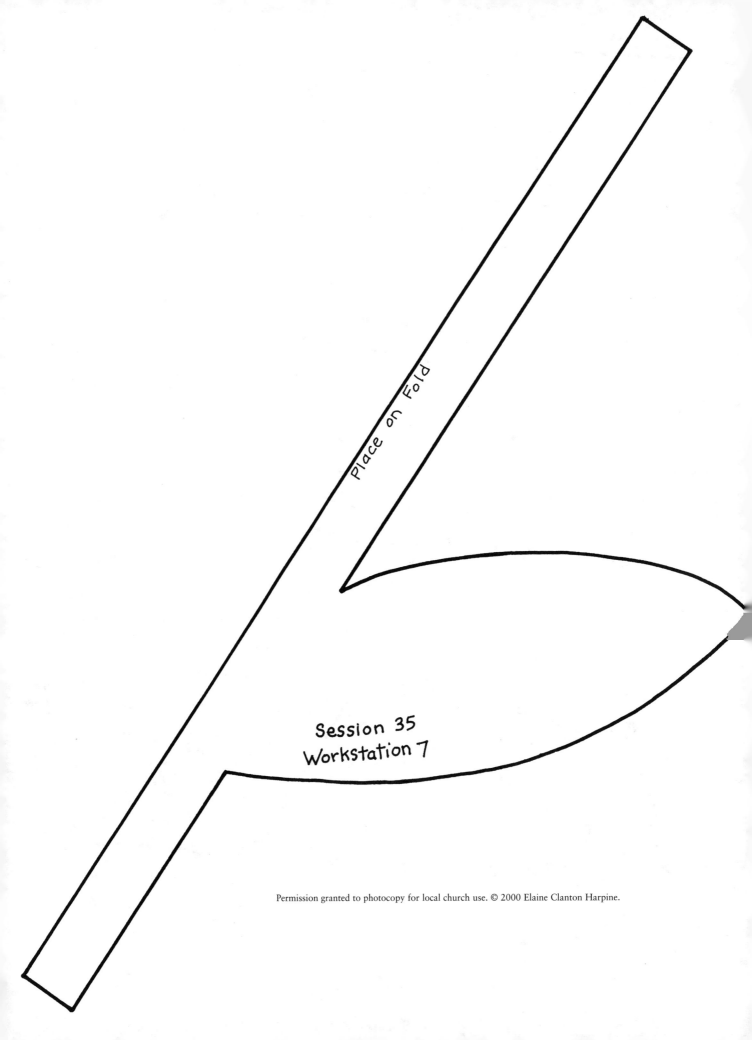

Place on Fold

Session 35
Workstation 7

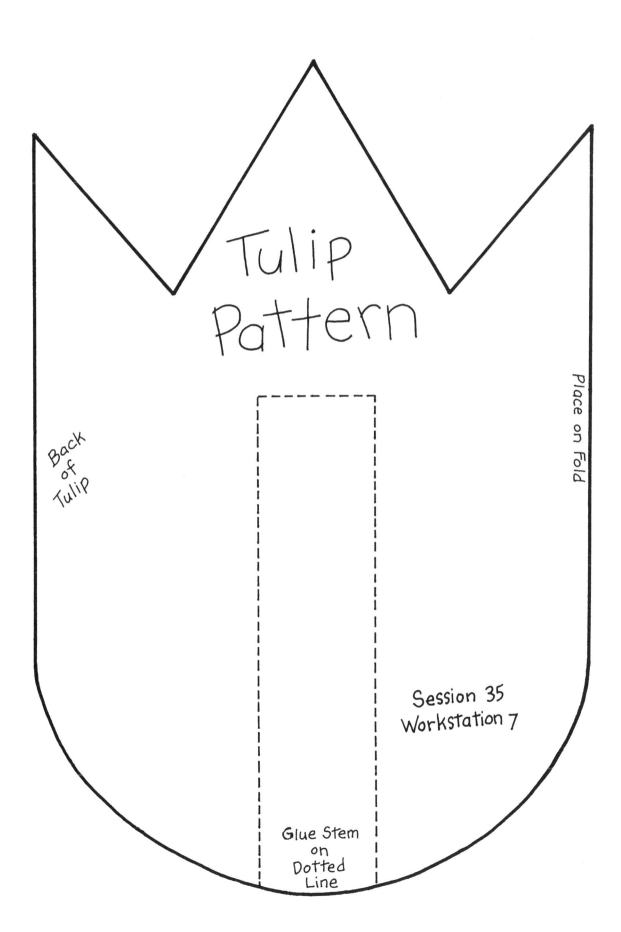

Tulip
Pattern

Place on Fold

Back
of
Tulip

Session 35
Workstation 7

Glue Stem
on
Dotted
Line

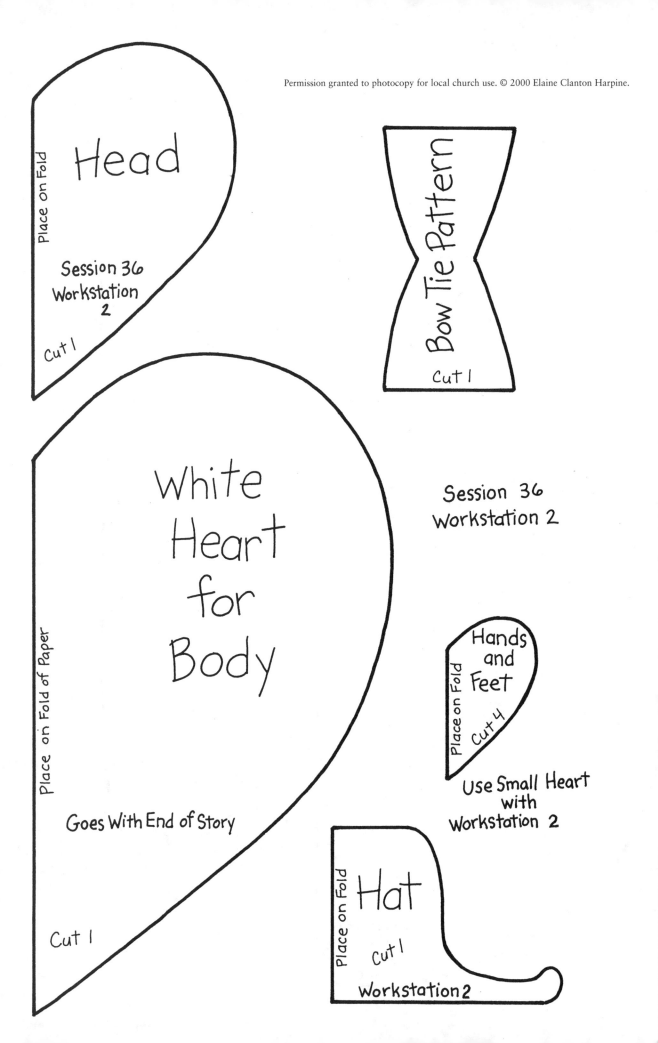

Head

Place on Fold

Session 36
Workstation
2

Cut 1

Bow Tie Pattern

Cut 1

Session 36
Workstation 2

White
Heart
for
Body

Place on Fold of Paper

Goes With End of Story

Cut 1

Hands
and
Feet

Place on Fold

Cut 4

Use Small Heart
with
Workstation 2

Hat

Place on Fold

Cut 1

Workstation 2

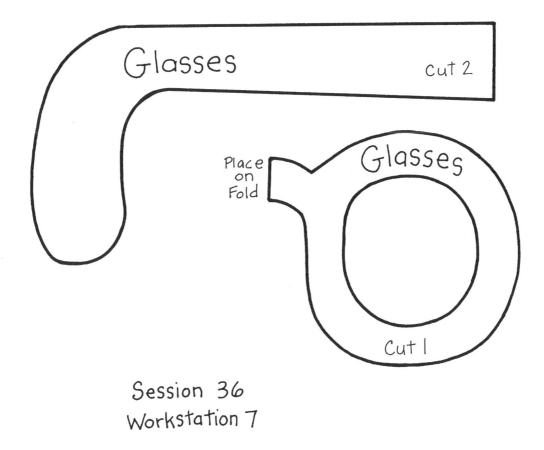

Glasses

cut 2

Place
on
Fold

Glasses

Cut 1

Session 36
Workstation 7

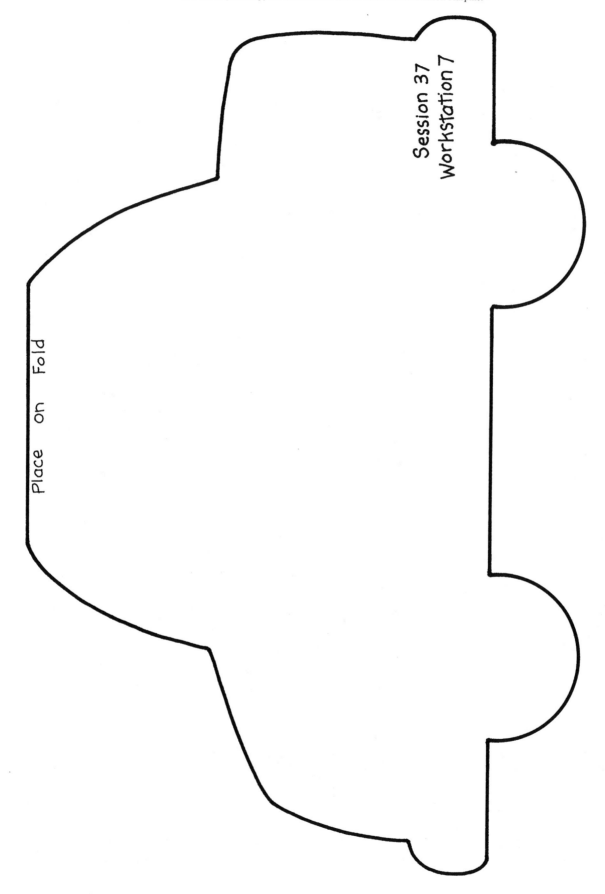

Session 37
Workstation 7

Place on Fold

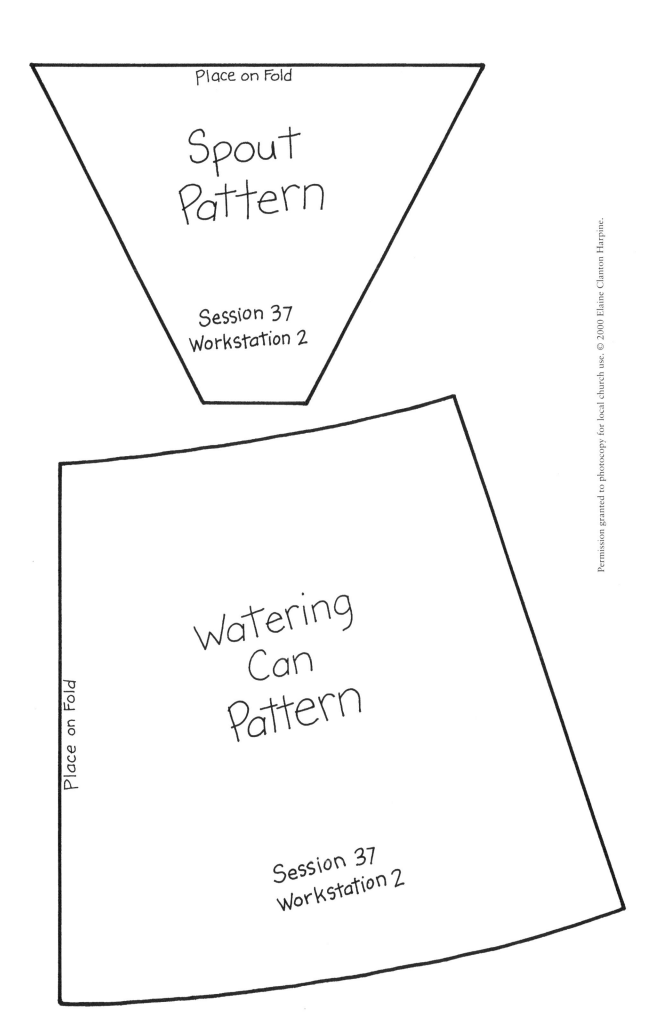

Place on Fold

Spout
Pattern

Session 37
Workstation 2

Watering
Can
Pattern

Place on Fold

Session 37
Workstation 2

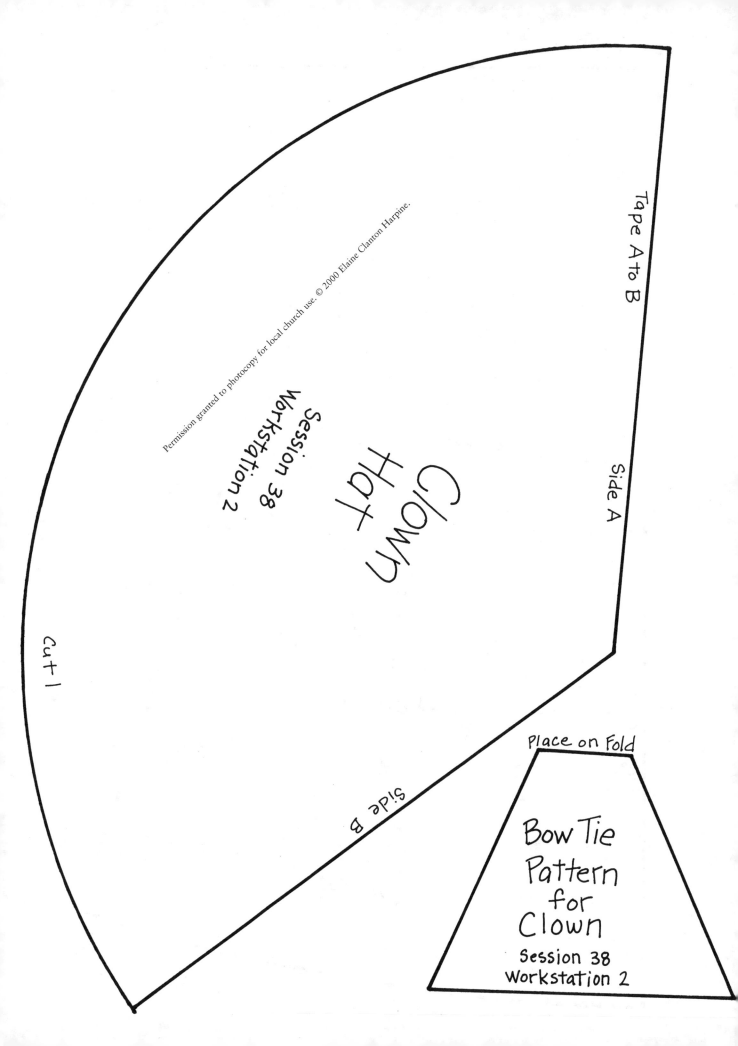

Tape A to B

Side A

Side B

Cut 1

Clown
Hat

Session 38
Workstation 2

Place on Fold

Bow Tie
Pattern
for
Clown

Session 38
Workstation 2

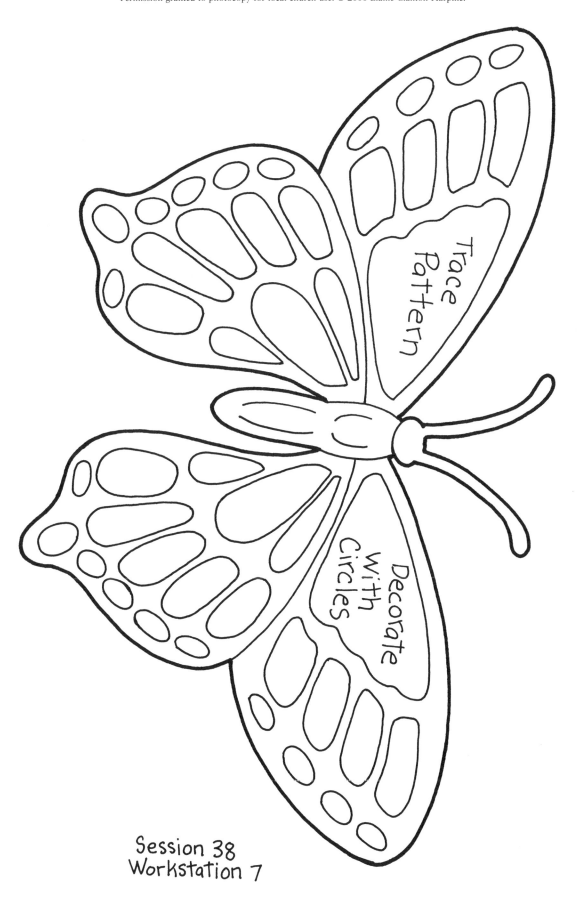

Trace Pattern

Decorate With Circles

Session 38
Workstation 7

Rose Window
Pattern
for
Front
Cover

Roof
for
Steeple

Top

Fold

Cut
Window for
White Front Cover

Place on Fold

Window

Cut 2

Cut out fish only on
Red Piece of paper

Place on Fold

Bell

Church
Pattern

cut 3

1 Red
2 White

Cut on Solid Line

Cut
Doors
on
White
Front
Cover
Only

Fold on Dotted Line for Front Cover

Cut 2

Door Pattern

Cut Front Cover Only

Session 40
Workstation 2

Place on Fold

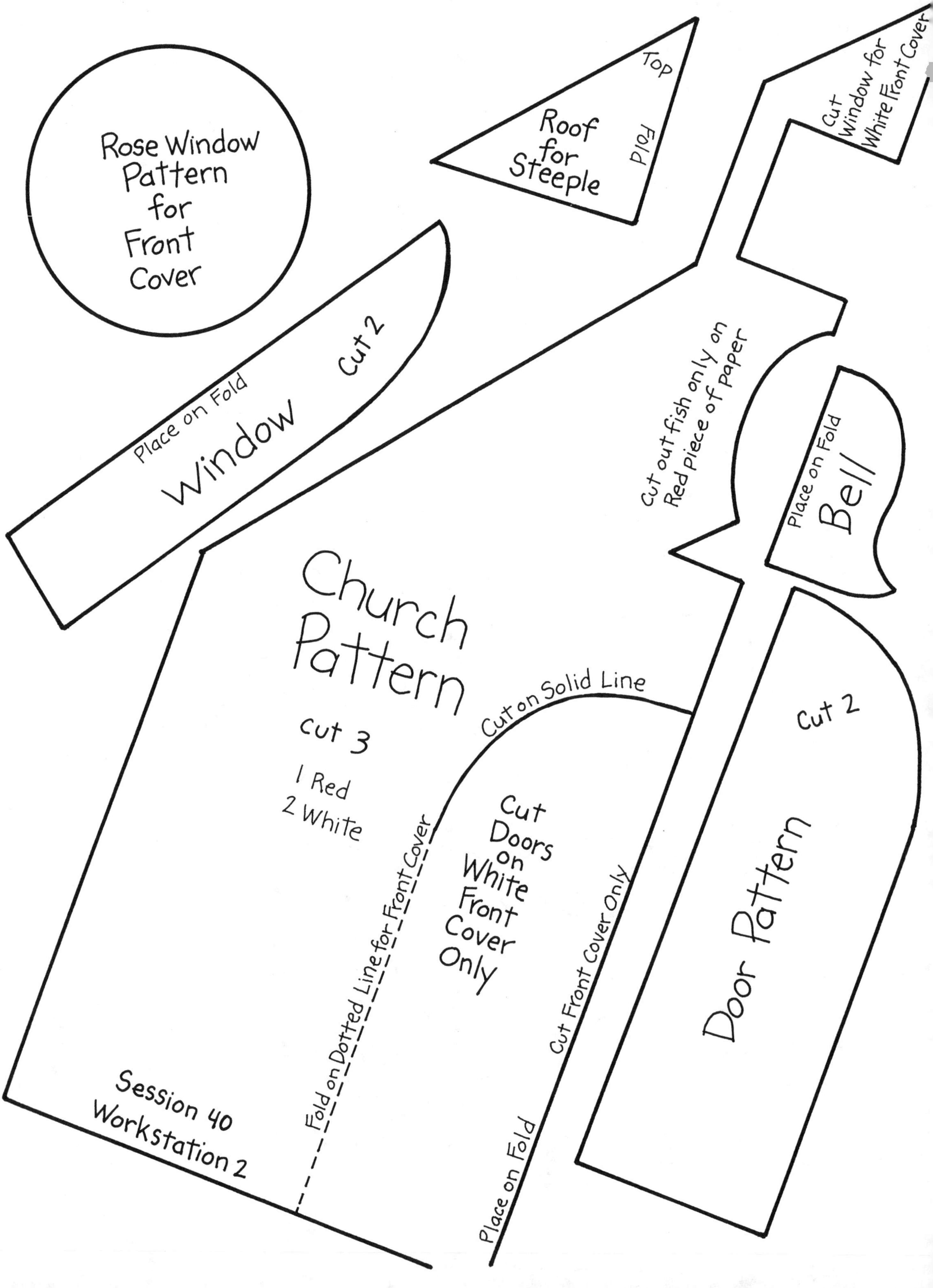

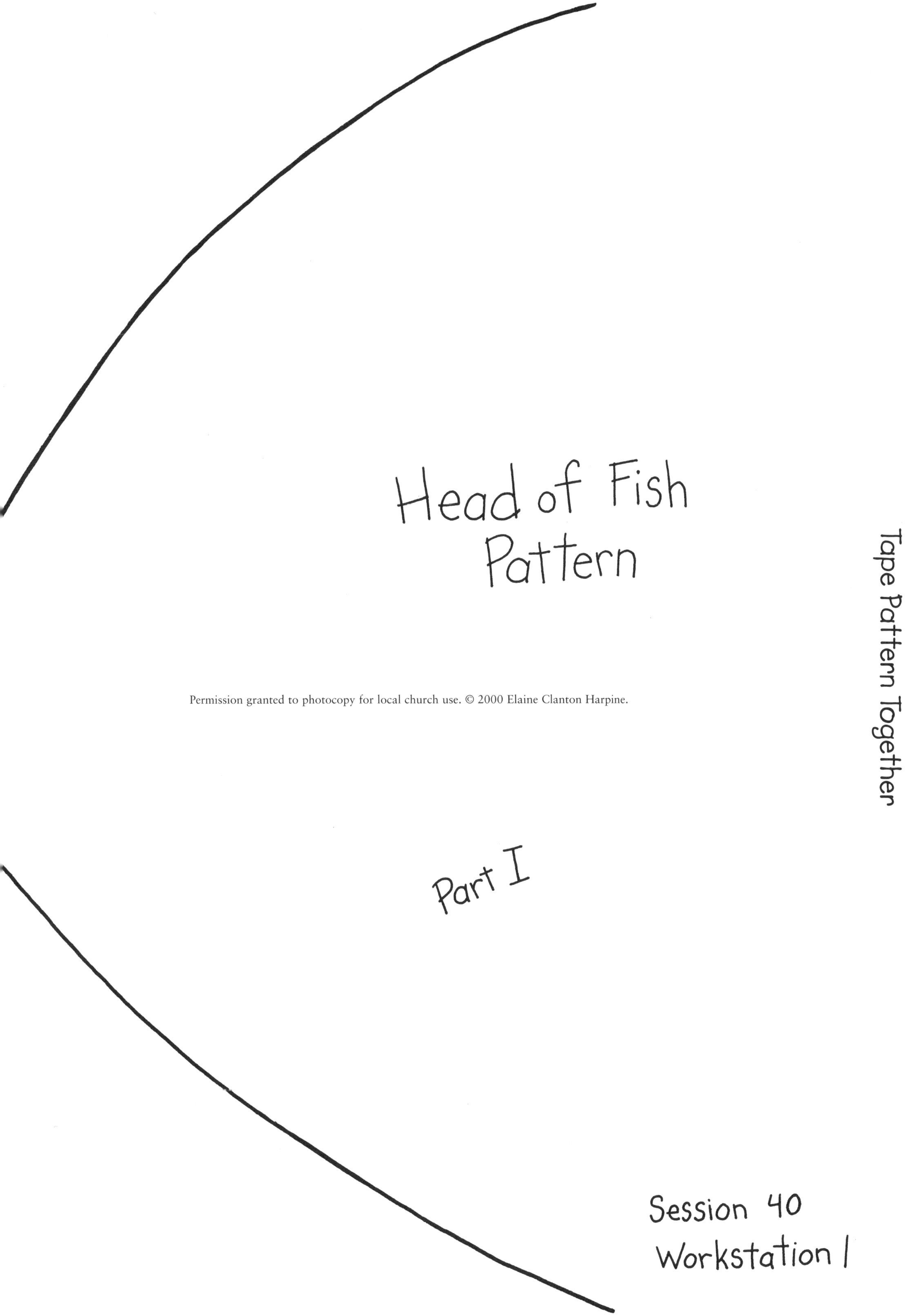

Head of Fish
Pattern

Part I

Tape Pattern Together

Session 40
Workstation 1

Nose Cone
for
Peace
Rocket

Session 41
Workstation 3

Cut 1 from Cardboard
or Thick Paper

Second Half
of
Fish Pattern

Part II

Fold
Bottom
of
Paper
Sack
to
Form
Tail

Session 40
Workstation 1

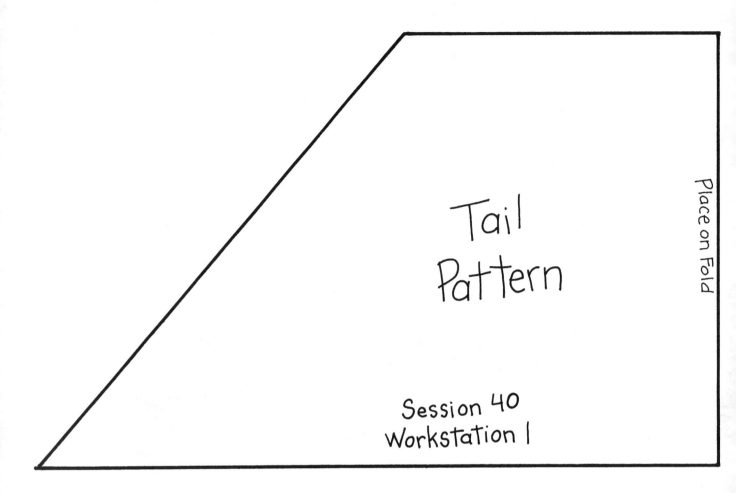

Tail
Pattern

Place on Fold

Session 40
Workstation 1

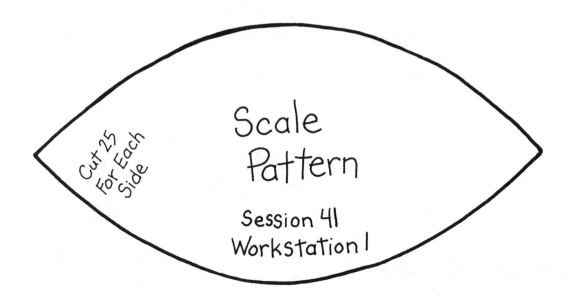

Scale
Pattern

Cut 25
For Each
Side

Session 41
Workstation 1

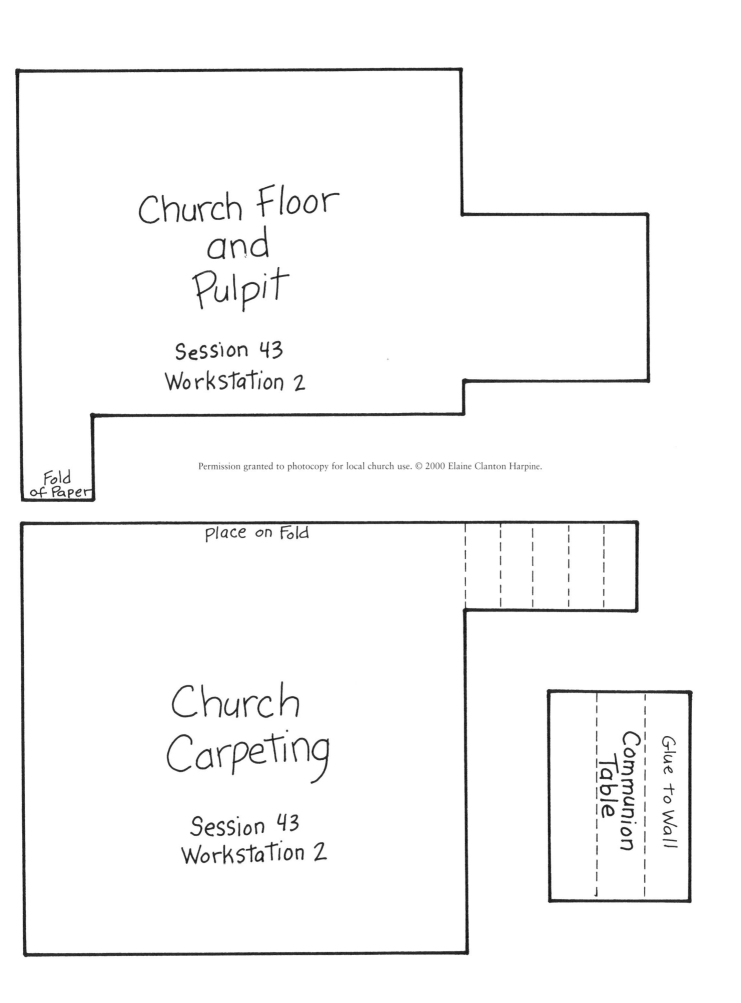

Church Floor
and
Pulpit

Session 43
Workstation 2

Fold
of Paper

Place on Fold

Church
Carpeting

Session 43
Workstation 2

Communion Table

Glue to Wall

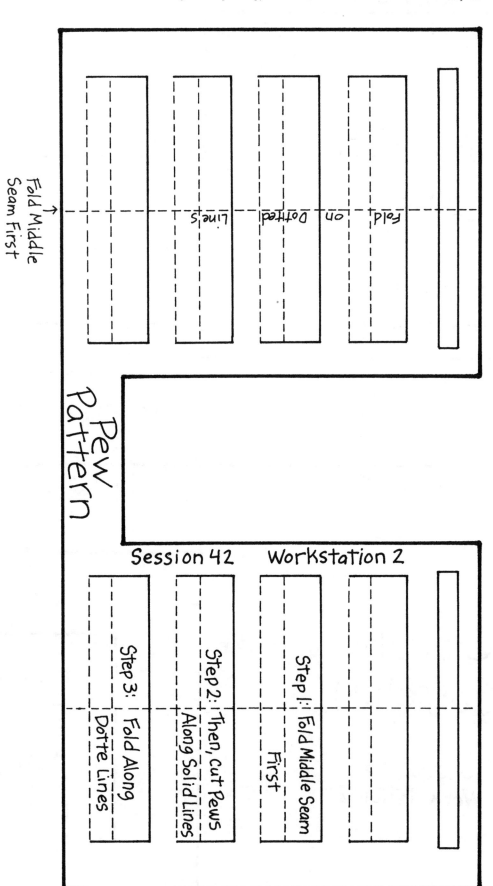

Cut 1 from Yellow Paper for Pews.
Cut 1 from Brown Paper. Glue to Back of Pews.

Fold Middle
Seam First

Fold on Dotted Lines

Pew Pattern

Session 42   Workstation 2

Step 1: Fold Middle Seam First

Step 2: Then, Cut Pews Along Solid Lines

Step 3: Fold Along Dotted Lines

Place on Fold

Mouth Pattern

Session 42
Workstation 1

Fin

Fold Back

Session 42
Workstation 1

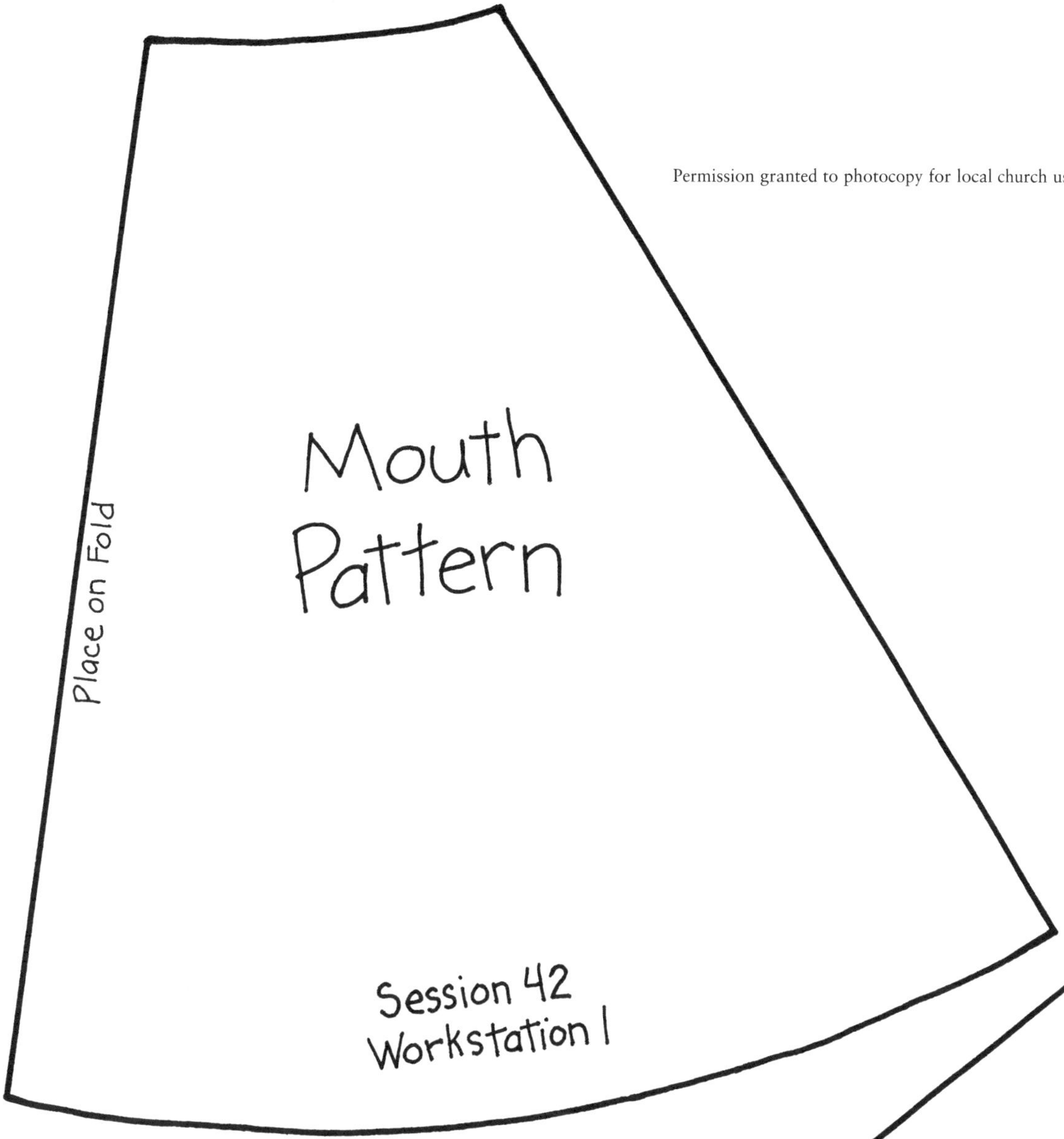

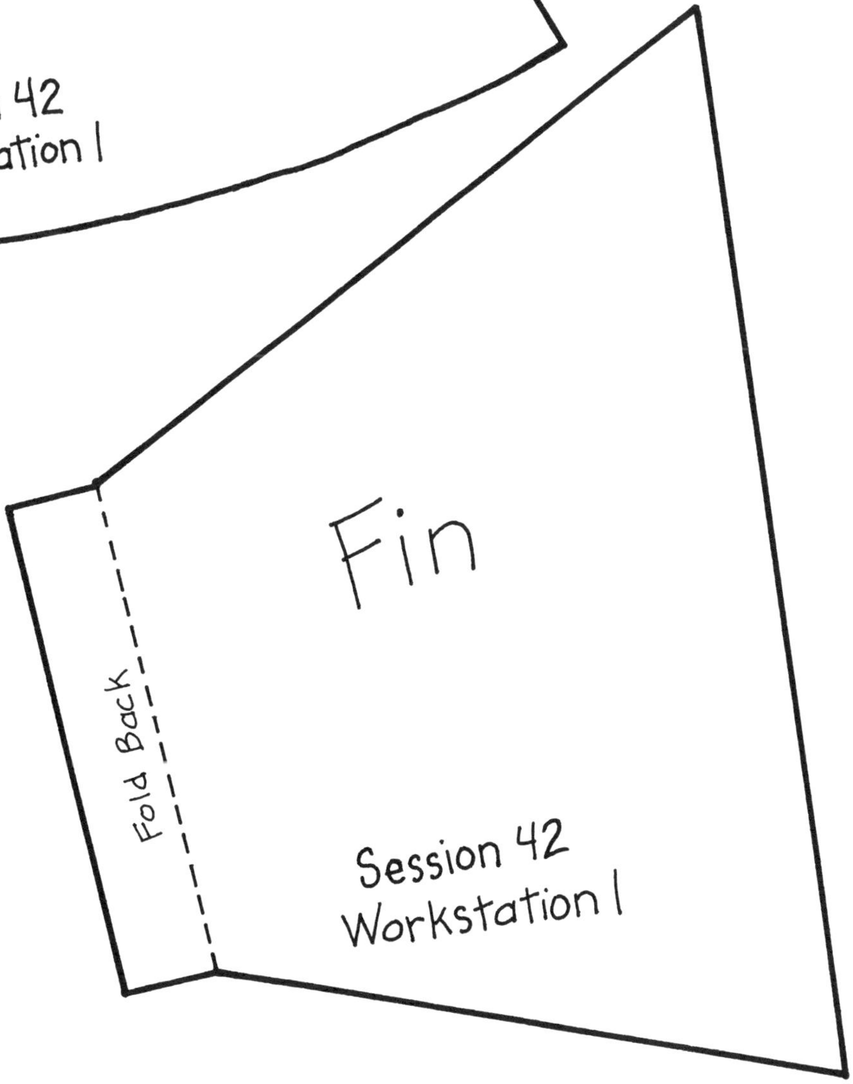

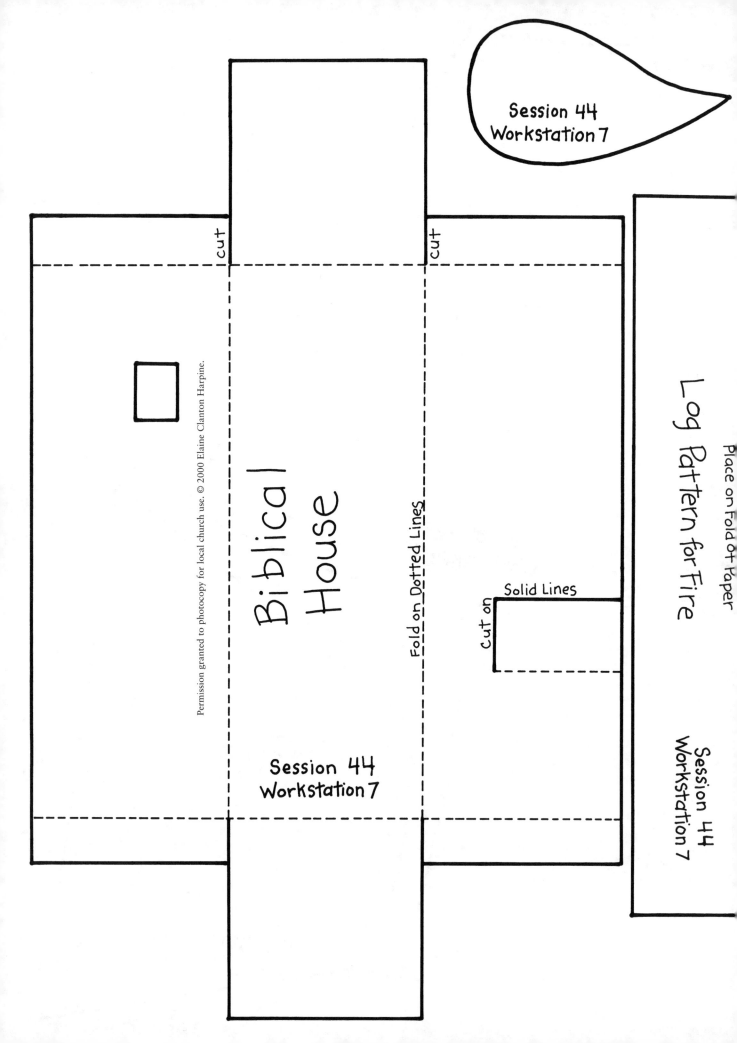

Session 44
Workstation 7

Place on Fold of Paper

Log Pattern for Fire

Session 44
Workstation 7

cut

cut

Solid Lines

Cut on

Fold on Dotted Lines

Biblical
House

Permission granted to photocopy for local church use. © 2000 Elaine Clanton Harpine.

Session 44
Workstation 7

Leg Pattern

Cut 2

Session 46
Workstation 5

Place on Fold

Place on Fold

Sleeve Pattern

Cut 2

Session 46   Workstation 5

Hand Pattern

Session 46
Workstation 5   Cut 2

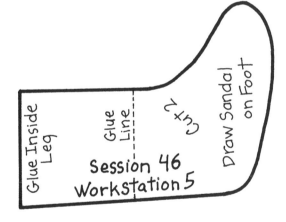

Glue Inside Leg

Glue Line

Cut 2

Session 46
Workstation 5

Draw Sandal on Foot

Bookmark Pattern

Session 45
Workstation 6

Step 2: Push Back to Make Awning Stand Out

Cut on Solid Lines
Fold on Dotted Lines

Step 1: Cut all Solid Lines

Fold This
Section Out to
Make Awning

Place on Fold

Place on Fold

Market Place Pattern

Step 3:
Push This
Section Inside

Session 46
workstation 7

Session 46 Workstation 7

If paper is thin, add extra sheet for thickness and support.

Table
Slide Table Top Into Slit

Fold Forward

Step 4: Fold

Fold This Section
Out to Make
Table

Cut 1

Scroll Pattern

Cut 1

Session 46
Workstation 6

Place on Fold

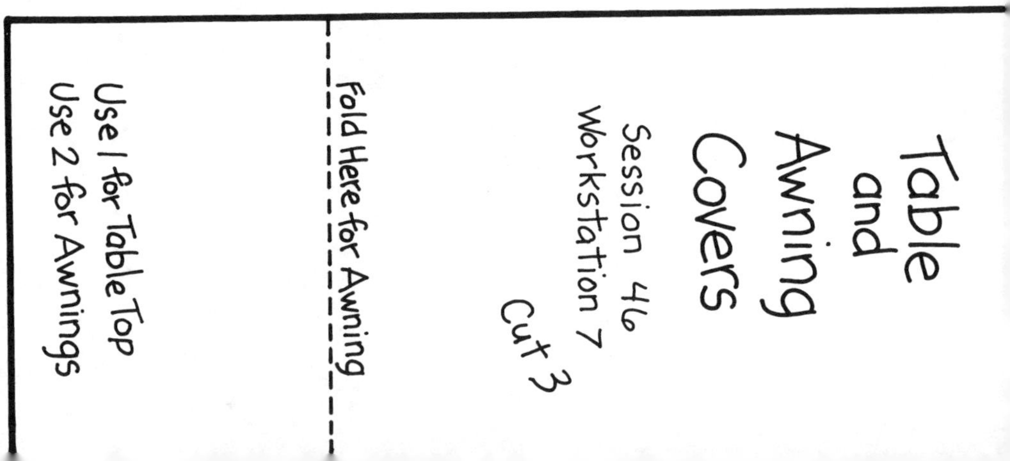

Use 1 for Table Top
Use 2 for Awnings

Fold Here for Awning

Session 46
Workstation 7

Cut 3

Table and Awning Covers

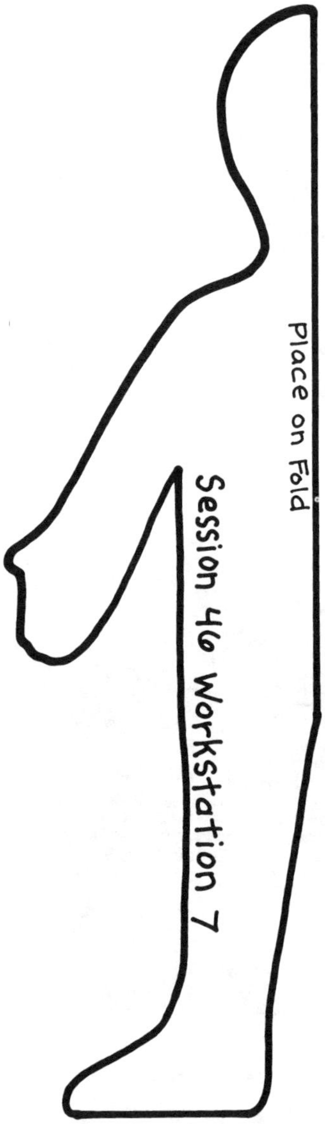

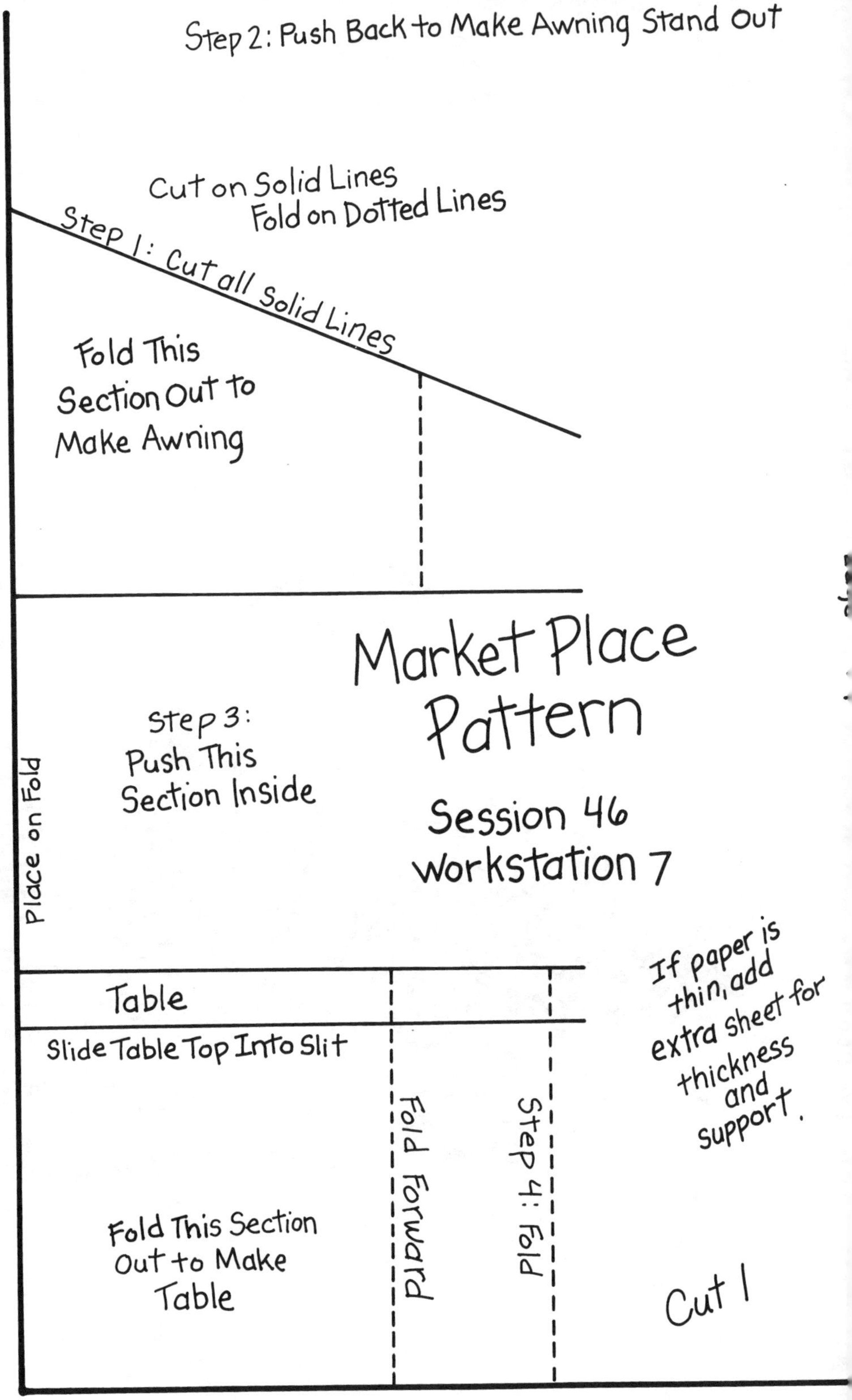

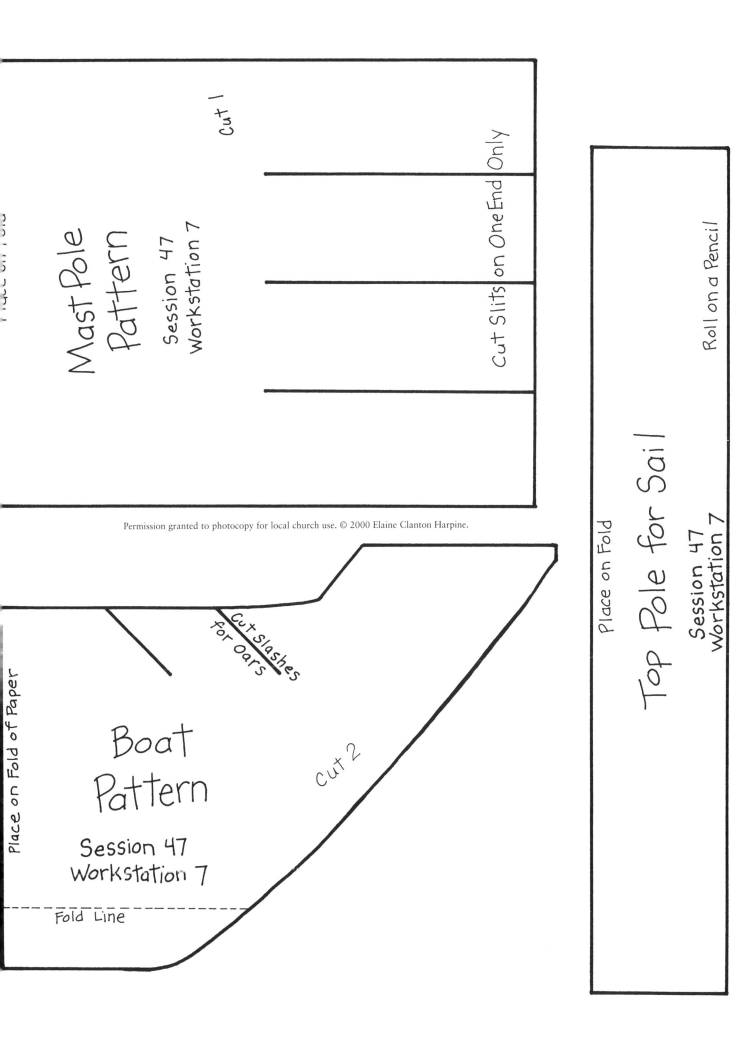

Mast Pole
Pattern

Session 47
Workstation 7

Cut 1

Cut Slits on One End Only

Boat
Pattern

Session 47
Workstation 7

Cut 2

Place on Fold of Paper

Cut Slashes
for Oars

Fold Line

Top Pole for Sail

Session 47
Workstation 7

Place on Fold

Roll on a Pencil

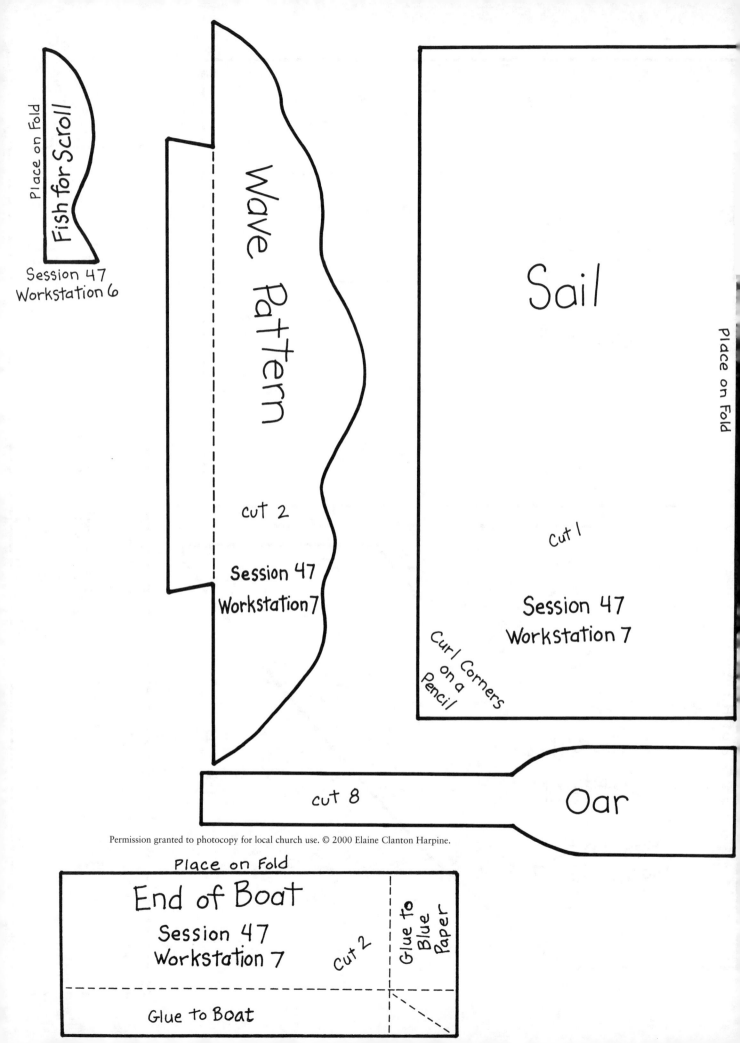

Place on Fold

Fish for Scroll

Session 47
Workstation 6

Wave Pattern

cut 2

Session 47

Workstation 7

Sail

Place on Fold

Cut 1

Session 47

Workstation 7

Curl Corners
on a
Pencil

cut 8

Oar

Permission granted to photocopy for local church use. © 2000 Elaine Clanton Harpine.

Place on Fold

End of Boat
Session 47
Workstation 7

Cut 2

Glue to
Blue
Paper

Glue to Boat

Tail for Lamb
Session 47
Place on Fold
Workstation 1
Use Cardboard

Ear for Lamb
Session 47
Workstation 1
Place on Fold

Cut 4 Ears

2 Black
2 white

Then Glue Together

Water
for
Boat
Pattern

Glue Wave Here
Cut on this Line.

Glue Boat Here
Cut on this Line.

Place on Fold of Paper

Boat
Cut on this Line.

wave
Cut on this Line.

Place on Fold

Winnowing
Fork
Pattern

Session 48
Workstation 7

Lamb Pattern

Session 48
Workstation 6

Lamb
Pattern

Session 49
Workstation 6 and 7

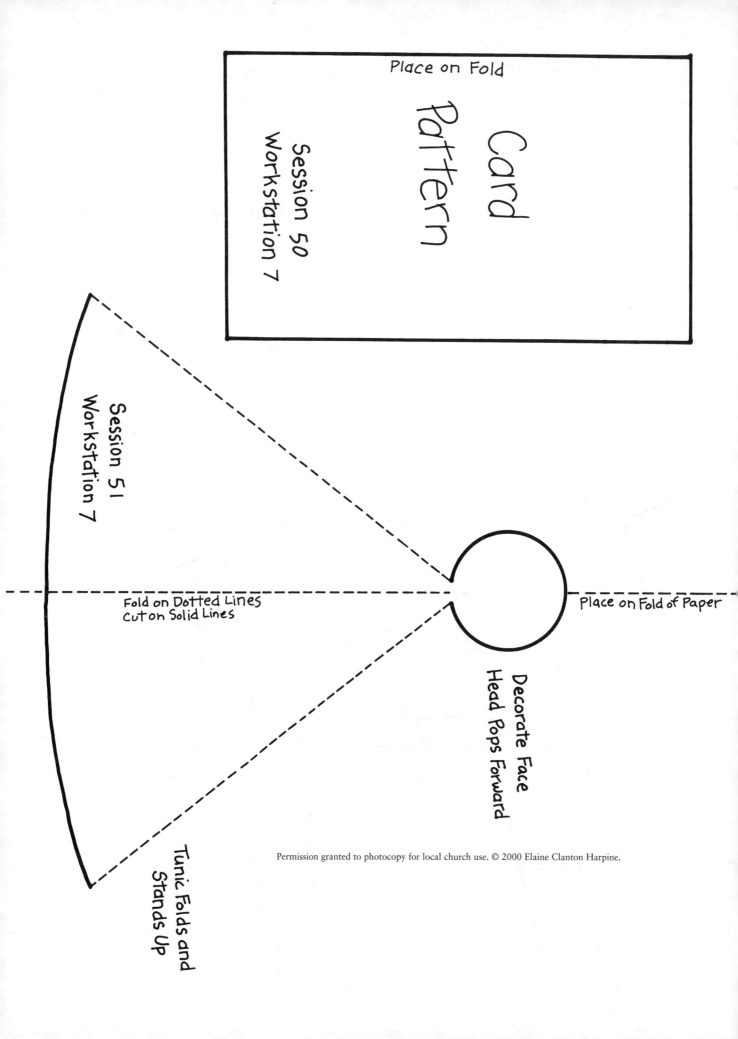

Place on Fold

Card
Pattern

Session 50
Workstation 7

Session 51
Workstation 7

Fold on Dotted Lines
Cut on Solid Lines

Place on Fold of Paper

Decorate Face
Head Pops Forward

Tunic Folds and
Stands Up

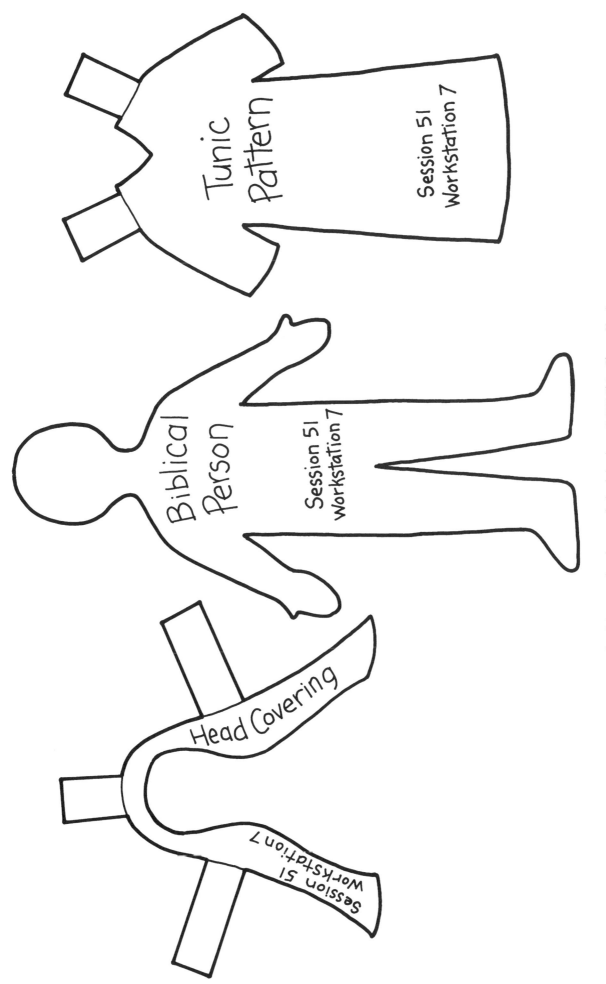

Tunic Pattern

Session 51 Workstation 7

Biblical Person

Session 51 workstation 7

Head Covering

Session 51 Workstation 7

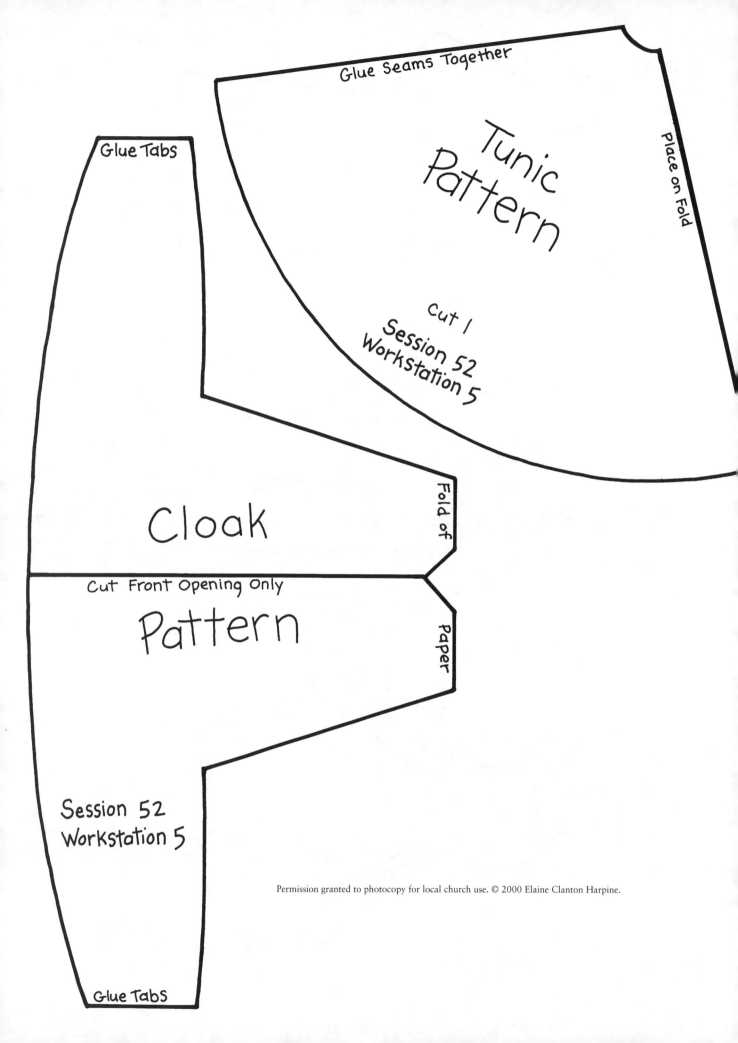

Glue Seams Together

Tunic
Pattern

Place on Fold

Cut 1
Session 52
Workstation 5

Glue Tabs

Cloak

Fold of

Cut Front Opening Only

Paper

Pattern

Session 52
Workstation 5

Glue Tabs

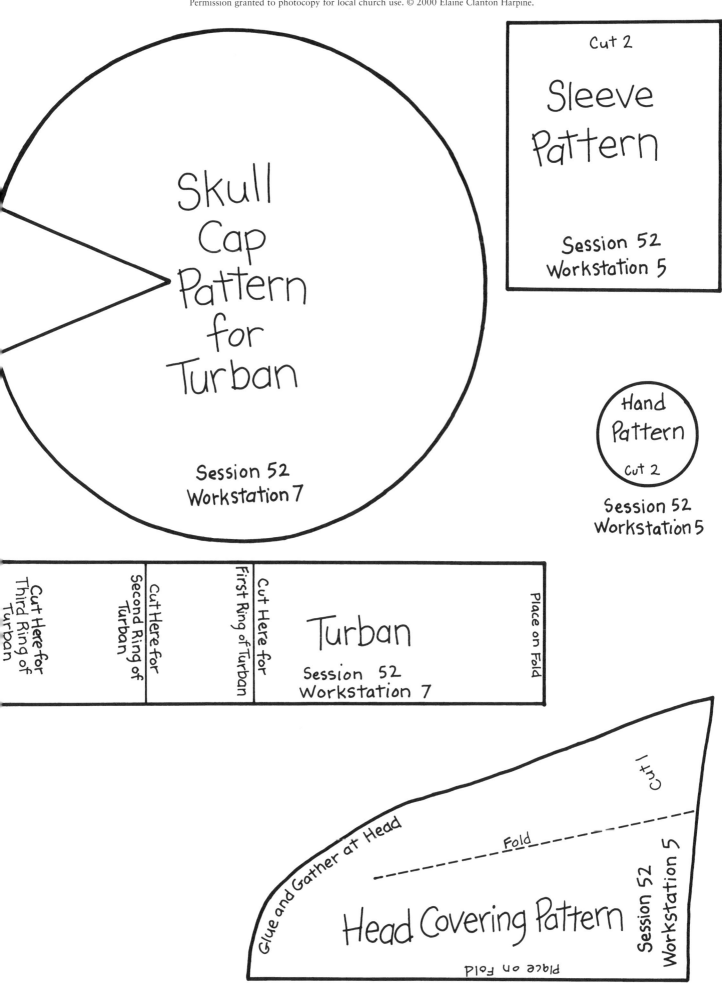

Skull
Cap
Pattern
for
Turban

Session 52
Workstation 7

Cut 2

Sleeve
Pattern

Session 52
Workstation 5

Hand
Pattern

Cut 2

Session 52
Workstation 5

Cut Here for
Third Ring of
Turban

Second Ring of
Turban

Cut Here for

First Ring of Turban

Cut Here for

Turban

Session 52
Workstation 7

Place on Fold

Glue and Gather at Head

Fold

Cut 1

Head Covering Pattern

Place on Fold

Session 52
Workstation 5

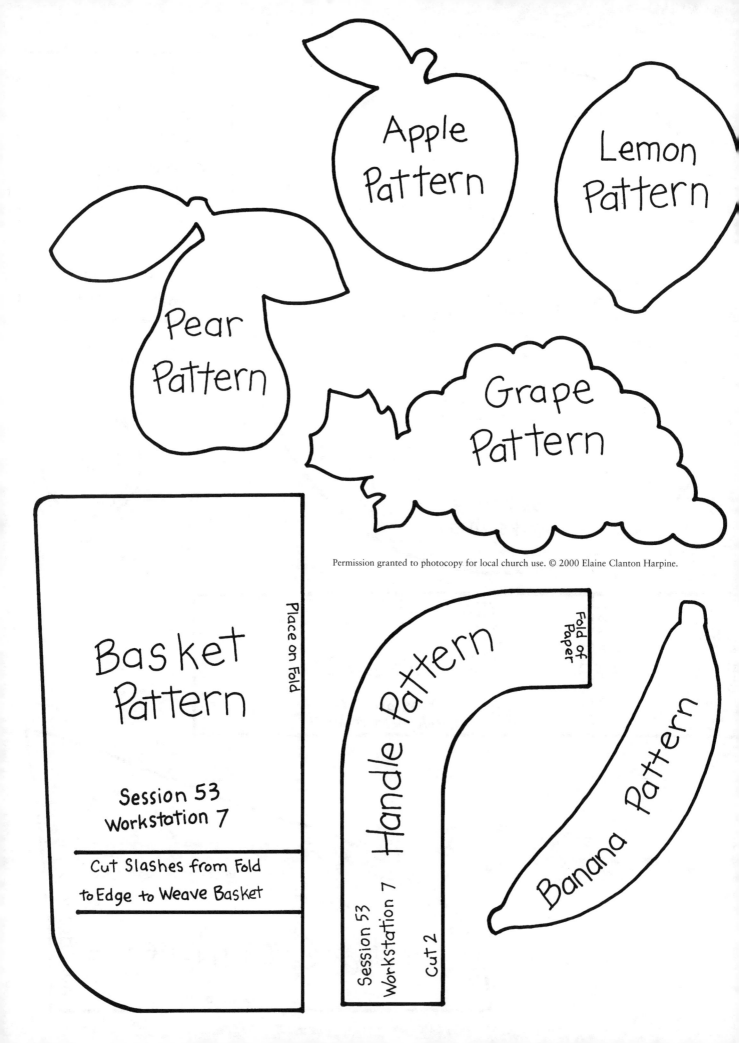

Apple
Pattern

Lemon
Pattern

Pear
Pattern

Grape
Pattern

Permission granted to photocopy for local church use. © 2000 Elaine Clanton Harpine.

Basket
Pattern

Place on Fold

Session 53
Workstation 7

Cut Slashes from Fold
to Edge to Weave Basket

Handle Pattern

Fold of Paper

Session 53
Workstation 7

Cut 2

Banana Pattern

Our

Thy   **Kingdom**   **come.**

Give   **us**   **this**

debts,   **as**   **we**

And   **lead**   **us**

for   **Thine**   **is**

Father   **Who**   **art**   **in Heaven,**

Thy   **will**   **be**   **done**

day   **our**   **daily**   **bread.**

forgive   **our debtors.**   **(those**

not   **into**   **temptation,**   **but**

the Kingdom,   **and**   **the power,**

hallowed be Thy name.

on earth, as it is in Heaven.

And forgive us our

who sin against us)

deliver us from evil:

and the glory, forever. Amen.

This is a sample permission form and letter you may wish to use to
announce your hospital or nursing home visit to parents.

Dear Parents:

One of our Outreach Ministry Projects in Children's Worship this month is to visit

_____ on _____.

The children have been learning about clown ministry and practicing ways to share
God's love. All children are welcome to participate. Yes, we still need drivers.

We will meet at _____.

Return to the church by _____.

Parents are definitely needed and invited to participate. We must know today if your
child would like to participate so that we can arrange transportation.

Clown ministry allows young people the freedom to express God's love more openly.
All clown costumes must be positive. No scary costumes. Old dress-up clothes work fine.

The children will have the option to wear clown make-up. The makeup is water based and
washes off with soap and water. Those who choose to wear makeup will be coming home with
their makeup on. A bath or shower will easily remove the makeup. The children may also choose
to clown without makeup.

Please sign the attached permission form and return today or call me at _____.

Thank you for allowing us the pleasure of working with your daughter or son.

Peace and love,

* *

_____ may accompany the Children's Worship group clowning at

_____ in _____ on _____.

My daughter or son (does or does not) have permission to wear clown make-up.

Parent's Name _____

Address _____
Phone _____

If needed, I can be reached on the day of the trip at : _____phone number

Please note any known allergies to makeup or face paint.

Diagram of Boat

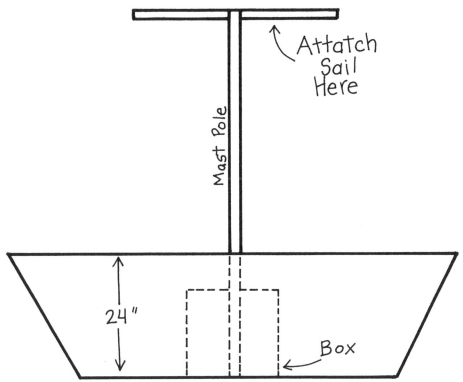

Mast Pole

Attatch Sail Here

24"

Box

Step 1: Cut plywood for sides of boat. Cut 2.

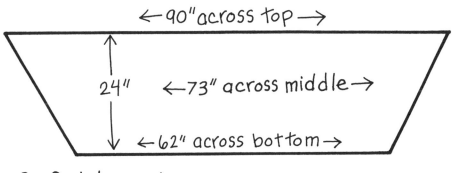

← 90" across top →

24" ← 73" across middle →

← 62" across bottom →

Step 2: Cut boards for base. Glue and nail boards together to make two blocks.

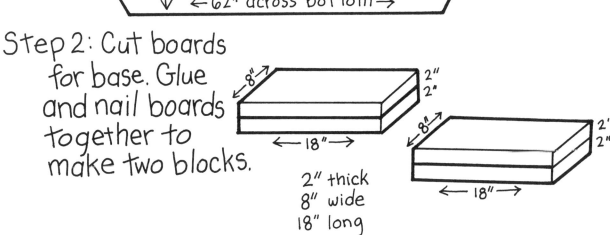

8"   2" 2"

18"

8"   2" 2"

18"

2" thick
8" wide
18" long

Step 3: Cut boards for sides of box.

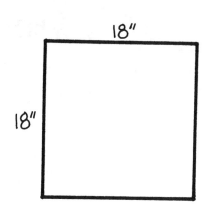

18"

18"

Step 4: Cut braces for box and mast pole.

2"

72" Long

Mast Pole

Braces for Box.

2x4's

8" Long

2x4's

18" Long

2x4's

12" Long

Step 5: Check length of dowel rod. Cut if necessary.

Step 6: Nail boards from Step 2 if you haven't done so yet.

Step 7: Glue and nail mast pole to base.

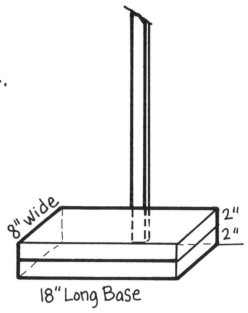

8" Wide

2"
2"

18" Long Base

Step 8: Glue and nail other base block against mast pole. <u>Wedge 8" long 2×4's</u> beside mast pole for a snug fit.

Step 9: Nail and glue 4 18" long braces across top. Make sure that there is a brace on each side of mast pole.

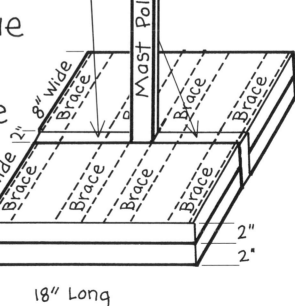

8" Wide

8" Wide 2"

Brace   Brace   Brace   Brace   Brace   Brace   Brace   Brace

Mast Pole

2"
2"

18" Long

Step 10: Nail braces in place. Drill hole for bolt.

Step 11: Repeat process for other side of boat.

Step 12: Nail sides of box to base.

Step 13: Use glue for all seams.

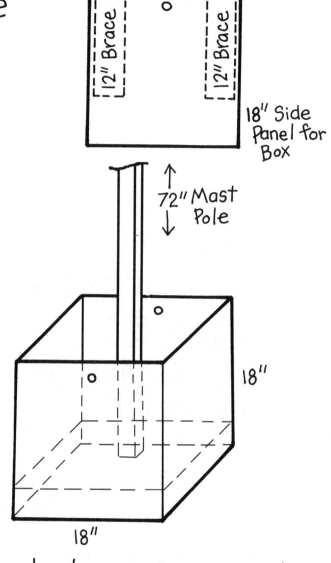

18" Side Panel for Box

12" Brace

12" Brace

72" Mast Pole

18"

18"

Step 14: Drill matching holes in side panels of boat. Holes must line up with holes in box.

Step 15: See main diagram for assembling boat.

ABOUT THE AUTHOR

Elaine Clanton Harpine, Ph.D., is a program design specialist and group training consultant specializing in conducting and evaluating youth and children's group programs. A Methodist minister's daughter, Dr. Clanton Harpine has spent the last twenty-seven years working in both volunteer and staff positions in The United Methodist Church.

She earned her doctorate in Educational Psychology and Counseling from the University of Illinois, where her research focused on leadership development in The United Methodist Church. She has worked as a Director of Christian Education and as a Youth Coordinator.

Dr. Clanton Harpine's published writings include: *The Christmas Tree: How to Make Christian Ornaments for your Christmas Tree, Pattern Book,* Volume I and II (1998); *The Christmas Tree: A Tree-trimming Workshop and Program Using Christ-centered Ornaments* (1994); *No Expeience Necessary!: A "Learn by Doing" Guide for Creating Children's Worship* (1992) (selected as one of the top five worship curriculums in the nationwide survey, 1995); *Youth-Led Meetings: 10 Step-by-Step Meeting Plans Designed for Teenagers to Lead Themselves* (1989); and "A Creative Retreat: Popularity Pursuit," reprinted in *More Group Retreats* (1987), edited by Cindy Hansen. Other programs published in *Directions in Faith* (Graded Press, 1986–87) deal with peer pressure, coping with failure, witnessing, alcohol abuse, parental pressure, suicide, and leading your friends to Christ.